Journeys into the Heart and Heartland of Islam

by

Marvin W. Heyboer

DORRANCE PUBLISHING CO., INC.
PITTSBURGH, PENNSYLVANIA 15222

For more information or to order additional books, please contact:
Dorrance Publishing Co., Inc.
701 Smithfield Street
Pittsburgh, Pennsylvania 15222
U.S.A.
1-800-788-7654
www.dorrancebookstore.com

To Bassam and Shirley Madany

STILL SHINING THE LIGHT

FOREWORD

Publicly and privately, many Americans are asking these questions; "How do I relate to Islam? How does my faith relate to Islam? How does Islam relate to my faith? How does Islam relate to the United States? We are increasingly part of a global village. Islam is my neighbor, a great big neighbor, as 20-25 percent of the world population. How do we relate to each other?" These are the questions and issues of the day, affecting the next century, and possibly the next millennium.

Journeys into the Heart and Heartland of Islam explores answers to those questions. While many American scholars, in consultation with Muslim commentators, peek at Islam from behind library walls, Heyboer independently ventures into the real world to examine the evidence. His exploration cautiously sidesteps the trap of explaining Islam, by way of moderate Muslims versus radical Muslims. To that explanation he emphatically says, "That is so much not the point." It is not about good Muslims or bad Muslims. It is about Islam. Islam is not accurately defined by observing the behavior of a Muslim anymore than democracy is defined by observing the behavior of an American.

Heyboer's method of exploration is uncomplicated and unforgiving. He proficiently explores and summarizes the two major authorities positioned at the very heart of Islam to uncover their instructions on appropriate attitudes and behaviors toward Jews, Christians, and other non-Muslims. First, he explores and identifies Muhammad's models of conduct toward unbelievers, gathered from the writings of Ibn Ishaq, primary biographer of the prophet, honored and trusted throughout the Muslim culture. Second, he explores, identifies, and explains specific teachings of *Allah* toward unbelievers as they are recorded in the Koran. When Heyboer clearly establishes terror behavior against unbelievers as the official policy of Islam, he then advances to his second stage, journeys into the heartland of Islam.

In Nigeria, Sudan, and Egypt, he explores whether the official policy of terror war (*jihad*) and terror subjugation (*dhimmitude*) coordinates with the attitudes and behaviors currently exhibited by Muslims against Christians. In his visits, he discovers a consistent practice of killing Christians, burning their homes, and destroying their churches. Christian women are threatened, manipulated and abused physically and sexually. When husbands and fathers object, they are beaten and sometimes killed. They have no legal standing within the judicial system of Islam. Muslim teachers terrorize Christian children with threats of hell. In areas of northern Nigeria, they are forced to convert to Islam in order to officially register as students within the public schools. In Egypt Christian children are forced to participate in Islam whether they attend public schools or private schools. Everywhere terror behavior is used to dehumanize non-Muslim peoples and force them to convert to Islam.

In my youth, I lived under the shackles of Islam in Egypt, my motherland. The oppression of Christians has worsened every year since my departure. Every day I hear of new atrocities and the cries of my people. Fifteen million Christian Copts, the indigenous peoples of Egypt, have no freedom within their native land. They are persecuted as a subjugated people by the holy laws (*sharia*) of Islam. Heyboer—Bishop Marvin, as he is known in Egyptian circles—visited, observed, and heard testimonies of hundreds of Christian victims trapped within the oppressive terror network of Islam.

I thank him from the bottom of my heart for his compassion and courage. When he visited Bishop Wissa in Upper Egypt, I feared for his life. At international conferences in Newark and Zurich, I heard his crisp, clear, passionate defenses of Christian victims suffering at the hands of Islam. In his book, *Journeys into the Heart and Heartland of Islam,* he brings the same clarity and passion. Prepare for an intelligent, instructive emotional read.

Monir Dawoud, MD.
Monir Dawoud, M.D., F.R.C.S, General, Vascular and Trauma Surgeon
President of the International Christian Union (Main Headquarters in USA)
President of the American Coptic Association
President of the Arab American Physician Foundation
Saddle River, New Jersey

References and quotations from the Bible are taken from: *The New International Version* (NIV) *of the Holy Bible* (Worship Bible). Grand Rapids, Michigan: Zondervan Bible Publishers, 1988.

References and quotations from the Koran are taken from *The Quran*, translated by George Sale in the year 1761 and is currently available online at http://arthursclassic novels.com/Arthur/Koran/koransale11.html. President Thomas Jefferson is said to have reviewed Sale's translation when he came to office, shortly before he sent U.S. troops to war against Muslin sailors along the Barbary coast (Tripoli), North Africa (1801-1805). Prior administrations had apparently paid a form of the *jizya* (protection money) to the Islamic caliphate in order to secure safe passage for American cargo ships.

For the sake of clarity and understanding, the author occasionally provides words or phrases within the texts of the Koran, but distinguishes them within parentheses' marks (—-). Translations are routinely similar, but readers are encouraged to compare and contrast translations. To simplify the task, the numerical identity of the texts are not annotated at the end of the chapter but printed with the quoted text. Occasionally, the numerical identity of the text may differ from one translation to another. If so, the text is generally only several texts before or after. For comparisons the reader may wish to use *The Holy Quran Text, Translation and Commentary* by A. Yusuf Ali, and *The Holy Quran with English Translation and Commentary* by Maulana Muhammad Ali.

Names, scenes, and locations of many individuals within this study have been changed to ensure their anonymity and safety. Throughout history to this very day, Christians and Jews who are legally subjugated by Islamic holy law behind the Crescent curtain are forbidden to speak words, true or false, that may damage the glory of Islam at home or abroad. Punishment can mean beatings and even death for them, their families, and their tribal believers. The author's promise of anonymity to protect them, their families, and their places of worship remains absolute.

Quotations from victims are provided when possible. At times remarks are reworded for the reason of clarity. The ideas, opinions, and sentiments expressed by the victims are their own.

INTRODUCTION

I f I express any doubts about the integrity of Islam, my colleagues are quick to counter with a challenge about the "sins of the church." I appreciate the spirit that we who live in glass houses should not throw stones. Yet my objective is not to throw stones, but to explore urgent concerns about relentless violence perpetrated by numerous followers of Islam against non-Muslim peoples in critical regions throughout the world. For satisfactory answers, I need more than the confusion of political opinions, which seem to prevail in the Western world. *I need a trustworthy review of reliable sources from which I can make wise and informed decisions about Islam and future interactions with Islam.*

As a Christian, I do not pretend that the church is innocent of evil behavior. With degrees from Calvin Theological Seminary and San Francisco Theological Seminary, I am very aware of ugly chapters in church history. I know the repulsive church behavior expressed through oppressive acts of violence under the leadership of the Holy Roman Emperors. I know the horrors of the Thirty Years War (1618–1648). I know the sporadic persecutions of non-orthodox Christians. I know the church's persecution of the Jews throughout the Middle East,

North Africa, and Eastern and Western Europe for sixteen hundred years. I know the persecutions of Anabaptist Christians by the state churches of Europe. I also know that all of these were disgraceful acts of disobedience to the teachings of the "Good Samaritan" and other biblical mandates. "Love your enemies, do good to them, and lend to them without expecting to get anything back. Then your reward will be great, and you will be sons of the Most High, because he is kind to the ungrateful and wicked. Be merciful, just as your Father is merciful" (Luke 6:35–36).

As an ordained minister in the church for thirty-nine years, I am also aware of its current failures. Contrary to biblical injunctions, there are still many so-called Christians unwilling to share themselves with the suffering and the poor, in our nation and our world. The health care crisis for the poor and elderly continues to escalate. Worse, in recent years our police and prosecutors have been employed to pursue and punish certain church clergy for sexual abuses of women and young boys.

The negative church story is not fully told by a few illustrations. I also witness the struggles within churches to value each person in a spirit of community. "Submit to one another out of reverence for Christ" (Ephesians 5:21). Inner church cultural conflicts continue to rip the harmony among church people, whether the issue involves the sharing of the Supper or the singing of a song. As I begin my journey to explore the meaning of terror behavior in Islam, I do sadly acknowledge the presence of evil among members of the fractured church. The church can be no greater than the community of its people, forgiven or unforgiven.

However, a trashing of the church for its failures ought not be a means to excuse a legitimate search to understand terror behavior within Islam, misleading us from the hard realities of the world around us. We cannot sanctify Islam by cataloging the failures of the church. *We **know** evil behaviors carried out*

within the church are in disobedience to the teachings of its ulti-
mate authority, the Bible. **We do not know** *that the evil behaviors*
practiced in the name of Islam are in disobedience to its ultimate
authority, the Koran. **We need to know.**

Several personal experiences with Islam raise serious questions for me about its claims of tolerance and peace. In my college years (1960–1965), the headlines of a leadership scuffle
within the Nation of Islam between Elijah Muhammad and
Malcolm X caught my attention. As I followed the story, I discovered that the Black Muslims (a street name for the Nation
of Islam) had a storefront mission several miles from my alma
mater, Calvin College, in Grand Rapids, Michigan. To that
point in my life, Islam had been little more than an occasional
footnote in my formal education. When curiosity got the better of me, I set out to visit the small mosque located on South
Division Avenue.

When I arrived late morning, the doorway light from the
morning sun had already shifted south. The meeting hall was
dark and windowless. There was no music to ease the presence
of a heavy, angry spirit. The stench of garbage filled the air, and
I sat alone, the only white man in the building. I was not greeted. I was not welcome in that place. The sermon was racist. It
was supremacist. I walked out before the official closure to
avoid a disorderly confrontation. In the months that followed,
I learned that the Nation of Islam had adopted its supremacist
teachings from the Near Eastern religion of Islam. In those days
of the early sixties, the teaching of a religious superiority was a
colossal contrast to the ecumenical spirit spreading among most
mainline churches across America. I never really gave much of
my mind or time to that experience. Only now, after Islam
whacked America in the face on 9/11, does that memory strike
me as a warning.

Several years after, I signed a teaching contract with the
Department of Education in Nigeria and joined the faculty at

Bristow Secondary School in the small city of Gboko. The religious commitments of the Nigerian peoples in that particular region were animist and Christian. However, as a secondary school, qualified students came from a broader geographical area, and several students were of a Muslim persuasion. They mixed well among the student body, but that may have been related to the ongoing Nigerian Civil War, the Biafran War (1967–1968), a conflict that seemed to unite all of the northerners.

Nonetheless, I do remember stories of anxiety among our Muslim students when they returned to school following vacation breaks. One afternoon shortly after such a break, I stepped into the administration's office, and by coincidence, overheard a young woman in tears talking to the principal about threats from her family if she should leave the religion of Islam. Her face was bruised, and her spirit seemed broken. Later I learned that the Koran instructs the Muslim community to censure and even execute apostates. I began to think of Islam as very narrow-minded.

In 1974, during the years of the great "sub-Sahara" famines, the World Relief Committee of my denomination, the Christin Reformed Church of North America, assigned Eugene Rubingh and myself to do a needs assessment in two West African nations then known as Upper Volta and Niger. At the time of our arrival, I thought very little about the fact that Christian relief organizations were bringing assistance to a mostly Muslim population. What I remember best of that tour was my visit into a refugee camp populated by Mali peoples who had fled the famine of their homeland and migrated into Niger.

Shortly after entering camp, armed soldiers engaged us, forced us to spread-eagle, searched, and arrested us. Earlier that morning in the city of Niamey, we had obtained clearance to visit the site through a personal interview with our United States Ambassador, L. Douglas Heck. I learned more about Islam. Even though ours was a goodwill mission to feed starving (Muslim) peoples, we were perceived as an offense and a threat. When the Muslim leaders were offered a choice, strangely enough, they preferred hunger and death to aid and assistance from us, "the Christian West."

Afterwards, I learned that the Red Cross had experienced similar problems with their assistance to needy Muslims in other regions of Islam. The cultural resistance is probably rooted in the Koran's teaching that the Christian cross is evil and a crime against *Allah*, the deity of Islam. Eventually, the Red Cross renamed itself the "Red Crescent" in locations where relief aid was administered to Muslims. For Islam the name change eliminated the blasphemy of the cross, replaced the cross with the crescent, and helped to facilitate a fallacy that relief distributions for Muslims originate from Islam. I concluded that the local leaders' intolerance was routed in the fear the Christian acts of mercy might win the hearts of hungry Muslims and undermine the claims of Islamic supremacy.

For me these experiences, the hard realities of 9/11, and the constant drumbeat of worldwide terrorism have seriously weakened my faith in the declarations of my political and religious leaders that Islam is a religion of peace and tolerance. To me they illustrate a great need in America to do some serious independent explorations to uncover the legitimate or illegitimate place of terror behavior in Islam.

Is there a sound methodology by which Americans can obtain that understanding? With difficult challenges like this in the past, Americans have acceded to the expertise of their scholars. They learned together. They shared political and religious insights. They publicly debated the pros and cons with colleagues. America was the melting pot. Consequently, they ascertained some form of satisfaction on issues. But not this time! *This time, ironically, they appear dependent on seeking instruction on Islam from Islam.*

Currently, American schools, grammar to college, invite well-trained missionaries of Islam (*dawa*), often scholars of academia and medical professionals, to educate students and faculty alike. Churches and synagogues do the same. Muslims instruct our government officials, publicly and privately. The American media also seems to have lost its independence and freedom. Leading newspapers regularly rely on Muslims to describe incidents of terrorism within the Islamic heartland. Journalists, committed to the allegedly oppressive religion, report their opinions from the field about acts of violence against non-Muslim victims. Their storyline is told to America. Is that an effort at objective journalism, or is it yellow journalism? With odd exceptions, our educators, ecclesiastics, politicians, and correspondents seem stuck on learning about terror behavior *in Islam from Islam*. What does that really mean for America? As best I am able to understand, that means America consults their alleged enemy for instructions on their alleged enemy.

What is wrong with this approach? Followers of Islam lie! They too are part of the human family. The missionary professionals (*dawa*) who often present their religion in our schools, churches, and libraries spread false propaganda. For example, in a number of cases, people from their audiences informed me that the practice of *jihad* was dismissed as no more than a Muslim's personal struggle against sin and evil. They also explained that the Muslim *dawa* taught them that Christians and Muslims worship the same God. These are only two illustrations of many half-truths taught to America—misinformation—which in reality is absolutely false according to the ultimate authority of Islam, the Koran. We can argue that everybody lies. But then that is precisely the point. In a case so critical to our security and well-being, to how much risk do we wish to expose ourselves? Are we trapped, with no independent sources of knowledge on Islam? Are we to simply trust an alleged enemy, cross our fingers, and follow the non-sighted?

In this strange circumstance of life, I chose to personally pursue an independent exploration on the place of terror behavior toward non-Muslim peoples in the religion of Islam. I do so with prayers and hopes that in some way my efforts may contribute to (1) a *greater* **OPENNESS TOWARD PUBLIC DISCUSSIONS** *on the actual teachings and behaviors of Islam, (2) an increased **awareness of America's need to secure the protection of our individual freedoms,** (3) an increased **assistance to non-Muslim victims** of Islamic violence abroad, and (4) **an awakening and emancipation of Muslim peoples** who have been enslaved by the legalistic tyranny of Islam (sharia), a bondage that seems to have haunted them since the death of Muhammad.*

CHAPTER ONE

In Defense of My Need To Explore Terror Behavior in Islam

I find myself facing some distressingly troublesome obstacles as I begin my independent journey to explore the realities of Islamic terror behavior amongst non-Muslim peoples. The *first obstruction* comes from sympathizers and advocates of Islam in America who insist that the most reliable way to understand terror behavior in Islam is to ask Islam. Independent journeys to explore the teachings and behaviors of Islam are described by them as acts of fear, paranoia, and prejudice. The *second obstruction* is rooted in the exclusive character of Islam. Only faithful Muslims do justly possess the privilege to assess and review Islam. A search to understand Islam by a non-Muslim person is unwanted and generally viewed as intrusive, offensive, and criminal. The *third obstruction* comes from seventh century sacred prohibitions, which have historically protected Muhammad and the Koran from any negative commentary. In fact Muslim spiritual leaders may issue *fatwas* charging critical reporters blasphemers, on some occasions demanding their executions. The *fourth obstruction* is from American church leaders who increasingly practice an inclusive policy toward other religions. In a frank departure from the past, some pastors and priests now seem boldly committed to the inclusion of other religions as co-equals of Christianity. American Christians who adhere to such a policy are proving to be more troublesome to critical investigations into the religion of Islam than American Muslims.

Obstruction One – Ask Islam

My commitment to independently explore the place of terror behavior in the religion of Islam is consistently challenged by sympathizers for Islam, and even more so by Western advocates of Islam, Western Muslims and their non-Muslim supporters. They view my pursuit as offensive and futile. They say, "Why not ask Islam? Who is more qualified to speak on terror behavior in Islam than Islam? But in my life experience, that practice was never honored as a legitimate method of scientific research. The critical method was understood as an exploration, collection, and evaluation of reliable sources. Never before was I instructed to terminate a critical study of a subject with a simply silly statement such as, *who is more qualified to speak on Christianity than Christians, on Communism than Communists, or on Nazism than Nazis?*

Would we rush to Cuba to ask its communist leaders to provide us with an understanding of the evils of Marxism? We do not visit the local pastor of the Presbyterian Church as our authority for understanding *negative elements of divine predestination*. Would we question members of the Ku Klux Klan to ascertain their views on the *wrongs of racism*? Nonetheless, as Americans we invite followers of Islam to lecterns in our classrooms to ask them to explain terror behavior in Islam. We interview them in our congressional committees. We enthusiastically parade them into our churches and synagogues, although we have no yardstick by which to measure the accuracy of what they say about violence and terror in Islam.

With no independent means of verification, how can we honestly defend and promote their testimonies? Some unwitting inquirers may even accept their words as descriptions of objective realities. In this vacuum of knowledge, we ourselves may mistakenly substitute our religious values for their religious values. How do we know the difference?

Some visits and dialogues with Muslim people may be worthwhile in a serious effort to understand the place of terror behavior in Islam, but our search to understand, honestly and intelligently, demands much more. Any other ideology, system of thought, or religion in America is subject to serious independent examinations and criticism. To merely "ask Islam" is not our way of learning and certainly fails our standards for the critical method of knowing. Legitimate **primary sources** on Islam are still available. Why do we not investigate them? English translations of the Koran and the biographical traditions of Muhammad are prepared for our reading. Why do we not read them? Many alleged victims of Islam are still able to speak. Why do we not listen to them?

As we ask Islam about Islam, the most common words we hear them speak are claims of "tolerance and peace." I do understand some of the defensive talk by Islam, post 9/11, but what I do not understand is the persistent parroting of that phrase by some of us from America. Why are we so eager to say, *"Islam is a religion of tolerance and peace"? We confess that we know little or nothing about Islam, yet some of us enthusiastically testify that Islam is a tolerant and peaceful religion. How does our lack of knowledge qualify us to make that judgment?* According to any form of legitimate scholarship, commentary *from* Islam *on* Islam needs independent verification. The way I reason is this: if Islam is our enemy, then we may expect what we normally collect from an enemy: deception. "Peace, peace... when there is no peace" (Jeremiah 6:14). Does America still know that?

Naturally, Western advocates of Islam who visit our schools, churches, synagogues, and political committees paint the very brightest pictures possible of the Islamic religion. We as Americans do the same to promote our political ideology and religion. It would be exceedingly disingenuous for us to scold them for doing what we always have done so well. That is marketing in our Western world. *But why would we, cynics that many of us are, trust Islam any more than we trust our politicians, CEOs, and stockbrokers, or ourselves, for that matter?* Our real problems with the self-promotion of Islam in America is our inability to accurately evaluate its presentations. *We must do more than ask Islam about Islam. We must independently explore the teachings and behaviors of Islam.*

Of course, Western advocates of Islam prefer that we only listen to them, our limited knowledge keeps us within their radar screen of "indoctrination." Like mother bird, Islam dutifully piecemeals choice bits of palatable pro-Islamic information. In turn, we eagerly swallow juicy romances of their film, *Islam: Empire of Faith.* We chirp enthusiastic approval of heartwarming distortions of Islam by the book *Approaching the Koran: The Early Revelations.* These are only two of many effective tools of deception that promote Islam as a peaceful religion and are distributed to educate adults and children in our schools, libraries, homes, and churches.

Obstruction Two – Exclusivity of Islam

In an effort to control commentary and criticism, Islam challenges and attempts to weaken influences of non-Muslim students of Islam. Bernard Lewis, Emeritus Professor of Near East Studies at Princeton, shares an objection to his studious pursuit of Islamic history in his book, *Islam and the West.* He recalls an article from a Kuwaiti newspaper stating that a Western historian, obviously Lewis, is not qualified to write history on the

Middle East because "he is not an Arab, he is not a Muslim and he is a Jew."[1]

To attack the ability of Bernard Lewis, historian *par excellence*, and his right to study the history of Islam because he is a non-Muslim, non-Arab, Jew, absolutely slams the door on any other American who wishes to pursue an independent understanding of Islam. Obviously, the Kuwati journalist no longer hides behind the word "tolerance," but on the bases of race and religion, proceeds with prejudice to undermine the qualifications of a world-famous scholar and his lifelong achievements in Near Eastern studies.

Do American political, religious, and educational leaders support such obstructive efforts as that in the Kuwati newspaper (a current international façade to cover evil corruption)? If so, do they realize how they defile the integrity of non-Muslim scholars who diligently search for firsthand information concerning the authentic character of Islam and its teachings of terror behavior?

Islamic scholars reject non-Muslim investigations of their cultures, religions, and even governments. Not only is every independent non-Muslim scholar rejected, so is his scientific methodology in an analysis of Islam.[2] We are not invited or welcome to independently explore the teachings, behaviors, and terror behaviors of Islam because we are not adherents of Islam. Islam insists that the only legitimate source of information on Islam is Islam. America must trust Islam! Do our leaders believe that?

Independent, non-Muslim efforts by Americans to explore and understand terror in Islam are viewed as that of a foreign predator. If anyone finds the teaching and the conduct of terror behavior in the life of Muhammad and the Koran, then the study is considered an invasion of privacy. If anyone files negative charges against the teachings of Muhammad and the Koran, then the indictments are called blasphemous. If anyone discovers the practice of terror behavior in the history of Islam, the findings are seen as interference in their religious and political heritage. If anyone visits the lands of Islam to listen to alleged victims of terror war, *jihad,* and terror subjugation, *dhimmitude,* then the explorations are described as that of an intruder spying on their cultural habitat.

When I evaluate these objections, I acknowledge that I am a non-Muslim. I am an American of Dutch extraction. I am a Christian. Therefore Islam depicts me as an illegitimate actor in Islam's theater to America. But Islam must recognize that I did not move into their world. On 9/11 Islam made a radical move into my world. Islam has been moving into my world for decades. In my world, freedom of critical review and the scientific method are sacred rights. Why should I, as an American, forfeit that *fundamental freedom, that heritage,* to please the exclusivist claims of Islam? America ought to reject any ideologists that enter its nation with instructions to obstruct freedom to explore and to assess them, their histories, teachings, and values.

How are American college communities teaching Islam? Do they maintain balance in their presentations by exercising independent studies of Islam along with the practice of listening to commentary *from* Islam *on* Islam? Certainly, I trust, they will not suspend the freedom of critical thought to befriend the religion of Islam. Critical thinking is the heartbeat of freedom and a major source of knowledge in America. Islam, on the other hand, is an unknown in the twenty-first century in part because Islam is viewed by its adherents as the flawless, supreme religion. So its ideology and behavior are seldom, if ever, subjected to independent, critical review. That exemption is part of the reason why Islam remains a religious and political dinosaur after fourteen hundred years of existence.

As students from the West, we have the freedom and the moral obligation to examine the teachings and behaviors of Islam as much as we do any other public subject. If Islam insists on living in the West, then let Islam submit to the freedoms of the West. We ought not sacrifice our methods of leaning and freedom of under-standing to some third world courtesies, or to coercive threats root-ed in seventh century sacred prohibitions, or, for that matter, to safe-shelters for Islam at our colleges and universities to pacify Islamic adherents and their lifelong academic cronies.

America needs to confront advocates of Islam who make efforts to intimidate non-Muslim students seeking to explore the legitimate place of terror behavior in Islam. In addition, Americans need to join the Europeans who boldly challenge scholars of Islam who are attempting to cover over centuries of violence and rewrite their history of terror behavior. Currently, the more notable example is the Muslim Turks' persistent denials of their efforts to exterminate Armenian Christians (1885–1915). In Turkey today, any person who speaks publicly about Islam's effort at Armenian genocide can be sentenced to three years in prison. In response, the French Parliament has defied the Turks' efforts at historical distortion and proposed laws to criminalize denials of the Armenian genocide by anyone on French soil. Why is America looking the other way?

Probably the most glaring distortion of history by Islam is the portrayal of the European Crusades (Christian Crusades) as Western imperialism. How many college students learn that tale of fiction as actual history? That distortion in the minds of Western youth is huge. It is as if the West is the primary offend-er of Islam. In many colleges, students embrace the above-men-tioned distortion rather than viewing the Crusades as defensive retaliations against the religion of Islam after four hundred sixty-six years of Islamic aggression (630–1096). With little knowledge of the historical context, Americans tend to repeat that fiction. The distortion damages their ability to accurately perceive current terror behavior by Islam because they are unschooled in its terror behavior of the past. As the myth has gone unchecked, it has gathered its own credibility within many American schools and churches.

Think about it. Islam began shedding the blood of its enemies in the early seventh century (623). In the year of Muhammad's death (632), Christians and Jews were already living in subjugation to the Muslims of Medina. Muhammad's followers, led by the caliphs, proceeded to subjugate the Christian lands of Syria, Iraq, Persia, Armenia, Palestine, Egypt, North Africa, Spain, and parts of France. As a matter of historical record, Islam was halted in its military subjugation of Western Europe by the army of Charles Martel in Tours, France, in the year 732. That describes the first one hundred years of Islam's subjugation of non-Muslim peoples of the West. In the following three hundred years, Islam devastated Sicily, islands of the Mediterranean, invaded the lands of the papacy, and extended its conquests of Persia and Armenia farther north into Russia. Nobody needs a history degree to understand who was the real imperialist aggressor. Until the creation of the myth, neither the Europeans nor Islam viewed the Crusades as Western imperialism.

The Muslims, not Europe, were the imperialists for a thousand years. From the Moors' conquests in Spain (seventh century) until the Turks' final siege of Vienna (seventeenth century), Christian Europe was under assault.[3] In the sixteenth and seventeenth centuries, Islam advanced militarily into areas known today as Russia, Hungary, Poland, Austria, Bosnia, and Serbia. These military conquests explain the roots of current tension and conflict taking place near Chechnya, Bosnia, and Kosovo.

In the sixteenth century, Elizabethan historians viewed Islam as a religion of terror and a threat to the whole of Europe. Nonetheless, Islam is not held accountable for its imperialistic militarism of thirteen hundred years. Why is that? If Islam is unwilling to honestly own its imperialistic behavior in the past, often in the forms of terror *jihad* against non-Muslim peoples, why do Americans choose to believe their talk of "peace and tolerance" toward non-Muslim peoples in the present?

In the Middle East, critics of Islam fear imprisonment and torture. Should America be concerned that such threats are beginning to intimidate non-Muslim critics from the West into a fearful silence? Consider the murder of Dutch filmmaker Theo van Gogh and the carving of his body parts on the streets of Amsterdam on November 2, 2004. A twenty-six-year-old Muslim, born in the Netherlands to parents of Moroccan descent, murdered van Gogh because of his critical film exposing the maltreatment of women by adherents of Islam. According to Egyptian journalist Manal Abdul Aziz, the film was televised in the Netherlands in August, much to the consternation of Muslim residents.[4]

Aziz went on to describe the murder as a random act of rage, and he then condemned the Dutch for overreacting to the crime. His dismissal of the murder as a random act ignores the deliberate nature of the crime and its intent to coerce submission and silence of non-Muslim peoples to protect the glory of Islam. It was not a random act; it was an act of terrorism. It was a calculated execution with identifiable connections to the Islamic Hofstad terror unit. Its intent was to silence a very vocal critic and others as well.

The maltreatment of women by Islam needs exposure, not only in Amsterdam with its non-Western majority population, but throughout the civilized world. In particular, the West must condemn the mutilation of female genitalia, which destroys a woman's natural right of sexual pleasure. A major source of information to van Gogh on this perverted practice was a former Somali immigrant, Hirsi Ali. After executing van Gogh, the killer knifed to his chest a letter in which the life of Hirsi Ali was also threatened.

Critic's van Gogh and Ali are offensive to many followers of Islam, like Manal Abdul Aziz, but does that mean criticism of

Islam should be silenced? While in the Netherlands, I came across a leading Dutch magazine in which one journalist described the van Gogh murder as a justifiable response induced by a critic that had gone too far. In other words, van Gogh provoked his own murder. The writer concluded that the violent execution of van Gogh could be more or less excused.

As I consider the implications of that article, I begin to wonder if there is a safe place to stand in the Western world from which persons may report their negative findings as they explore the issues of terror and violence in Islam. Does the convoluted philosophy of the Dutch journalist mean that Islam has already won the mind of the West? How exactly are Europeans and Americans to publicly present a criticism of Islam should they find one? By what mechanism are non-Muslim peoples to measure a critical report and the style of a critical report so that they are not guilty of provoking excused hate and murder by the hands of Islam? Does the Dutch journalist sacrifice freedom of speech in order to please some very subjective, supremacist issues of Islam? Is this some new process of political politeness by which we strip away the freedom of speech from Western liberties? If American journalists submit critical reviews which do not conform to the undefined, subjective wishes of Islam, for example the popular Danish cartoons of Muhammad, then may their murders be viewed as justifiable homicides?

Islam has entered our Western world and has a choice to isolate or to integrate. But Islam ought not be welcome to immigrate into the Western world with social, political, and legal protection from public critical reviews. Of course, Islam does not wish to be the subject of any critical study. Neither does any other ideology, nor did Christianity or Judaism

As for myself, I do not wish to go back to the absolute authority of the medieval church and its efforts to control religious and political thought. I certainly do not want to substitute the cultural, legalistic, and religious controls of Islam—not today, or on any other day in the future. The West has been there! Many Americans fled persecution by state-controlled religions of Europe. Exclusivist policies of religion have no place in America. They do not belong in any world. Religion is a choice.

In the West, we have learned painfully from experience, and are still learning, that religion is better used as an opportunity to exercise personal freedoms than to forbid them. *Islam has not.* Followers of Islam have very limited experiences in freedom, if any, in critical reviews of their religion. Salmon Rushdie serves as a famous example in the 1980s and 1990s. After the publication of *The Satanic Verses,* Ayatollah Khomeini issued a *fatwa* demanding his execution. Millions of dollars were offered in reward. Out of fear for his life, Rushdie lived under-cover in America. Sacred prohibitions of Islam forbid criticism of Muhammad and the Koran.

Do the sacred prohibitions of Islam now control the Netherlands? Sadly enough, the philosophy of excused murder, coupled with fear, won the day among the Dutch. The Hofstad terror unit remains active in its threats against critics of Islam, but Hirsi Ali finally fled for safety to the United States.

Obstruction Four – The Inclusive Spirit of the West

In the immediate aftermath of the 9/11 tragedies, the political leaders and religious leaders of America began to describe Islam as a religion of peace and tolerance. I suppose we will never be able to measure how profoundly that simple declaration defined Islam in the American psyche. Ever there after, Islam became known as a religion of tolerance and peace. Many American cit-izens marched in lockstep to that declaration. After all, who at that time was sufficiently schooled in the religion and behavior of Islam to legitimately challenge their political, and ecclesiasti-cal advisors?

Even seven years later, we hear the same phrase of peace and tolerance. What is disturbing, however, as the years pass, is that these leaders still seem unable or unwilling to provide a clear basis for their public pronouncements. When I visit with pastors and they defend Islam as a religion of peace, I ask them, "What is your evaluation of the teachings of Koran IX (29) or II (191,192)?" They have had no understanding of what I was asking them. To this date, I have yet to meet a pastor who has studied or seriously read the Koran.

The same is true with regard to the biographical traditions of Muhammad. When I ask pastors their opinions about Muhammad's supervision of the beheadings of six to nine hundred captive Jewish men in the village of Qurayza, near Medina, they confess that they never heard of it before. Why? Why no due diligence? How can pastors, priests and rabbis guide their people on this serious journey that Americans are asked to take with Islam when they have never taken the time to consult the road map? That unverified guidance of peace and tolerance is worse that hypocrisy. It conspires against the basic values of life, truth, justice, goodness, and decency. People have trusted religious leaders with their lives and their children's future, and in return, they get undocumented lingo.

One pastor angrily reacted to my questions with the question, "What do you want to do, kill all of them?" Why does a simple inquiry into the undocumented, unsubstantiated claims that Islam is a religion of peace and tolerance provoke such deep anxiety and anger among some church leaders? I think it is primarily a religious issue. Why are so many American religious leaders hiding under their church pews? Am I unreasonable to look to them and their churches for an evaluation of Islam?

How do I relate to Islam? How does the church relate to Islam? How does the United States relate to Islam? These are important questions. Equally important are the questions from the other side. How does Islam relate to me? How does Islam relate to the church? How does Islam relate to the United States? We are increasingly a global village. Islam is my neighbor—a great big neighbor—as 20-25 percent of the world population. How do we relate to each other? These are the critical questions of the day, affecting the next century and the next millennium.

What are the attitudes and behaviors of Islam toward Christians, Jews, and the non-Muslim peoples? What can we learn about these relationships from the Koran and the life of the prophet Muhammad? What can we learn about these relationships by observing the behaviors of Islam toward Christians, Jews, and other non-Muslim peoples from within the Islamic heartland?

As American church leaders expand in orientation and scope, are they really ready to acknowledge Islam as the religion of truth without an independent, critical evaluation? For centuries religion controlled the thought and behaviors of people within the Western world. Millions of human lives were lost in order to free us from religious tyranny and gain individual freedoms. Does the religion of Islam threaten those costly freedoms? Have our religious leaders examined the alleged legal prohibitions of individual freedoms by Islamic holy law (*sharia*)? If so, where are the public evaluations from church synods and councils? *Religions have power. Power to free or control.*

For centuries people of the West were under the control of the Roman Catholic papacy. By the pope's claim to be God's ultimate authority on earth (Petrine Theory), he declared his rule over all people. He could dispense heaven or hell by granting or withholding holy Eucharist. For example, in the year 1076, Pope Gregory VII condemned to hell the most powerful monarch of the West, Henry IV, and commanded his subjects to revolt against his rule. The authority of the pope was so great that King Henry rushed to Italy in the dead of winter and stood in the garb of a penitent for three days barefoot in the snow, begging forgiveness.

In the West, our struggle for freedom from religious control was long and painful. Creative thinkers like Jon Scotus and William of Occam planted the early seeds of individual freedom. At later dates, contributions by Descartes, Locke, and others elevated the value of the individual and individual freedoms. For four centuries (1450–1850), the value of the individual was lifted up throughout Europe. With the rise of the individual came the critical voices of protest by Martin Luther and John Calvin, who courageously challenged the church to free individual thought, faith, and behavior. Gradually, reform garnered support from political leaders as well. Protestant princes, Lutheran and Reformed, served the protestors as protectorates. Eventually the authoritative regime of the religious and the political tyrannies of Northern Europe—the Holy Roman Pontiff and the Holy Roman Emperor—toppled.

With the religious and political success of the Protestants, the value attributed to each individual continued to rise. Men and women were increasingly viewed as image bearers of God: "So God created man in his own image, in the image of God he created him; male and female he created them" (Genesis 1:27). The New Testament further enriched the creation account by teaching that the image of God is redeemed through the Gospel of Jesus Christ: "Put on the new self, created to be like God in true righteousness and holiness" (Ephesians 4:24). In direct proportion to the ascribed value of the individual or the appraised value of the individual, personal choices and personal freedoms also increased. In other words, individual freedoms flow from the appraised value of the individual. Honor, reverence, and esteem for the value of the individual then became the sanctuary of individual freedoms, the home for protest and critical review.

As Americans, we are heirs of that sanctuary. We have received an inheritance from the blood of generations past, which acknowledges that each of us has a independent value simply because each one of us is an individual. As individuals we are free to make choices. Unlike the Muslim world, we may choose our laws. We may choose our religions, or no religion. We may choose our diets. We may choose our dress. We may choose our political, educational, and religious leaders. We may choose to praise or to criticize them. We received the inheritance of freedom. Each individual is considered to be of equal value to every other individual. On that basis, each individual is to possess equal individual rights and equal individual freedoms. But are those freedoms at risk under the authority of Islam? Do those individual freedoms of non-Muslim peoples remain secure within a majority culture of Islam? Where on the world map is such a practice located as a reality?

We need independent evaluations of Islam to provide us the answers to legitimate questions. Does Islam practice terror behavior against non-Muslim peoples who are living under its cultural, religious, and political authority? Does Islam still abide by its seventh-century teachings, which have been translated into Islamic holy law (*sharia*), to control the lives of both Muslim and non-Muslim peoples? Is obedience to Islamic holy law still enforced by divine terror prescriptions in the form of physical and mental cruelties? Are individual freedoms so limited in Islam that a person is forbidden to disbelieve Islam? May such persons be executed as apostates to protect the honor of the families, communities, and the religion of Islam?

Do the legal strictures of Islam limit serious commitment to individual value and subsequent individual freedoms? Is the value of an individual voided to the supremacy of Islamic community? When we see 9/11, do we see nineteen young, intelligent individuals kill themselves for the community of Islam? When we see Muslim boys and girls become weapons of war as suicide bombers, do we see them on Islamic *jihads* to expand and protect the Islamic community?

Journeys Into Islam

Political leaders, educational leaders, and religious leaders in America cautiously endorse Islam as a religion of peace and tolerance, but they do so without proposing a sound basis for such belief. Most of them furnish information and perspective gathered from devout advocates of Islam. When an occasional challenge or inquiry arises, Western Muslim scholars and their non-Muslim cronies defend the peace and tolerance of Islam.

Meanwhile our small planet experiences incessant eruptions of Islamic violence, which are often dismissed as the actions of fundamentalists, radicals, and fanatics. So America finds itself in the middle of a world being torn apart by a people who are radically committed to the fundamentals of a religion of peace and tolerance. How reasonable is that? Watch those perpetrators of terror behavior. They move in and out of their villages and their mosques without an accusation, an apprehension, or an arrest. Where are the adherents of peace and tolerance? Does anyone see them restricting the behaviors of the so-called radical fundamentalists?

Once I was sitting in a crowded theater to view a celebrated film. The show began, but I heard no sound. I waited for a few moments and asked my wife. "Where is the sound?" I waited another minute or so. Everybody sat and listened to nothing. Finally, I got up and went to the sound booth. The operator apologized and turned on the sound.

Today, I keep asking myself, "How long will we listen to no sound? Is someone going to the sound booth?" As the years pass, American crowds seem pleased with the baffling silence. Where is the audio on the independent political and ecclesiastical investigations of terror behavior by Islam? Are their no independent, published investigations by church and/or state? Really?

So I begin my journey into the heart and the heartland of Islam to explore the realities of terror behavior. I set out to implement a critical search as to whether two alleged terror teachings, the doctrine of terror war (jihad) and the doctrine of terror subjugation (dhimmitude), are really taught and practiced in Islam. What do the ancient authorities really teach? What does the culture really practice?

On my first journey, I pursue a simple, critical review of the life of Muhammad. For that purpose, I choose to review **as a primary source** the first written biography of Muhammad by Ibn Ishaq (circa A.D. 750). He wrote his biography of Muhammad in the mid-eighth century, and it remains a primary source of reliable information about Islam and its prophet within the Muslim world today. Other biographical sources, recorded at later dates, tend to build and expand on the Ishaq material. For centuries, his presentation of Muhammad has been accepted as the cornerstone for understanding the origins and the teachings of Islam and has become deeply embedded within the Muslim culture. Ishaq's collection of Muhammad's sayings and experiences are generally affirmed by the work of biographer al-Bukhari (circa A.D. 850) and by many other biographers, some as recent as that of John Glubb (2001).

On my second journey, I explore **as a primary source** the Koran, the most authoritative voice in Islam, the voice of Allah. What do the imams read to their audiences at Friday prayers as to how a real Muslim is to address and relate to Jews and Christians? My additional journeys explore whether terror behavior by Islam, terror war (*jihad*) and terror subjugation (*dhimmitude*), is currently a practice within the Islamic heartland. I employ **as crucial, primary sources** the testimonies of non-Muslim peoples who live near or under the authority of cultural, religious, and political Islam.

For these journeys, I did the following:

1. I visited, listened, and on occasion recorded (with permission) non-Muslim peoples in central and northern Nigeria, a micro-world laboratory of interactions between non-Muslim peoples and the followers of Islam.
2. I also visited and interviewed non-Muslim peoples in the nation of Egypt, including the Christian Copts. The indigenous Copts claim to have suffered under the authority of Islam since the year 641.
3. In spite of obstructions by the Islamic bureaucrats, I finally gained entry into Sudan and listened to the testimonies of non-Muslim peoples from southern Sudan. Throughout twenty years of terror *jihad* (1983–2004), victims of the south testified to the United Nations and the World Council of Churches of their imprisonment, enslavement, displacement, and executions at the hands of Islam under the religious and political leadership of Islamic cleric, Sheik Hassan al-Turabi.

On the bases of these journeys (and others), my critical review describes the behavior of Islam toward non-Muslim peoples who live near or under its cultural, religious, and political authority. To identify any consistent pattern of behavior, I compare the results of my discoveries between Nigeria, Egypt, and Sudan. Along the way, I occasionally explain and compare my discoveries to various historical accounts of Islamic behavior acknowledged and recorded by non-Muslim historians.

Summary

In the West, we celebrate the freedom to critically examine any and all ideologies, philosophies, and theologies. However, in the culture of Islam, critical commentaries and reviews of Muhammad and the Koran are unlawful. The West must make a decision. We can agree that Islam, by divine authority, stands above our laws and our freedoms. Or, we can claim our freedoms and use them to examine the alleged terror teachings and behaviors of Islam. The choice is ours. *If we bow to disinformation and coercive forces, and therefore maintain silence on the violence, then we choose to walk a road into the unknown. On that journey, we may eventually risk our children's heritage of individual freedom in an exchange for living life under the tyranny of Islamic holy law (sharia). Do we know what that means?*

We *know* Islam is not spreading truth about "the Christian West." Why would we *believe* Islam spreads the truth about Islam? We *know* that Islam is actively re-creating and re-writing its history to remove its violent past from Western scrutiny. Why would we *believe* the re-writes and ignore the realities of terror behavior presently practiced against indigenous Christians (Armenians, Chaldeans, Assyrians, Egyptians, Berbers, Lebanese, Serbians and Sudanese)? We *know* that the laws of Islam restrict personal freedoms, from diet to dress. Why would we *believe* they respect our personal freedoms? We *know* that the heart of Islam, Iran (Shiite) and Saudi Arabia (Sunni), prohibits the freedom of religion, even the possession of a Bible. Why would we *believe* they respect our freedom of religion? We *know* women may not drive automobiles and in many cases enjoy the pleasure of sex, within orthodox regions of Islam. Why would we *believe* they respect the freedom of women in the Western world? We *know* Islam ascribes no significant value to the individual, apart from the Islamic community. Why would we *believe* they respect the value we assign to individuals and subsequent individual freedoms?

As I begin my explorations in the religion of Islam, I search to know for a fact whether the terror offenses are prescribed and designed in its ancient authorities or are spontaneous crimes of passion. If terror behavior by Islam is advised and enjoined by the Koran and modeled by Muhammad, then we must defend ourselves and confront Islam for its teachings of terror behavior against non-Muslim peoples. On the other hand, if terror behavior is a more recent impulsive form of behavior, then we may join with those of Islam who wish to fight against terror behavior. What do the life of Muhammad and the text of the Koran really teach about the views and relationships of Islam toward non-Muslim people?

CHAPTER TWO

Journeys into the Heart of Islam
The Life of Muhammad

Western advocates of Islam tell America that terror behavior has no legitimate place in Islam, and that Islam is a religion of peace and tolerance. Nonetheless, faithful followers of Islam constantly rock the world with acts of violence. Americans seem confused. Can they work with Islam against terrorism? Or is Islam the cause of terrorism? To avoid a colossal error in judgment with permanent consequences, Americans need to determine which of these is the actual case. They can begin by reaching into the heart of Islam to monitor the instructions of its ancient authorities.

Does the life of Muhammad model, and do the texts of the Koran teach, terror behavior against non-Muslim peoples? Islamic radicals say, "Yes." Western advocates of Islam say, "No." Want confusion? Even more puzzling, Western advocates of Islam call the radical terrorists, "fundamentalists." But can they have it both ways? Think about it. The Western advocates charge that the fundamental of the radical terrorists is the fundamental teaching of terror behavior, then how can the

Western advocates turn around and deny the existence of terror behavior as a fundamental of Islam? How absolutely bizarre! What kind of nonsense do they propagate? If there is any reasonable explanation for this unbelievable contradiction alleged by Western advocates of Islam, other than lies, it can only be that terror behavior was once a legitimate, fundamental principle of Islam, but that principle at some point has been officially abrogated.

As Americans explore Islam, it is important for them to determine whether or not terror behavior is really taught in the ancient authorities of Islam. When and if they uncover such instructions, then they must also explore whether or not any legitimate authoritative events, words, persons, or divinity cancelled those fundamental principles of terrorism. If they can clearly identify an actual abrogation, the Western advocates of Islam and non-Muslim peoples of America have a common ground on which to stand, resist, and defeat terror behavior by radical Islamic fundamentalists.

What is the reality? We know that terror behavior against non-Muslim people of the West was very limited for a lengthy stretch of time from region to region between the years 1850–1970, but was that time of peace out of character for Islam? Was the peaceful era simply a result of European military occupations of Islamic lands? For centuries the Turks led the Islamic terror *jihad* against the Western world, conquering Hungary, coercing Bosnia, besieging Austria, and annihilating Armenia. But when the Ottoman Turks finally submitted to the European powers, the Western world seems to have lost sight of Islamic *jihad* and even the religion of Islam itself.

What are the Western advocates of Islam really saying about terror behavior? The promotional works of Western Muslim scholars are readily available at most significant book stores across America. Many of them argue that militant Islam is merely a myth and that terror behavior by Islam never existed.

For example, one Muslim scholar writes that Islam exercised great tolerance toward Judaism and Christianity, unlike typical military behavior in the medieval era. He claims that the Muslim cavalry behaved with honor and integrity in its *jihad* to extend the colonial authority of Islam into Western and Eastern Europe.

Such pompous descriptions of a benevolent Islamic military have no historical authenticity and are the common expressions of victorious armies of all stripes. The conquered seldom write the history of the victorious. Sadly enough, some Americans think such fabrications credible and put off earnest independent explorations to know the models of Muhammad and the teachings of the Koran. *Exactly how do the ancient authorities of Islam teach Muslims to view non-Muslim peoples?* In the West, whether adhered to or not, the Judeo-Christian commandment is to "love your neighbor as yourself," but what are the actual instructions to Muslims as to attitudes toward and relationships with non-Muslim peoples?

As I explore for answers in the life of Muhammad and the Koran, I define terror as "a state of intense fear" and terrorism as "the systematic use of terror especially as a means of coercion" *(Merriam-Webster's Collegiate Dictionary).* In other words, terrorism (or terror behavior) is the systematic use of intense fear to manipulate the behavior of a person, community, or institution. Some of the non-judgmental, political community of the twenty-first century has chosen to ban the use of the words "terror behavior" and/or "terrorism" as inappropriate descriptions of violent actions of hostility that penalize Islam. They strictly prefer to substitute the term "violence." In that way, they argue that there is no prejudice of violence.

In the Iraqi War, for example, the behavior of the Sunni insurgents and Shiite militias are viewed as behaviors of violence not unlike the behaviors of violence by the American military. If we wish to put the subject in the historical framework of World War II, then the behaviors of the Nazis would be viewed as comparable to those of the Americans: violent. In essence, they argue that persons, communities, and institutions do not possess the moral capacity to make valid judgments as to any rights or wrongs of violent behaviors. Today we may understand such reservations as "moral relativism," or as it is put in the classrooms of America, "Who's to say?"

In my review, I plan to continue to use the word "terrorism" (terror behavior) because it accurately describes *coercive violence*, not *violence*. Furthermore, the concept of coercion and the words "terror" and "terrorism" are indigenous to the historical development of Islam. For example, the God of Islam in the year 622 instructed the followers of Islam with the admonition, "Strike terror into the enemies of God..." (Koran VIII (60)). At another point, *Allah* defined himself as a terrorist: "I will cast dread into the hearts of unbelievers. Therefore strike off their heads and strike off all the ends of their fingers" (Koran VIII (12)). In both of these texts, as is the case with a number of others, the coercive purpose of the terror behavior is eventually described as "conversion" or "subjugation."

On the basis of the indigenousness of terror behavior (*jihad* and *dhimmitude*) to Islam and its development, imposing a ban on the words "terrorism" or "terror behavior" is an unprincipled prejudice of critical review! Such an omission misleads and misguides an independent search to understand any coercive teachings and behaviors of Islam in its ancient authorities and its behaviors in our world today.

In my search for terror behavior in the life of Muhammad, I use as my biographical source the works of Ibn Ishaq. This is the earliest (circa A.D. 750) and the best-known biography of Muhammad. Any words and/or actions of Muhammad that I reference from Ibn Ishaq are common knowledge within the culture of Islam and are generally acknowledged by other Muslim and non-Muslim biographers.

The life of Muhammad as a prophet may easily be divided by the reader into five stages: (1) Muhammad the *pacifist*, the early years of pre-terror (612–622); (2) Muhammad the *defender*, the flight and settlement in Medina, when *Allah* grants permission to Muhammad to shed the blood of the polytheists (622–623); (3) Muhammad the *protector*, the years of raids to increase the Muslim treasury, to feed, clothe, house, and arm his followers (623–627); (4) Muhammad the *antagonist*, the years of perpetrating systematic coercive violence against the Jews and others (627–632); and (5) Muhammad the *subjugator*, the years of terror war (*jihad*) threats to intimidate and to subjugate Jews and Christians (629–632).

Those stages of division enable us to better understand the gradual escalation of violence in the ministry of the prophet Muhammad and also facilitate an explanation of how the Ishaq account may be used to support the sharply divergent views of Islam currently active in our Western world. For example, since the Western advocates of Islam wish to present Islam as a peaceful religion, they can draw chiefly on resources from the early years of pre-terror, stages one through three, with portrayals of Muslims as a persecuted people. On the other hand, since the Islamic fundamentalists wish to portray Islam as "terror active," they can draw more heavily on resources from stages three though five, with models of terror war (*jihad*) and terror subjugation (*dhimmitude*).

Muhammad the Pacifist

Muhammad was born into a polytheistic culture in the year A.D. 570. Stones represented the spirits of his gods. The most precious stone was a large, sacred, black stone, protected in a square building, called the Kaba, in the vicinity of Mecca. Followers of his pagan religion made long pilgrimages to Mecca to honor the great, black stone. In contrast to the worship of many gods of his culture, he probably gained an awareness of monotheistic worship from the Jews who lived in settlements scattered throughout Arabia. In addition, he may have dialogued with Jews and Christians as he journeyed in a trading caravan to and from Syria.

His first wife, Khadija, championed his monotheistic understanding of God. While I visited at a monastery in southern Egypt, several Christian monks of the Orthodox Copts shared with conviction their opinions that Khadija was a Christian. As a relatively wealthy woman who ran trade caravans into Christian Syria, they reasoned that her link in Syria was probably with those of her own faith, other Arab Christians. They noted that unlike the polytheistic Arab culture, the Christian tradition is monogamous, and that during their twenty-five years of marriage, Muhammad took no other wives, even though Khadija was older and had failed to provide him with a surviving son.

Their argument is compelling and opens the door to another consideration—that Khadija's ancestors may have fled to Arabia as persecuted followers of the non-orthodox theologian, Arius, who had rejected the deity of Christ and the plurality of persons in the Godhead. From that perspective, Khadija may have been pro-active and supportive of Muhammad's conception and formation of his deity, *Allah*. Whichever the case, Muhammad grew in his antagonism toward polytheism. Increasingly, he appeared open to a theology in which the greatest attribute of *Allah* was the absolute oneness of his being.

When Muhammad began hearing the voice of angel Gabriel (610), he was in the area of Mount Hira, a region to which he often retreated for solace and meditation. At first he was hesitant to share his experience, but Khadija encouraged him. When angel Gabriel ordered Muhammad to publicly proclaim his revelation, he was remarkably faithful to his calling. Immediately, he was ridiculed and scorned by his family and tribe. Some even accused him of stealing his religion ideas from Judaism. As he preached his view of *Allah*, his converts were few, and mostly from among destitute Arabs. It is noteworthy in the early years, with the slow growth of converts, Muhammad's character reflected qualities of sorrow and grief. He was portrayed as a man of a humble and honorable spirit. Moreover, his words under oppression displayed a character of devotion and submission. He spoke of *Allah* as his sovereign Lord and testified that he preferred persecution to Allah's wrath. Muhammad claimed that *Allah* alone held all the power and provided his people light in the darkness.

The polytheists (worshippers of many gods) of Mecca, his initial enemies, continued to persecute Muhammad and his small community of believers. Their oppressive behavior raises the question, why did they persecute a man of their own family and tribe? According to Ibn Ishaq, Muhammad was known as an inordinately pleasant and exceedingly honest man. Did his ministry for the absolute oneness of *Allah* threaten anyone?

There are two obvious answers to that question. First, he was creating a division within the Quraysh tribe. Among the tribes of Arabia, that was no small issue, for there was no established government to provide safety and protection. Members of the tribe relied upon each other, and Muhammad was destroying that union by introducing a completely new form of allegiance between his new believers.

The second answer is that his preaching generated fear of economic loss to the Quraysh tribe. The circumstances were comparable to those recorded in the Bible six hundred years earlier in the mission expansion of Christianity. In the city of Ephesus, Demetrius, the silversmith, called the idol makers and craftsmen together and lectured them as to the economic losses in store if the Apostle Paul's ministry about the unity and oneness of God was to continue.

Men, you know we receive a good income from this business. And you see and hear how this fellow Paul has convinced and led astray large numbers of people here in Ephesus and in practically the whole province of Asia. He says that man-made gods are no gods at all. There is danger not only that our trade will lose its good name, but also that the temple of the great goddess Artemis will be discredited, and the goddess herself, who is worshiped throughout the province of Asia and the world, will be robbed of her divine majesty. (Acts 19:25–27)

Likewise if Muhammad's campaign against polytheistic forms of worship were to be successful, Mecca could lose the financial enrichments it had been receiving for decades—if not centuries—from polytheistic pilgrims who came from across Arabia to worship the gods at the black stone of the Kaba. These primary concerns, economic loss and tribal division, set in motion an ever-increasing oppression of the prophet. Throughout those early years of his ministry, in the face of persecution, biographer Ibn Ishaq presents Muhammad as a leader who exhibited a sincere capacity for non-violence (610–622). He demonstrated the character of a genuine pacifist.

Muhammad the Defender

Out of concern, Muhammad eventually advised approximately one hundred of his converts to flee for protection to the Christians of Abyssinia (Ethiopia). Some time later, he ordered the other half of his followers to flee from Mecca to Medina (622), but he remained behind. In those last days, the people of Mecca, the Quraysh tribe, attempted to murder him in his sleep. He escaped and took flight to Medina (*hegira*). Muhammad's departure in 622 brought to a close the innocent years—the peaceful years of Islam, between 610–622. With his departure from Mecca, a major transition toward violence began to take place: the beginning of terror war (*jihad*) in Islam.

Ibn Ishaq records that *Allah* permitted Muhammad to *jihad* in defense of his followers since they had been oppressed by the Quraysh tribe for declaring *Allah* is Lord. Previous to this declaration, the followers of Muhammad had understood the Arabic word, *jihad*, as a description of confrontational preaching to the polytheists to convert to the new religion Islam, meaning "submission to *Allah*." Muhammad boldly preached the words received from Gabriel to the people of Mecca.

We can safely say, on the basis of Ibn Ishaq's writings on the life of Muhammad, that his leading objective, throughout his lifetime, was his desire to convert non-Muslim peoples. But at this juncture, a whole new element of violence was introduced to Islam: to spill blood, the blood of the non-Muslim peoples, and in this particular case, the blood of the polytheists of Mecca (*mushrikun*). For the previous twelve years, Muhammad's non-violent behavior toward his persecutors seems to have been similar to that of Jesus Christ in the Gospels. This abrupt transition of Islam, from non-violence to violence, demands serious evaluation.

In this transition event, *we witness a dramatic change in the leaderships style and probably the character of Muhammad. He changed from twelve years of suffering persecution to a radically new resolve to kill his oppressors.* This transformation of character probably occurred over a period of several years. It began in the year 621 with his advice to some of his followers to flee from oppression. By October of 623, Muslims shed the first blood of non-Muslim peoples in a caravan raid. In striking contrast to his former pacifism, the God of Islam led Muhammad to defend Islam by the sword.

As to why Muhammad waited through twelve long years of

suffering before taking the sword to his oppressors, we do not know. One intriguing possibility for his change may have been the death of his blessed supporter and encourager, wife Khadija. Did the death of his wife (619–620) strip him of his capacity to suffer and make him vulnerable to the leading of some new antagonistic, monotheistic, militant, possibly non-orthodox Christian leader (an Arian) in the camouflage of the angel Gabriel?

According to Ibn Ishaq's account, the declaration of *jihad* was not even Muhammad's decision. It was presented as an act of *Allah* (Koran II (190–1)). *Allah* commanded believers to execute militant *jihad*. That methodology of transposition of responsibility for behavior, from Muhammad to *Allah*, was employed frequently in resolutions of social and political crises in Muhammad's ministry. Muhammad obviously used the God of Islam to order and bless his pragmatic decisions as he developed the religion of Islam. In due course, he taught them that he and *Allah* spoke with equal authority: "Whoever obeyeth the Apostle, obeyeth God" (Koran IV (80)).

To avoid a common error in America, to substitute stated values of one religion for the stated values of another religion, we need to observe at this point a sharp distinction, which emerges between the God of Muhammad as the founder of Islam and the God of Jesus of Nazareth as "the founder" of Christianity. The God of Islam granted an oppressed and persecuted Muhammad permission to *jihad* and to shed blood in defense against his oppressors. In contrast, the God of Christianity was begged by Jesus Christ to be released from his humiliation, persecution, and crucifixion: "My Father, if it is possible, may this cup be taken from me" (Matthew 26:42). But the God of Christianity granted Jesus no escape, and subsequently, he submitted to his passion under the authority of Governor Pontius Pilate.

So the God of Islam granted Muhammad a lifetime reprieve from oppression by use of the sword (*jihad*); thereby, the God of Islam established through Muhammad a military authority to rule the world (Koran IX (29)), the Islamic perspective. In contrast, the God of Christianity insisted on the suffering, crucifixion, and death of Jesus; thereby, the God of Christianity established through Jesus a substitutionary atonement to redeem the world (John 3:16), the Christian perspective. Today, Muhammad and Jesus stand as value models of thought and behavior for their sincere adherents to replicate.

This sanction to wage war and shed blood is the most critical juncture in the development of Islam. Ibn Ishaq records in the spirit of the day that true Muslims are to fight against the false believers until the only religion still standing is that of Allah and no other deity is worshiped.[1] In this context, *jihad* (war) is presented as a reaction to the aggressive, oppressive behavior of the polytheists of Mecca. Followers of Muhammad had been imprisoned, tortured, starved, and forced to live under social and economic sanctions. Initial *jihad* then was ordered by *Allah* in the context of oppression as a defensive response to protect and to prosecute (as in the case of war) Islam as a viable religion.

Today Islamic leaders still justify terror behavior against non-Muslim peoples as defensive reactions against their so-called "crusader" offenses and/or their "colonial" occupations. Terror behavior must always be justified as defensive in the culture/religion of Islam. In contrast, however, Western advocates of Islam argue that war declared under the circumstances of oppression was only meant to apply to war against the polytheists (*mushrikun*) at that time and was never intended against any others, Jews or Christians. Militant Islam, they say, is no more than a myth.

Americans must understand that initially *jihad* referred to a style of confrontational preaching for people to fight against evil and convert to Islam. But as they can clearly see, even at the early stages of Ishaq's account, the meaning of *jihad* was already being protracted to include violence. *Allah* permitted

Muhammad to kill. Such violence was ordered in the context of oppression and therefore was initially viewed as defensive in nature. However, the meaning of defensive *jihad* is a very subjective issue. Tragically, Muslim preachers at local mosques are often the authorities that clarify its application. In Islam, the definition of defensive war is very confusing and misleading and may be impulsively declared on the grounds of a simple rumor.

The claim by Western Muslim scholars that violence was limited to terror war against the polytheists of Mecca has no substance. Ibn Ishaq's account implies that terrorism or coercive violence was to continue in Islam until only the God of Muhammad was worshipped, and no other God. The idea that terror war was abrogated after Muhammad's conquest of the polytheists of Mecca is untrue according to Ibn Ishaq.

Muhammad the Protector

Certainly we can see from the Ishaq account that Muhammad was on the defensive when he fled from Mecca and settled in Medina (622). Once in Medina, he confronted two major obstacles, the threat of war from Mecca and the poverty of his people. Many of his followers in Medina, migrants from Mecca, had no money, no family, and no shelter. Muhammad needed the financial means to care for his poorest people and arm his abject warriors. An obvious answer to his problem was to raid and rob caravans of enemy tribes, which was typical of tribal life in the trade-ways of Arabia. Tribal wars were common, and the warriors' behaviors impulsive. Their ultimate objective was to keep the loot. Eighteen months after his arrival in Medina, Muhammad sent Abdullah b. Jahsh and eight migrants to scout out a caravan near Mecca. On this expedition, it is recorded that Muslims took their first booty and killed their first victim. The shares of booty were split 80 percent for the warriors and 20 percent for the Islamic community. The division of booty provided essentials for women and children of Islam and increased the size of the militia. *Allah* instructed his cavalry to use the loot to purchase stronger and faster horses and camels for *jihad*.

We can surely imagine that the effectiveness of booty on Muhammad's impoverished warriors was similar to its effects on any other desert raiders. Booty puts a glitter in the covetous eye and energy into the sword. That is true not only of followers of Islam, but warriors of other faiths as well. The Bolsheviks' plunder of the Russian aristocrats was more than a blind faith in Marxism. It too was led by the proletariats' covetous yearnings to wear the robe of the tsar. Such seems the nature of the human mind. Western history tells us that in the millennium that followed, Islam fed its covetousness by raids on the possessions of its Jewish and Christian neighbors, their money, wives, children, houses, vineyards, cattle, sheep, farms, libraries, and cathedrals.

Certainly the Muslim community of Medina was desperate for the bare essentials of life, and Muhammad demonstrated his uncanny knack to fix such tribulations for those faithful to his religion. He actively pursued means by which he could fill the needs of his believing community (*umma*), to enlarge its purse, to feed its poor, and to arm and motivate its warriors. With his eyes on the riches of caravans and the lands of neighboring Jewish tribes, his defensive posture of war became less defensive. In his transition method to abandon a former principle to pursue another, Muhammad used *Allah*. Previously *Allah* had permitted Muhammad to kill oppressors in the place of pacifism. Now *Allah* grants permission to raid caravans for booty to feed and arm the faithful—a subtly more offensive form of violence. "Whoever obeyeth the Apostle, obeyeth God" (Koran IV (80)).

Muhammad preached another incentive for his warriors to fight with the sword (*jihad*) for Islam, namely paradise. He maneuvered this very skillfully in Medina after his defeat by the warriors of Mecca at the battle of Uhud. Muhammad made clear that only true believers fight to the death. He instructed his warriors that the only way *Allah* knows the genuineness of their faith is when he sees them earnestly and consistently engaged in combat against the enemy.[2]

Muhammad taught his warriors that those who die in battle would truly enjoy the wonders of paradise because they had waged holy war in the name of *Allah*. He described paradise as a place with colorful birds and beautiful rivers. He also seems to have accessed language from the "Revelation of Jesus Christ" in the New Testament as he spoke about paradise with golden candlesticks around the throne of God.

Muhammad's paradise portrays some peculiar aspects for those of us from a Judeo-Christian milieu. Nonetheless, the compelling influence of his paradise reached into the hearts of his warriors then as well as today. The nineteen young men complicit in the 9/11 murders were awarded paradise in the same manner as the warriors at the battle of Uhud. In both cases, they are viewed as martyrs for Islam. Although some Western advocates of Islam have rejected the 9/11 attacks on America as violations of civilian innocents, sadly enough, they have not yet been so bold as to reject the so-called "magnificent nineteen" as martyrs of Islam.

Pragmatic Muhammad, former pacifist, used his experiences of conflict with the polytheists of Mecca as instructive exercise from which to learn lessons of war and the use of war for the expansion of Islam. By the year 624, the teachings of terror war (*jihad*) appear to have taken a firm hold within Islam. With the incentives of booty and paradise, Muhammad increased his wealth for military armor and gained additional military support from neighboring tribes. According to Ibn Ishaq's account, he also began to focus greater attention on the Jews.

When he fled oppression in 622, he settled into Medina, fearful of the military strength of the warriors from Mecca. In organization of his defense, he drafted a very practical defensive alliance, which he planned to offer to the Jewish tribes of Medina. Some critical tenets of the alliance mentioned by Muhammad according to the Ishaq account are as follows: (1) Jews were to be granted equality without oppression or war, (2) Jews were to split the military costs when they fought a common enemy, (3) Jews may maintain their own religion, (4) Jews must respect Medina as sacred territory, (5) Jews must share and consult with Muhammad (the believers) when and if war is imminent and visa versa, (6) if the Jews call for peace, Muhammad (the believers) must also call for peace and visa versa except for the cause of a holy war, and (7) Jewish warriors are to be rewarded by the Jews, and Muhammad's warriors are to be rewarded by Muhammad.

In view of the threat of war from the polytheists of Mecca, the proposed alliance with the Jews of Medina demonstrated the pragmatic resolve of Muhammad to defend his followers with the sword. Such inter-tribal alliances were ordinarily common in Arabia at that time and frequently alternated between tribes as they struggled to maintain a balance of power. Muhammad's proposed alliance with the Jews also coordinated with his long-term desire that the Jews accept his message from angel Gabriel as authentic, and *thereby honor him as an equal to their former prophets of divine revelation.*

The response of the Jews of Medina to a military alliance is unclear in Ishaq's account. Other students of Islam have made the point that there is no record of agreement by the Jewish tribes. Even if there was, it was short lived. The Jewish tribes were not open to the preaching of Muhammad. They ridiculed his calling to be a prophet in their religion. In anger, Muhammad described them as arrogant. When he claimed himself as *Allah's* appointed fulfillment of the futuristic prophecy of Moses recorded in the Torah, they scorned his ignorance: "The Lord your God will raise up for you a prophet like me from among your own brothers. You must listen to him" (Deuteronomy 18:15).

Obviously Muhammad misunderstood the teaching of the laws and the prophets within the religion of Judaism. For the prophecy in which he claimed himself as the fulfillment, it clearly applied to a prophet who was to come from the lineage of Isaac, "your own brother." Formerly Muhammad, rightly or wrongly, had claimed to be from the line of Ishmael, the other son of Abraham. When the Jews rejected his claims as a prophet of God, foretold in the religion of Judaism, Muhammad took the rejection as a personal offense to his honor and credibility, as well as that of *Allah*.

Jews were charged as blasphemers, criminals of distortion, and guilty of the crime to "cover over" (*kafirun*) a futuristic prophecy of Muhammad in the Torah. From nearly the beginning, A.D. 622–625, Ishaq's account consistently portrays the Jews as headstrong unbelievers of Islam. Numerous anecdotal illustrations in the biographical traditions describe them as pompous and misled in the ways of God. The anecdotes reflect surface signs of deep bad blood that existed between Muhammad and the Jews.

For example, Muhammad visited a Jewish school and preached to the students that they should believe in *Allah*. When he was asked about his religion, he told them that he believed in the religion of Abraham. The students informed him that Abraham was a Jew. Muhammad disagreed and told them to bring him a Torah and let that decide. But the Jews refused. The illustration portrays the Jews to the followers of Islam as a people of evil disgrace who even rejected their divine revelation of the Torah.

In another situation, Muhammad went into a Jewish village and threatened them with the wrath of *Allah* if they did not accept the religion of Islam. But the Jews rejected Muhammad's preaching and told him that they preferred to follow the religion of their fathers who were righteous and learned men. Then Muhammad condemned them. He stated that their fathers knew nothing and were not properly guided by *Allah*.

As Muhammad witnessed the collapse of his dreams for the conversions of the Jews, as early as 623, he made another serious transition of principle in Islam. He cancelled two public identifications he had formerly made between Islam and Judaism, honor of the Jewish Sabbath and prostration toward Jerusalem in Muslim prayers (*qibla*). Both of these had been the active practice of Islam until that time and probably served as enticements for the Jews to adapt to the ways of Islam.

Muhammad substituted Friday prayers for Sabbath worship and replaced Jerusalem with Mecca as the *qibla*. The notice of these public formal changes signaled a serious shift in Muhammad's objectives toward the Jews. They clearly became the enemy and a future target of revenue for Islam. Here again, Muhammad used the God of Islam for an official closure to any relationships with the Jews. When the Jews questioned Muhammad about the change of the *qibla*. He responded with words from *Allah*. Muslims, no matter where they dwell, are to turn their faces to the Kaba (Mecca) when they pray.

As Muhammad developed his military skills within the new framework of violence, *Allah's* command to kill, he appeared to gain some significant insight into human nature, in particular, the human fear of death. In his negative engagements with the Jews, he learned their fears. He sensed their willingness to sacrifice anything for life. In the process, he gathered an understanding of the power of death, and, it seems, the power of the fear of death, as a means by which to coerce specific behaviors from not only a person, but a whole community. His insights into the fear of death are reflected in *Allah's* harsh words for the Jews.

> Say, if the future mansion with God be prepared peculiarly for you, exclusive of the rest of mankind, wish for death, if ye say truth. But they

will never wish for it...and thou shall surely find them of all men most covetous of life, even more than the idolaters. One of them would desire his life to be prolonged by a thousand years, but none shall reprieve himself from punishment, that his life may be prolonged: God seeth that which they do. (Koran II (94–96))

Muhammad saw clearly that the ultimate proof of a person's faith was his willingness to die. Whether or not he merely conceptualized that insight or pragmatically used that insight to develop a methodology of terror behavior to convert or to subjugate non-Muslim peoples is unclear. However, his use of terror and threats of terror in his attacks on non-Muslim peoples indicate that he knew the power and effectiveness of the terror of death and terror threats of death on the minds of Muslim and non-Muslim peoples alike. "Say, O ye who follow the Jewish religion, if ye say that ye are the friends of God above other men, wish for death, if ye seek truth...death from which ye fly will surely meet you" (Koran LXII (6–8)).

With the threat of imminent death, a hypocrite could soon be a happy convert. In coordination with these fear/force conversions, *Allah* put in effect a law to prohibit converts to apostatize their new religion: "If they turn back from the faith, take them, and kill them wherever ye find them, and take no friend from among them" (Koran IV (89)). A well-respected commentator in the Muslim world, Baydawi, insists that the execution of apostates is not only legitimate but required according to Koran IV (89).[3]

In 625 the God of Islam led Muhammad to lay siege against the Jews of Banu al-Nadir. He informed Muhammad that the Jews plotted to kill him. Again *Allah* blessed violence. The coercion and intimidation of terror *jihad* against the Jews had begun. Muhammad and his warriors surrounded al-Nadir six nights. Allah terrorized them. Vulnerable, the Jews negotiated to take away as many of their possessions as they could load on their camels and horses. Upon departure, Muhammad divided their fields, houses, groves, and orchards between the suffering migrants who had fled persecution. According to biographer John Glubb, the impoverished Muslims of Mecca were becoming exceedingly wealthy.[4]

In the siege against the Jews of Banu al-Nadir, two significant incidents occurred that may assist us in understanding certain aspects of terror behavior in Islam. The first is the power of rumor. According to Ishaq's account, the justification for the siege was a rumor that the Jews of Banu al-Nadir had attempted to assassinate Muhammad. Rumors of assassinations were common talk among the Muslims of Medina. For example, Ibn Ishaq mentions that Muhammad himself had hired assassins to kill Abu Sufyan, military leader of Mecca.

Today rumors remain a moving power in the world of Islam. For example, when the Muslim preachers fetch rumors about evils of America and circulate them from their pulpit, they inflame Muslim men into acts of violence. Take a story from *Newsweek* magazine, regarding the flushing of a Koran down a toilet at Guantanamo Bay. As the Muslim preachers proclaimed that Americans placed the sacred Koran with human dung, madness erupted, hundreds were wounded, and many died. Later the rumor printed by *Newsweek* proved to be untrue. *Rumors are very effective in the efforts of terrorism to protect, promote, and expand Islam.*

The other significant incident, in the siege of Banu al-Nadir, was the effectiveness of coercive threats that led to the conversion of two Jews. Two Jews professed Islam and were granted the right to retain possession of their property. These conversions were important enough to become a part of oral tradition until Ibn Ishaq recorded them in his biography of Muhammad. These were the first conversions harvested from terror war and did not go unnoticed. They became a regular feature in terror behavior ministry as Islam developed laws that encouraged and protected such converts. Some military *jihads* regularly announced at or before opening exercises, publicly and behind the scenes, that conversion privileges were available to Jews and Christians who were willing to forsake their faiths. Beginning with Banu al-Nadir, the Islamic objective toward Jews (and Christians) was clearly conversion, deportation, or subjugation.

In the very face of the conflict between the Jews and Islam as presented in Ibn Ishaq's account, Western advocates of Islam defiantly argue that the Jews of Medina and the Muslims of Medina functioned as joint forces of *jihad* against common enemies. Imagine that! They deliberately isolate the proposed military alliance prepared by Muhammad, stripping the proposal from its context of threat by Mecca and the Muslim's displacement of the Jews at Banu al-Nadir. They argue that Muslims and Jews cooperated militarily for common protection as if they were a unified people. In their argument, they completely ignore the hostility by Islam toward the Jews for the rejection of Muhammad as a prophet in the tradition of Judaism. They completely ignore the deportation and killings of the Jewish tribes in the vicinity of Medina. Still the great wonder is that American scholars fail to call these Muslim scholars to account for their outrageous manipulations of Ishaq's text. They proceed with these lies under total impunity.

In this case, the Western advocates of Islam have deliberately distorted the historical account of Ibn Ishaq. Yes, Ishaq did record Muhammad's draft of an alliance he planned to offer to the Jews of Medina in 622–623. But it is uncertain as to whether or not the Jews accepted the alliance. Clearly when Muhammad offered his proposed alliance to the Jews, he was in a very desperate situation, fearing military attacks from the Mecca warriors. Contrary to claims by Western advocates of Islam, in the accounts of Ibn Ishaq and Al-Bukhari there are no records of Jews and Muslims fighting sides by side as one (*umma wahida*) in a war (*jihad*) against a common enemy. In fact, according to the earliest sources (Ibn Ishaq), any relationship between the Jews and Islam was completely broken beyond repair within eighteen months after Muhammad's arrival in Medina. For *Western advocates of Islam to seriously misrepresent the biographical tradition to foster a non-existent relationship between Muslims and Jews is disheartening and demoralizing for any Americans searching for the facts about terror behavior in Islam.* The intentional spread of misinformation to the American people ought to raise serious doubts about the message and the messengers.

Muhammad the Antagonist

In the year 627, a rumor spread that the Jews of the Banu Qurayza tribe of Medina had encouraged the Quraysh tribe of Mecca to attack Muhammad. The warriors of Mecca under the command of Sufyan placed Medina under siege. As the days passed, the pact or the rumor of a pact between Mecca and the Jews unraveled and Sufyan and his troops returned home. Upon his departure, Muhammad's army gathered and stored their weapons.

The claim that Muhammad's army gathered and stored their weapons is significant for it demonstrates that the major propagator of terror war against the Jews in Islam was the God of Islam. By way of Gabriel, *Allah* ordered the Muslims to retrieve their weapons and to march against the Jewish tribe of Banu Qurayza. On the streets of Medina, Gabriel, riding his donkey with sword in hand, prophesied that he would make the Jews of Qurayza tremble. The clear message of Ishaq's account is that the God of Islam is the God of terror to non-Muslim peoples, especially Jews and Christians. The army of Muhammad faithfully followed *Allah's* orders to holy war (*jihad*).

After the Muslim warriors rearmed themselves, Ishaq describes in detail Allah's guidance of Muhammad in the terrorist executions of the Qurayza Jews of Medina. After he imprisoned the Jews, he instructed his followers to dig trenches in the marketplace. Then he ordered the Jewish men, in small groups, single file, to march into the marketplace along the trenches, instructing his executors to strike off their heads so that they would fall into the trenches. The total number of executions was somewhere between six and seven hundred. Other Muslim biographers run the count as high as nine hundred.

Muhammad divided the property, women, and children of the Banu Qurayza tribe among the Muslims. He maintained one-fifth for himself. According to the record, the prisoners were sent to Najd to barter them as slaves in exchange for horses and camels in order to strengthen his cavalry for future *jihads*.[5,6]

These killings were not committed in battle, but they were executions of captives for the purpose of coercion. The terror/coercion factor is clearly stated in Islam: "Say unto the unbelievers…if they return to attack thee, the exemplary punishment of the former opposers of the prophet is already past, and the like shall be inflicted on them" (Koran VIII (38)). In the twenty-first century, America has witnessed murders with similar objectives, e.g., that of Daniel Pearle. The effectiveness of Pearle's execution on American journalists is difficult to measure.

Of course some argue that Muhammad's behavior was within the context of a normally violent era. Certainly no antiseptic policies of twenty-first century war (e.g., the Iraq War, a case in which the victor pays the cost to rebuild the defeated nation) were in place in the seventh century. Still the significance of these murders may not be overlooked. They were deliberate. They were executed according to the will of *Allah*, under the supervision of his prophet, to spread intense terror and submission among Jews and Christians of Arabia. The coercive intent of these terror executions is certainly clear from future threats by *Allah* (Koran VIII (38)).

The annihilation of the Banu Qurayza tribe enriched Islam and enabled it toward fiercer confrontations with Jews and eventually Christians. In the year 628, Muhammad gathered his warriors to attack the Jewish tribe of Khaybar, about one hundred miles from Medina. Again, Islam was at war for *Allah*. With *Allah* and war hitched together, war continued to gather a sacramental value in the religion of Islam. "Holy War" in that regard is compared to the "Holy Supper" celebrated by the church, often described as the Lord's Supper. In both cases, "holy" means that "God" is in the mix.

For the Western advocates of Islam to call Muhammad's military attack on Khaybar, one hundred miles from Medina, a defensive war, exhausts the human imagination. The wealth and riches of the Khaybar Valley served as a far more palpable justification for the attack. Furthermore, and not to be ignored, the Jews of Khaybar had previously refused a written invitation from Muhammad to convert to Islam.[7] The terror attack on Khaybar Valley expanded the horizons of war to include attacks on those who had previously received divine scripture (people of the book) in order to enrich Islam with converts and material wealth. In this, another transition, Muhammad again used the sacred hands of Allah to expand the war against the polytheists of Mecca into shedding the blood of Jews and Christians.

Outside the city gates, following his prayer of terror *jihad*, when Muhammad heard no Muslim call to prayer, no sign of conversion coming from the Jews of Khaybar, he attacked, proclaiming *"Allahu Akbar."* Once again war was modeled as a sacred duty, a rite with *Allah*, a holy war. After the conquest, Muhammad divided the booty, taking Safiya, the wife of the Khaybar chief, for his own. He had taken many other wives and slave women since the death of his beloved Khadija. He ordered his men to torture her husband to divulge the location of the treasury and then strike off his head.

At this juncture, the argument by Western prophets of Islam that Islam only fought against the polytheists of Mecca is indefensible. Muhammad and his warriors besieged nearly every Jewish fort through the Hejaz region of Arabia. As students analyze the attack by Islam on the Jews of Khaybar, they must consider two factors that began to be used to justify holy war: (1) the Jews' rejection of Muhammad's call to convert to Islam, and (2) the Jews' rejection of Muhammad's claim to be a legitimate prophet in the religion of Judaism. From this juncture forward, the justification of terror war and the threats of terror war continued. Soon Christian villages were subject to attack as well. Power, paradise, booty, coerced converts, (and eventually the subjugation of unbelievers to the authority of *Allah*) became the driving forces of Islam.

As the terror of Islam spread throughout the region, the lessons of fear learned in Khaybar aided in the development of another major form of terror behavior in Islam, that of subjugation. The word, "subjugation," most accurately described the condition of non-Muslim peoples who submit to the authority of Islam. The Arabic word, which is used to describe the way of life for such people, is *dhimmitude*. When a Jewish or Christian community was unable to face a military *jihad* by Islam or chose peace over war. It could surrender and covenant to live in submission to the supremacy of Islam.

The covenant was called a *dhimma*. The Muslim ruler covenanted to protect the non-Muslim peoples from any non-Muslim military aggression, a promise he could suspend. In turn the non-Muslim community covenanted to acknowledge the supremacy of Islam and to subjugate themselves as an inferior people. With limited religious rights stipulated by Islam, they could retain their religion (but in silence), humbly acknowledge their inferior status, obey

Muslim prohibitions, and pay taxes (*jizya*) imposed by their Muslim conquerors.

The terrified Jews of Khaybar and neighboring Fadak initially proposed this religious, military, and political system of Islamic supremacy, the life of *dhimmitude*. When the Jews of Fadak heard of the violence by Islam in their attack on neighboring Khaybar, they were filled with terror. Unable to defend themselves, they sent delegates to Muhammad with a proposal that he spare their lives, and they, in turn, would forfeit to him their property. Meanwhile, the survivors of Khaybar also requested that they be allowed to remain in their former houses and cultivate the lands, divide the produce fifty percent to themselves and fifty percent to Islam. Muhammad agreed, but made clear that the covenant (*dhimma*) was tentative.

Initially, the terrors of subjugation meant servitude. The shamed victims lost authority to control their possessions, families, and lives. They served Islam on their former property. Fifty percent of their production was used to improve the war machine of Islam, *jizya for jihad*. As the years passed, Muslim scholars developed a system of detailed legalistic degradation, which governed almost every aspect of the subjugated Christian or Jewish victim's life.

In degrees which varied from place to place and from time to time, the Jews and Christians (*dhimmis*) were ordered as to which clothes to wear, which animal to ride, which side of the street to walk on, which direction to face in the presence of a Muslim, which Muslim warrior to board in their homes, where to publicly pay their tax, and how Islam could shame, ridicule, and physically abuse them when the tax collector ordered them to come forward to pay their taxes before a crowd of gloating Muslims. They were forbidden to weep aloud at funerals or gravesides; to speak, act or hold authority over any Muslim person; to have equal defense in court; or to repair their place of worship, even when destroyed by Muslims. All the while they lived at risk of deportation, slavery, and death.[8]

The purpose of abusive subjugation (*dhimmitude*) was to coerce the non-Muslim person to convert to Islam. In Islam, conversion is not difficult. There is no catechism or lengthy preparation. The only requirement is a declaration: "There is no God but Allah and Muhammad is his prophet." Thereafter, the convert is allegedly granted the rights and privileges of his former Islamic supremacists. Conversion to Islam is simple. Muhammad never lost his zeal for the conversion of Jews and Christians to Islam.

Muhammad the Subjugator

In the days of Muhammad (570–632), Christians and Jews were similar in several respects. Both were monotheists, both adhered to the moral law as revealed through Moses, and both laid claim to some of the ancient Scriptures. Otherwise, they were age-old enemies. The early stages of enmity began with the Jewish religious leaders' rejection of Jesus of Nazareth as the Christ, their pursuit of his crucifixion, and the tenacious campaign to purify Judaism by exterminating Christians throughout Jewish enclaves within the Mediterranean basin (Luke and Acts of the Apostles). Jewish persecution of Christians was officially joined by the Roman Emperors as early as Nero and reached its greatest severity empire-wide during the reign of Decius in 250 and again under Diocletian in 290.

With the conversion of Emperor Constantine to Christianity in the year 313, the relationship between Jews and Christians took a dramatic twist. Already as early as 319, the Roman Senate supported tax laws that favored Christianity as the state religion. As the Empire officially embraced Christianity, other political advantages were also exerted, not the least of which was military protection,. Within a generation of Christians, the same sword that had threatened them sheltered them. Consequently, the church grew in numbers and expanded throughout the Empire.

The transition from the persecuted religion to the state religion, however, had innumerable negative ramifications inside and outside the church. Under the influence of some of the secular bishops, the governors of provinces were prodded to use their military to torture and imprison non-orthodox Christians to force change in their beliefs and to force non-Christian peoples to conform to the teachings of the church. Jews suffered more than most. Synagogues were plundered and burned.

The church not only became a persecutor, sporadic outbreaks of which continued into the seventeenth century, but new adherents joined for social, political, and economic advantage. As the years passed, a person became Christian simply by birth within the Empire. When Muhammad began hearing the voice of Gabriel in the year 610, the church appears to have been in serious moral and spiritual decline, vulnerable to the emergent force of Muhammad's consecrated warriors.

Several other factors exposed Christian communities to the military success of Islam. Nominal adherents easily converted to Islam as they had easily converted to Christianity. The non-orthodox Christians were probably more than open to military protection by Islam, with the hope that a new protector would provide them with greater kindness and safety. They had suffered severely under loathsome collusions between the Church and the Empire. Probably the worst possible circumstance for the church at that time, 500–650, was the crumbling of the Empire, allowing the orthodox and non-orthodox churches of the south and west to stand defenseless before the terror *jihad* of Islam.

In the Ibn Ishaq account, demeaning anecdotes inflamed Muslim animosity toward Christians, illustrating them as hypocrites, liars, and lovers of money and prestige. For example, a story is told that fourteen Christians from Najran came to visit Muhammad. The leader, Bishop Abu Haritha, supposedly professed that Muhammad was a legitimate prophet within the Christian religion. Nonetheless, he rejected Muhammad as a genuine prophet because it would have cost him his position of power, cultural refinements, and a life of luxury.

As the story was told, even the best Christians were portrayed as liars and hypocrites because they chose social and material gain over what they allegedly knew in their hearts as truth. In the choice of the good life, Islam viewed them as unworthy creatures, enemies of divine values, and duplicitous of character in their rejection of the calling of Muhammad. According to *Allah*, Christians knew from their own divine revelation that Muhammad was a legitimate prophet in the Christian religion. He was the "Counselor" foretold by Jesus Christ in the Gospels: "And I (Jesus) will ask the Father, and he will give you another Counselor to be with you forever—the Spirit of truth" (John 14:16).

In addition, Muhammad, in his zeal to protect the unity and absolute oneness of God, condemned Christians for their confession of God as Trinity and for their confession of the deity of Jesus Christ as a person of the Godhead. He prophesied that Christianity was broken and needed repair by Islam. He warned that future hell and other evils were incumbent on Christians because of their blasphemous pluralistic views of God. His God, *Allah*, also enjoined them.

In his condemnation of Christianity, Muhammad cut away the very heart of the Christian faith. According to the Ishaq account, he never seemed to grasp any significance of redemption through vicarious atonement of the cross and the life of Christ. In fact he eventually rejected that Jesus was even crucified. He saw the cross as an idolatrous object of worship. At one point he associates the evil of the cross with the evil of eating pig meat. He never seemed to understand the power of sin, as taught in the Christian tradition, and its control of the human mind: "everyone who sins is a slave to sin" (John 8:34). So, he never really comprehended the need for human redemption: "If the Son sets you free, you will be free indeed" (John 8:36).

Muhammad and his followers came to understand redemption as the divinely assigned duty to rescue the lands, possessions, and children of Christian and Jewish peoples, the *dar al-harb,* in order to restore them to the *dar al-Islam,* the territory of the Creator, *Allah,* the land of Islam. That is not to say that Muhammad failed to understand sin as disobedience to the will of *Allah.* In his practical, fix-it style, he saw obedience to the law as the great objective of the Muslim life. Furthermore, *Allah* led Muhammad to believe that obedience could be obtained by imposing more severe violent penalties for disobedience, e.g., stoning to death for adultery and physical disfigurement for less severe crimes.

Before Muhammad attacked Christian communities, he enriched his military purse by raids on caravans and Jewish settlements. When he attained sufficient military strength, he made a final and victorious attack on the polytheists of Mecca (630). He met with small resistance, probably due to his two former tactical incentives: (1) changing the *qibla* of Islam from Jerusalem to Mecca and (2) requiring Muslims to visit the Kaba in the vicinity of Mecca, the place of idol worship for his ancestors. Both tactics had proven to be a boon to the economy of Mecca as Islam increased in numbers.

After the defeat of the polytheists of Mecca, Muhammad used his new wealth from the Jews and polytheists to bribe his former enemies to join Islam. For example, he returned members of Malik's family that he held in hostage and gifted him one hundred camels to convince Malik to convert to Islam. He also gave one hundred camels to Abu Sufyan, the former commander of the Meccan warriors. The Ibn Ishaq account stated that Muhammad provided the bribes to make them good Muslims.

With his newly converted allies, Muhammad was ready to attack Christian communities several hundred miles from Medina. In September and October of the year 630, he began his broadest effort to expand Islam by way of terror war (*jihad*) and terror subjugation (*dhimmitude*). Christian communities mostly stood defenseless before Muhammad with the ongoing collapse of the Byzantine (Eastern Roman) Empire. When he and his warriors arrived at the Christian city of Tabuk, the only realistic alternative for Tabuk was to surrender and to pay the subjugation tax, *jizya*. A covenant (*dhimma*) was drafted and the Christians of Tabuk formerly humbled themselves to live as inferiors (*dhimmitude*) to the followers of Islam.

Muhammad sent Khalid, former warrior of the polytheists of Mecca and now a good Muslim, to arrest the Christian leader, Ukaydir, at Duma. He took him by surprise and brought him to the prophet, who spared his life when he promised to submit to Islam by paying the subjugation tax, *jizya*. Several years later, Khalid returned and murdered Ukaydir.

Life under the covenant of subjugation (*dhimmitude*) to Islam was punitive and volatile. Deportation was always the option of the local spiritual leader. The subjugation tax, *jizya*, was unfixed and subject to erratic changes, which at times meant poverty for women and children. Upon failure to pay the tax, family members were frequently taken and sold into slavery. There were also unregulated taxes imposed by nomadic Muslims who journeyed from place to place feeding themselves on the small resources of defenseless non-Muslim peoples.

When a charge was filed against a non-Muslim person for a crime, such as blasphemy against Allah, he was not permitted to defend himself against his Muslim accuser in court and was subject to execution. Christian and Jewish leaders were imprisoned to collect additional funds from the community. A *Dhimmi* life under the authority of Islam was terrifying. A simple accusation could mean the sentence of death, without recourse. A life of *dhimmitude* was filled with terror.[9]

When Muhammad surprised the Christians in the defenseless cities of Tabuk and Duma, they immediately surrendered and covenanted to pay the subjugation tax (the *jizya*), an acknowledgement of the supremacy of Islam. *Muhammad became the model subjugator of Christians as well as the model antagonist.* Incredibly, Western Muslim scholars ignore these initial terror *jihads* against Christians and Jewish communities. Of course they try to do the same with Islam's thousand years of terror behavior against Europe, beginning in the seventh century by attacking Spain and ending with the Turks' defeat at Vienna in 1683.

In fact the Muslim scholars go to such an extreme that they argue Christian soldiers fought side by side with Muslim soldiers in *jihads* against common enemies. Ironically, in their fictitious account they name the Christian soldiers as Armenians, the very people they later attempted to genocide between 1885–1915. Imagine that!

As evidence for their claim, the Muslim scholars say that a Muslim commander offered to the Armenians the opportunity to provide soldiers as mercenaries in place of the gold payments to Islam. The whole argument is worse than hyperbole. Either form of *jizya* payment, gold or mercenaries, symbolized subjugation to Islam. More importantly, why were Muslim forces already in Christian Armenia in the year 642, ten years after the death of Muhammad? The answer is that they were following the model of subjugation set by Muhammad. He led Islam three hundred miles from Medina to attack Christian Tabuk, and his emulators led Islam eleven hundred miles from Arabia to attack Christian Armenia, and on and on and on they marched. The incident powerfully declares that terror war (*jihad*) and terror subjugation (*dhimmitude*) in Islam were real and horrific tragedies.

After the covenant of subjugation (*dhimma*) in 642, the Christians of Armenia were not free to live their lives. They were controlled by subjugation terror behavior so that Islam could feed on their resources, produce, cattle, gold, wives, and children. In the year 704, a commander of the Islamic army gathered Armenian leaders into a cathedral in Naxcawan and a church on Araxes, locked the doors, and burned them all alive. That very form of terror *jihad* (burning Christians alive in churches) continues today as recent as March 2004 in Yelwa, Nigeria. Because I was in Nigeria at the time, I was able to obtain a videotape of the devastation of Yelwa and the villages on the plateau.

Are these not acts of terror behavior (terrorism) to excite fear and manipulate behavior? Imagine locking people into churches and then burning them alive. Why? The Armenian Christians resisted Muslim domination of their lands, cattle, wives, and children. The Armenians always fought back. The persistent fighting against Islam by the Armenian people is the reason the Muslim Sultan of the Ottomans finally decided, after twelve hundred fifty years, that the only way to deal with Armenians was simply to kill all of them (genocide). Now imagine this: After all those years of terror behavior against Armenia and the resistance of Armenians, a western Muslim scholar actually publishes an essay to Americans that Armenians and Muslims fought side by side in *jihad* against a common enemy. Want more? To know Americans who believe it.

Summary

The life of Muhammad written by Ibn Ishaq in the mid-eighth century remains one of the major sources of credible information about Islam and its prophet within the Muslim world. Other sources, recorded at later dates, have tended to build and expand on the Ishaq account. Obviously Ishaq's biographical materials do not meet critical standards of the twenty-first century. Nonetheless, his presentation of Muhammad has become the cornerstone for Muslim understanding of Islam's teachings and is deeply embedded within their culture. Hopefully my review enables us, as non-Muslim people of America, to view the life of Muhammad as Muslims view him, and also enables us to identify faithful followers of Islam who emulate his behavior models in our world today.

At the beginning of my review, I made note that the imperialistic reach of Islam was slowly but surely interrupted by Western military occupations (of Islamic regions) following the collapse of the Ottoman Empire. But once these regions regained their independence, the world began to witness the return of terror behavior reminiscent of the Muslim past. *As acts of terrorism continue to erupt around the world today, Islamic fundamentalists eagerly, boldly, and proudly state that terror jihad is a basic principle of Islam necessary for its development, preservation, and expansion. Clearly the Ishaq descriptions of terror behavior models practiced by Muhammad support that claim.*

In contrast, Western advocates of Islam declare that true Islam is a religion of tolerance and peace. *Initially the Ishaq account supports that claim, but when Allah permitted Muhammad to kill his enemies, terror behavior gradually became a significant factor in the development, preservation, and expansion of Islam. In the writings of Ishaq, there is no record of any abrogation on the teachings of terror violence.* In direct opposition to that view, Ishaq describes a gradual escalation of violence by Muhammad, reaching a crescendo at the time of his death. The reader can easily identify the significant transitions, the pacifist, the defender, the protector, the antagonist, and the subjugator.

Western advocates of Islam need to honestly look, and look again, at the raw terror behavior in the beheadings of captive Jews in Benu Qurayza. They need to look again at the attack and subjugation of Jews in Khaybar and Fadak and Christians in Tabuk and Duma. Western advocates of Islam deliberately mislead America when they state that the expansion of Islam was similar to the expansion of Christianity, i.e., through the non-violence of peace through the message of Jesus Christ (Matthew 28:18–20).

When facing the hard realities presented by Ibn Ishaq, such statements by Western advocates of Islam are unconscionable. Let them responsibly explain the specific escalations of violence in the life of the prophet. Let them explain the perpetration of that same policy of terror behavior by the caliphs who led Islam after the death of Muhammad, the executions and subjugations of Jews and Christians throughout the Middle East, Africa, and southern and western Europe. The West is confused about terror behavior in Islam, understandably so in the shadows of a methodology of misinformation persistently perpetrated by Western advocates of Islam.

Western Muslim scholars insult the intelligence of non-Muslim peoples in America by saying that Muhammad expanded Islam through non-violence. Think about it. *How did the so-called policy of non-violence work? It began with a terror threat by the warriors of Islam at the outskirts of the city. If the Jewish or Christian city fought the warriors of Islam, it was terribly violent, as in the case of Khaybar. If under the Islamic threat, Jews or Christians subjugated to the supremacy of Islam, as in the case of Tabuk, how is that a history that Western advocates of Islam want to crow about? More importantly, if they surrendered to the authority of Islam without a battle under the coercion of military jihad, how can that be seen as non-violent, especially as one begins to grasp the consequences of terror subjugation, a life of dhimmitude?*

Why do Western advocates of Islam brag about forcing Jews and Christians to live under dehumanizing, demeaning, and demoralizing subjugation? Why do they call dhimmitude a policy of non-violence?

Ibn Ishaq's biography of Muhammad fails to support Islam as a religion of peace and tolerance. In fact Ishaq's descriptions of terror behaviors raise some serious questions about the moral character of some of the Western advocates of Islam and challenges those of us from America as to whether we can conscientiously and confidently join them in their defense of Islam.

Ishaq's biography pushes us forward to examine the Koran. Does terror war (*jihad*) in the life of Muhammad comport with teachings of terror war in the Koran? What about terror subjugation (*dhimmitude*)? What are the current attitudes and behaviors of Muslims toward non-Muslim peoples who are trapped within their neighborhoods in Nigeria, Sudan, Egypt, Zamboanga in the Philippines, and elsewhere? When we journey into these neighborhoods, the very heartland of Islam, what will we witness? Will we observe a culture of terror war (*jihad*) and terror subjugation (*dhimmitude*) still faithful to the biographical traditions of the seventh century, or a policy of non-violence? But first, what are the teachings of terror war (*jihad*) and terror subjugation (*dhimmitude*) in the Koran?

CHAPTER THREE

Journeys into the Heart of Islam
The Holy Koran

Muslims generally view the Koran as a flawless record of Allah's sayings to his prophet Muhammad. According to Islam, angel Gabriel functioned as an intermediary to communicate each message, word for word, to the prophet. When Muhammad heard these messages, he committed them to memory, shared them with others, and later, by way of scribes, they were recorded into a book called the Koran. Today the Koran is considered the ultimate authority in the religion of Islam.

The simplicity of the Koran makes for easy understanding. In contrast to the Bible, the Koran claims only one messenger, Muhammad, who received all of his messages within the short time frame of twenty-two consecutive years, A.D. 610–632. The Bible on the other hand, claims a host of inspired messengers stretched out over hundreds of years. Similarly the simple verbatim dictation theory employed by most Muslim scholars to explain the words of the Koran is far less complex than the inspirational theory of biblical writers in the Judeo-Christian tradition.

In fact the Koran does describe itself as a "perspicuous" book, (Koran V (17)). The English word, "perspicuous," is a translation of the Arabic word, *mubin*. The idea is that the message is "plain and clear." In other words, imams, ayatollahs, and other privileged adherents of Islam are not necessary for a reader to understand the words of *Allah* recorded in the Koran.[1]

Although the Koran describes itself as perspicuous, it is imperative (already declared in eleventh century *hadiths*) that readers connect the messages to the appropriate corresponding events. Because the messages are not presented in chronological order in the Koran, the accurate dating of word with event does become a more difficult task. Certainly a prior perusal of the biographical traditions can assist readers in identifying messages with appropriate events. In my review of terror teachings in the Koran, I primarily rely on chronological designations provided for each chapter (*sura*) by renowned translator and commentator, the late Abdullah Yusuf Ali. As is the case in understanding any text, particularly ancient text, accurate dating contributes to the clearest possible interpretation and application of the message.

The other interpretation principle, not unique to Islam but significant, is called abrogation, or cancellation. The abrogation of a text applies when two texts of a common source are in apparent contradiction to one another. *The principle is that the latter text overrules the earlier text.* For example, an ancient biblical writing commands retaliation for an injured party, "...an eye for any eye and a tooth for a tooth, hand for hand..." (Exodus 21:24). But in contradiction, Jesus says, "But I tell you, do not resist an evil person. If someone strikes you on the right cheek, turn to him the other also" (Matthew 5:38). Abrogation means that the latter text of Matthew overrules the earlier text of Exodus. So the New Testament message of Jesus abrogates the Old Testament instruction of Moses.

In my brief review of terror teachings in the Koran, evaluations are separated into two sections. In the first, I identify and review texts that teach terror war (jihad)—i.e. threats to fight, kill, maim, or harm—and thereby coerce non-Muslim peoples to honor Islam as the religion of truth. In the second section, I identify texts that teach and encourage terror subjugation (*dhimmitude*) of non-Muslim peoples, i.e. to dehumanize them as inferior creatures so as to provide license for Muslims to exercise bigoted forms of violence to coerce them to abandon their faiths or conform to a life of inferior status within the culture of Islam as prescribed for them by the Islamic holy law.

Section One
Terror Behavior Jihad and Non-Muslim Peoples

Koran

Jihad is currently a hot topic in our Western world. It is one of the few Arabic words in our daily conversations. But do we understand the meaning of *jihad*? A literal translation of the word *jihad* is "striving in the path of God." Western advocates of Islam often teach America that *jihad* means the personal strivings of Muslims against evil while on their spiritual journeys. Christians of the West easily adapt to that explanation by simple association with the teachings of the Apostle Paul who calls them to fight against the evil practices of a sinful world: "Do not conform any longer to the pattern of this world but be transformed by the renewing of your mind" (Romans 12:2). The Christian life is a battle then against sin and evil. But is that an honest explanation of *jihad* in Islam?

How does the Koran describe *jihad*? Is it more than spiritual warfare? Is it also a physical warfare, fighting, killing, beheading, and crippling of so-called evil, unbelieving persons? From a historical point of view, Bernard Lewis writes that the "overwhelming majority" of ancient authorities address *jihad* in "military terms."[2] Likewise the Koran teaches that *jihad* means physical warfare against a physical enemy. It states that *jihad* is meant to be a significant military feature of Islam until the end of time. Its purpose is to subjugate the lands of unbelievers, the *dar al-harb,* under the authority of *Allah* as redeemed lands of Islam, the *dar al-Islam.* For a thousand years, militant *jihad* faithfully and successfully conquered large segments of the *dar al-harb,* stretching across north and central Africa, the Middle East, and Asia, along with strong enclaves in Eastern Europe and Russia. In 1683 the military force of the Hapsburgs finally crushed the *jihad* threatening Austria and central Europe. Much to the horror of devout Muslims, Christian Europe began to occupy and exert authority over the *dar al-Islam.*

Although Western advocates of Islam continue to describe *jihad* as spiritual warfare against evil, the Koran teaches that the purpose of *jihad* is also to conquer the unbelievers. At the tenth anniversary of the Iranian Revolution, 1989, the Ayatollah Morteza Mutahhari addressed the Muslim nation of Iran to affirm the necessity of *jihad* in order to fulfill the ambitious calling of *Allah* that Islam rule the world. In his anniversary address, he dismissed Christianity as a religion with no real purpose other than that of moralizing nice behavior. As such, he declared that Christians have no understanding or use for *jihad.* On the basis of Koran IX (29), Mutahhari challenged the Muslims of the world that *Allah* instructs them to organize an Islamic state! *Allah* instructs them to reform the world! For that purpose *jihad* is absolutely necessary.[3]

When we as Americans hear speeches by religious leaders such as Mutahhari and observe militant behavior by nations of Islam across the world, it becomes difficult to believe the words of Western Muslim scholars when they say *jihad* only means fighting a spiritual conflict. It also raises the question why we as Americans so quickly reject what we hear with our ears and see with our eyes to favor abstract words of tolerance and peace? Even more troubling, why do we encourage our grammar schools, colleges, churches, and libraries to invite Muslim missionaries (*dawa*) to share this very questionable information with our children? For a more accurate view, America could far better learn the legitimacy of terror *jihad* in Islam by reading the perspicuous Koran. It is far more trustworthy than the Western advocates of Islam.

Terror Behavior Jihad Protects Sacred Rites

Koran

According to Ibn Isahq's biography of Muhammad, violent forms of *jihad* began in Islam as a defensive behavior against the polytheists of Mecca. *Allah* approved the violence, granting Muhammad permission to fight and kill in order to protect and prosecute Islam as a viable religion: "Fight for the religion of God against those who fight you…kill (slay) them wherever ye find them…for temptation to idolatry is more grievous than slaughter. Yet fight not against them in the holy temple (mosque), until they attack you therein, but if they attack (fight) you, slay them. This shall be the reward of the infidels (or the persecutors who suppress the faith" (Koran II (190, 191)).

The text clearly illustrates violence as a legitimate feature in the religion of Islam. The words "kill," "slaughter," and "slay" permit no other reasonable understanding. The text also clearly states that the injunctions to fight the persecutors of Islam are from *Allah*. Under the circumstances, theses initial orders of *Allah* to "kill," "slaughter," and "slay" were obviously defensive in nature: "Permission is granted unto those who take arms against the unbelievers, for they have been unjustly persecuted by them…" (Koran XXII (39)).

In addition to the words used by *Allah* to describe defensive war as legitimate violence, physical *jihad*, a key factor in understanding Koran II (191) is to understand that the greatest evil of the persecuting polytheists is that they suppress faith. The actual objects of Islamic *jihad* (slaying, slaughtering, and killing) are the enemies who suppress the Islamic faith. Commentator Yusuf Ali describes the appropriate response by Islam to suppressors of faith when he teaches that if and when unbelievers obstruct the sacred rites of Muslims, it is an act of war on Islam. Therefore, it is the religious duty of Muslims to fight and destroy (slay, slaughter, kill) such despicable forms of oppression.[4]

The word "suppress," as well as Ali's commentary on the persecutors of faith, ought not slip away unnoted by those of us from the West. We are under a constant barrage of promotional rhetoric about *jihad only on defense* (only when attacked does Islam fight back), but we better take note that if any peoples suppress the faith or the practice of sacred rites, then in such cases terror *jihad* is considered defensive and a legitimate response, the duty of Islam. How does that work in America?

As Americans we must acknowledge the stark contrast between the freedoms of our secular culture to offend sacred rites and the prohibitions to offend sacred rites within the culture of Islam. When and if Americans exercise the freedoms of their secular culture to suppress the sacred rites of Islam, to Muslims that may be the same as a declaration of war, and as such it may verify within the minds of Muslims that Islamic *jihad* is an appropriate, legitimate, defensive reaction. Do we understand that? Do we understand how complex, subjective, diverse, and volatile are *fatwas* from within the culture of Islam for defensive *jihad* reaction against non-Muslim peoples?

Allah speaks to the suppression of a specific sacred rite of Islam, "fight not against them in the holy temple (the Kaba)" in Koran II (191). But Yusuf Ali expands that specific to include more than one sacred rite. He speaks of it in the plural, "sacred rites." So what are these sacred rites that unbelievers may suppress and thereby solicit the response of terror *jihad*? Certainly the five sacred pillars of Islam are considered sacred rites: confession, prayer, almsgiving, the fast of Ramadan, and the pilgrimage to Mecca. Sacred rites may also include other local religious holy days, cleansings, and cultural behaviors of Islam. That aside, even if sacred rites are limited to the aforementioned five sacred pillars, Islam may judge any obstruction to the performance of these rites as a suppression of faith.

That raises serious questions for us in America as to how our lawful separation between religion and state is to function with regard to the sacred rites of Islam. In our schools, for example, will we suppress the faith of Muslim children as we suppress the faith of Christian, Jewish, and Hindu children? When we hear the Muslim call to prayer, will we allow them to prostrate on the floors of our classrooms? Will we excuse them from class, or will we ignore the call? In our state-controlled setting, sacred rites are impermissible for religions. Even religious celebrations of Christmas and Thanksgiving are no longer legally legitimate within our public schools (other public institutions). In this setting, will we prohibit Muslim children and teachers from making confession and prayers in our schools, or will we allow them? Will we feel coerced to allow some religions to be more public in their sacred behaviors than others?

How effective will *jihad* or the threat of *jihad* be on the legal prohibitions of religion (spirituality) for children in public education for frightened people who desire peace more than equality and freedom? How will our leaders function as potential objects of slaying, slaughtering, and killing? Will they be guilty of prohibiting the prayers and/or cleansings of innocent children? Our political and religious leaders surely see this coming.

How proactive are our congresspersons in these matters with regard to immigration? If we maintain our policy of separation between religion and state, then who becomes the object of *jihad* for suppressing sacred rites? Will we simply allow Islam to burn churches and synagogues as a defensive, legitimate response, as they do in other regions of the world? What if the Muslim majority of a community in which sacred rites are suppressed votes by ballot to impose Islamic cleansings and prayers for their (or all) children in the public schools? In other words, they choose to follow Islamic *sharia* law as opposed to the Federal law of the United States of America. Got war? Who is willing to fight this war, in light of the fact that peace is the answer?

In America public education has become the responsibility of the state, and it is the duty of the state to enforce lawful prohibitions of sacred rites. However, in the culture and politics of Islam, the exact opposite is true. Promotion of sacred rites in public education is the lawful duty of the state. The two legal systems are exactly opposite, and when put together, they are on a collision course. If we suppress the sacred rites of Muslim children, ought we become objects of legitimate, defensive *jihad*? Is that the reason why the city of Minneapolis has built religious cleansing centers in publicly supported schools for Muslim children, but no worship centers for Christian and Jewish children? Is this a precedent for the nation?

Take another example, the Muslim call to prayer. For a clear understanding, the words described by Islam as "the call to prayer" are in fact more than a call to prayer. They are also a confession of faith. The words in the English language are, "There is one God, and his messenger is Muhammad." The confession serves a threefold purpose: (1) *it is a solicitation to others to believe in Islam,* (2) *it is a confession of faith in Islam, and* (3) *it is a call to prayer for Islam.* Certainly, this pillar of Islam is a sacred rite in the religion of Islam. For those who have not lived in the Muslim world, the call of prayer is terribly loud and obnoxious, three to five times per day beginning at sunrise and ending at sunset. Hopefully some Americans may object to having the religion of *Islam* rammed down their and their children's throats on a daily basis. Some of the open-minded people committed to the "whatever" creed could even view it as exceedingly offensive.

What if in our American politics we decide that we do not want public solicitations and confession of Islam three to five times every day? In the process, do we suppress the sacred rite of prayer? Will we permit the noisy, proselytizing call to prayer, but forbid the ringing of church bells? If New York City decides to suppress the calls to prayer from Arabic minarets on Times Square, then who in Islam may issue a defensive *fatwa* to "slay, slaughter, and fight"? Of course with the diversity of authority in Islam, almost any *imam* from anywhere in the world can issue a *fatwa* to *jihad*. In Islam *jihad* protects sacred rites and is considered legitimate defensive warfare (Koran II (190–1)).

Terror Behavior Jihad For Oppressors

Koran

The initial orders of Koran II (190–1) to fight against the persecutors from Mecca commenced officially at the battle of Badr, March 624. The God of Islam, through his prophet, commanded his believers to *jihad* against the polytheists of Mecca. At this battle, Islam, in spite of smaller numbers of warriors and camels, gained an amazing victory. In association with this particular battle, the central interest of our review is the instruction to the warrior, *mujahidun*, of Islam to commit terror war against non-Muslim peoples. For that purpose, it is important to observe the specific texts dated at the battle of Badr.

1. Say to the unbelievers, that if they desist from opposing you (from their unbelief), what is already past shall be forgiven them, but if they return to attack thee, the exemplary punishment of the former opposers of the prophets is already past, and the like shall be inflicted on

them. Therefore fight against them until there is no opposition in favor of idolatry, and the religion be wholly God's. (Koran VIII (38,39))

2. Therefore prepare against them what force you are able, what troops of horse, whereby ye may strike a terror into the enemy of God, your enemy, and into other infidels besides them, whom ye know not, but God knoweth them. And whatsoever ye shall expend in the defense of the religion of God, it shall be repaid unto you, and ye shall not be treated unjustly. And if they incline unto peace, do thou also incline therto... (Koran VIII (60,61))

3. Also when thy Lord spake unto the angels, saying "Verily I am with you; wherefore confirm those who believe. I will cast a dread (terror) into the hearts of unbelievers. Therefore strike off their heads. And strike off all the ends of their fingers. (Koran VIII (12))

In these texts of the Koran, one can see the community of Medina beginning to function as a small theocratic city-state. *Allah* and his prophet command the militia to *jihad* against the persecutors of Islam: "Strike a terror into the enemy of God..." (Koran VIII (60)). Here the critical word, *terror*, is a modifier used by *Allah* to further define *jihad*. In this context, terror *jihad* (war) was a response against the immediate threat to Islam, the polytheists of Mecca (*mushrikun*). It is important in one's effort to understand terror *jihad* to observe that in the middle of striking terror into the enemies of *Allah*, there is a peculiar offer of peace. Strangely enough, it seems to be peace in the context of terror: "If they incline unto peace, do thou also incline thereto..." (Koran VIII (61)).

However, with the persistent promotion that Islam is a religion of peace, it is important to see that the peace option proposed to non-Muslim people in Koran VIII (61) is not offered as a peace between equals. It is a peace offering that enfolds a special provision that entails conversion by the polytheists. The idea is similar to the previously quoted text, "Say to the unbelievers, if they desist from opposing you (from unbelief), what is already past shall be forgiven them" (Koran VIII (38)). Clearly the text says that the opposition is not the opposition rooted in warfare, but it is the opposition rooted in idolatry. From what are the unbelievers then to desist? Read the text. It says, "favor of idolatry." So the option of peace for the enemy of Islam is "fight against them until there is no opposition in favor of idolatry." So peace is offered to the polytheists if they reject their unbelief (favor of idolatry) in Islam.

At the very beginning, terror *jihad* was used to coerce terror-stricken polytheists to desist from unbelief (Koran VIII (38)), which in turn obviously meant belief in Islam, a QUID PRO QUO. These two elements of *jihad*, terror and belief, partner with each other in the expansion of Islam. To his warrior for the faith, *mujahidun*, the God of Islam promises the booty of plunder, but more important than appropriating other peoples' wealth, *Allah* says "fight…for truth and faith" (Koran C. (92)). Indeed the followers of Islam are instructed to *jihad* for faith. Faith is the most honored human quality in the religion of Islam. Terror *jihad* protects the faith and also produces faith in the hearts of former unbelievers. Terror *jihad* is justified as a legitimate means by which *the faith in Islam is defended*, but it is equally and arguably also justified as a means by which *faith in Islam is coerced* from terror-stricken, non-Muslim peoples; *"fight for truth and faith."*

Western advocates of Islam claim that terror *jihad* has no legitimate place in true Islam and that Islamic fundamentalists are the sponsors of terrorism. True Islam, they say, is a religion of submission to God and tolerance toward others. However, anyone can ready the Koran injunctions of terror *jihad*. *Allah* commanded his warriors to strike terror in the hearts of unbe-lievers. In fact, he himself says, "I will cast a dread (terror) into the hearts of unbelievers" (Koran VIII (12)). Western advo-cates of Islam try to dismiss these orders with the claim that they are limited actions of terror *jihad* that were only effective in defensive actions against the polytheists of Mecca, no other non-Muslim peoples.

It is true that terror war was initially defensive against the polytheists of Mecca. But terror *jihad* was in no way authori-tatively limited to the polytheists. In the Koran there is no abrogation, no stated exclusion for the use of terror *jihad* (ter-rorism) against other non-Muslim peoples, including Christians and Jews. In fact *Allah*, in the above quoted text, reveals a far broader idea of his enemies than those known by Muhammad when he says "...strike terror into the enemy of God, your enemy, and into infidels besides them, whom ye know not, but God knoweth them" (Koran VIII (60)). Here *Allah's* words imply that terror *jihad* addresses another regi-ment of non-Muslim peoples, "infidels besides them," these injunctions to strike terror in the hearts of non-Muslim peo-ples were never abrogated! If so, where? They continue to serve the purpose of prosecuting the expansion of faith in Islam by coercion.

Muhammad finally defeated the polytheists of Mecca in January 630. If the claim by Western advocates of Islam is true that Islam only warred against the polytheists of Mecca, then the defeat of the polytheists ended the reign of terror *jihad* by Islam. That obviously did not occur. In fact, to the contrary. The defeated leaders of the polytheists were blackmailed and then bribed by Muhammad to become good Muslims. They then joined him to threaten terror *jihad* against Christians in the defenseless cities of Tabuk and Duma, three hundred and fifty miles from Medina.

Terror Behavior Jihad Against All Unbelievers
Koran

Terror *jihad* is viewed by Islam as a legitimate defensive retaliation against any form of opposition. In other words, a declaration (*fatwa*) of war (*jihad*) is not limited to retaliations against a military assault, but may also be declared against rhetorical aggression, acts of "proselytization," suppressions of sacred rites, or any perceived criticism of Islam, even drawing cartoons of prophet Muhammad. *Jihad* may be declared to quash heretical teachings, as for example the terror *jihad* against African Muslims in Darfur. Terror *jihad* is a legitimate means to defend and protect Islam against a variety of threats. In essence, defensive terror *jihad* is legitimately posted against anyone or anything considered a threat to Islam, be it political, military, economic, educational, or religious. In one of *Allah's* last messages in the Koran, he did not limit terror *jihad*, but clearly stated that *jihad* is against all who reject the authenticity (truth) of the religion of Islam.

> Fight against them who believe not in God, nor the last day, and forbid not that which God and his Apostle have forbidden, and profess not the true religion, (including) those unto whom the Scriptures have been delivered (Jews and Christians), until they pay tribute (*jizya*) by the right of subjection (willing submission), and they be reduced low (feeling subdued). (Koran IX (29).

With the recording of theses words in the Koran, there exists no defensible argument that terror jihad by Islam was restricted to he polytheists of Mecca. This text declares *jihad* against all non-Muslim peoples. It is a declaration of the great divide between the world of Islam, *dar al-Islam*, and the world of war, *dar al-harb.* This declaration of war against the rest of the world is not a declaration by fundamentalists. But by the God of Islam. It is recorded as the final word of Allah in the ultimate authority of Islam, the Koran.

Contrary to the Western advocates of Islam, the declaration of war against the *dar al-harb* (Koran IX (29)) also includes Jews and Christians, people of "the Scriptures." Read the text! Why must Islam fight Jews and Christians? Because they reject Islam as "the religion of truth." They are unbelievers, the *kafirun.* They reject the teaching of the divine scriptures that in the mind of Muhammad prophesied his coming (Deuteronomy 15:18 and John 15:26). Therefore, they must convert or legitimately and necessarily be subjugated, by force if required, to live as inferior creatures under the supremacy of Islam, a life of *dhimmitude* under the authority of *Allah.*

The fact that these instructions of Koran IX (29) apply to Jews and Christians is also clarified by the broader context: (1) *Allah* condemns Jews and Christians, "The Jews say Ezra is the son of God and Christians say Christ is the son of God...God's curse be on them" (Koran IX (30)); (2) *Allah* rejects Christians and Jews and calls them equals of the polytheists (*mushrikun*). "...They take their priests and monks for their lords, beside God, and Christ the son of Mary" (Koran IX (31)); (3) *Allah* describes Christians as thieves whose wealth will produce the fire of hell, and that hell will be on their heads, backs, and legs, (Koran IX (35)). *In the closing words of the Koran, all non-Muslim peoples are at risk from terror jihad and terror subjugation.* The Koran is perspicuous. I can read the clear messages of terror *jihad* in the Koran and *so can anyone else.*

Section Two

Terror Subjugation of Non-Muslim Peoples
Koran

As we engage the subject of terror behavior, we may begin to believe that terror war (*jihad*) is the great negative within the religion of Islam. But is that really true? Or may, in fact, the same principles that drive a terror war policy, *jihad*, against non-Muslim peoples also be used for a *terror subjugation policy, dhimmitude,* in order to accentuate and exhibit the inferior character of conquered non-Muslim peoples, especially Jews, Christians, and their religions? What are the policy and the practice of Islam with regard to the supervision of subjugated peoples?

Bernard Lewis stated that *dhimmis*, Christians and Jews in subjugation to Islam, were portrayed as inferior human beings, a condition maintained and perpetrated by Muslim law as well as culture. *Dhimmi* dress, places of worship, means of transportation, and marriage were all rigidly regulated. *Dhimmis* were viewed as so untrustworthy, so unreliable, that they were not permitted to testify in Islamic courts. When in public, they were required to wear distinctive marks on their clothing to warn others around them of their defects.[5]

Precisely how does the Koran instruct the people of Islam to view Christians and Jews? Are they taught to love them like their own, as did Jesus Christ in the parable of the Good Samaritan (Luke 10:25–37)? Are they taught the Golden Rule? What are the instructions of the Koran regarding Muslim behavior toward Jews and Christians who live within the culture and authority of Islam? Have those instructions been abrogated or perpetuated in the culture, religion, and politics of Islam?

How did the concept of terror subjugation become a part of the teachings of the Koran and the culture of Islam? We know that *terror behavior* was introduced to Islam by the God of Islam and was initially aimed at the polytheists of Mecca. *Allah* commanded Muhammad, "... prepare against them what force you are able, what troops of horse, whereby ye may strike terror into (the hearts of) the enemy of God..." (Koran VIII (60,61)). Earlier *Allah* had endorsed the coercive use of fear when he testified, "I will cast dread (terror) into the hearts of unbelievers. Therefore strike off their heads. And strike off all the ends of their fingers" (Koran VIII (12)). Without question, the Koran instructed Muslims to terrorize and to kill the enemy polytheists unless they converted to Islam: "Therefore fight against them until there is no opposition in favor of idolatry, and the religion be wholly God's" (Koran VIII (30)).

So the polytheists had the choice to fight Islam or to convert to Islam, but what about the Jews and Christians? That question can no longer be ignored. To provide a clear answer, it is necessary to recap by way of a short review the early relationship between Muhammad and the religions of Judaism and Christianity. When Muhammad fled to Medina in the year 622, he made every effort to convince the Jews to believe that his prophecy was in keeping with Judaism. He developed specific points of doctrinal unity to encourage them to accept and endorse his new religion of Islam.

First, he declared that the God of the Jews (*YHWH*) was the same as the God of Islam (*Allah*): "...We believe in the revelation which hath been sent down unto us and also in that which hath been sent down unto you; our God and your God is one and unto him we are resigned" (Koran XXIX (46)).

Second, Muhammad claimed Judaism and Islam both came from the line of Abraham: Isaac of Israel and Ishmael (*Ismail*) of Islam. In fact, the Koran teaches that Abraham and Ishmael built the Kaba, the shelter of the great black stone near Mecca, as the mosque or temple of *Allah*. They "purified it to be a center of worship for all the world: for God is the God of all the prophets" (Koran C. (48)).

Third, Muhammad also taught that the Koran was an extension, although superior, of former scriptures such as the Torah of Moses, the Psalms of David, and the Gospel of Jesus; "The Koran is...a confirmation of that which was revealed before it, and an explanation of the Scripture; there is no doubt thereof; sent down from the Lord of all creatures" (Koran X (37)).

Fourth, Muhammad preached that he was the personal fulfillment of Moses' prophecy in the Torah, Deuteronomy 18:15.

In addition to these points of doctrinal unity, Muhammad endeavored to unite Judaism and Islam in several practical ways: (1) He offered them opportunity to unite in a military defensive alliance, (2) he taught his followers to respect and honor the Jewish Sabbath, and (3) he even instructed Muslims to prostrate toward Jerusalem as the *gibla* of their prayers. In the end, however, all of these efforts failed to convince the Jews of Arabia to believe in his preaching. As they persisted in their rejections of Islam, *paranoia, suspicions, rumors,* and *hostilities* swiftly infected Muslims' perceptions of the Jews.

With Judaism's rejection of Muhammad, Islamic policies of terror (*jihad*) and terror subjugation (*dhimmitude*) of Jews began to take shape. Although the words of the Koran, "let there be no compulsion in religion" (Koran II (256)), are often quoted by advocates of Islam around the world, *Allah* curses and condemns the Jews for their rejection of Muhammad as a legitimate prophet in the Jewish tradition: "But God hath cursed them with infidelity; therefore few shall believe" (Koran II (88)); "When that came to them which they knew to be from God, they would not believe therein: therefore the curse of

God shall be on the infidels: (Koran II (89)); Verily God is an enemy to the unbelievers" (Koran II (98)).

In reaction to the Jews' rejection of Muhammad, *Allah's* order to shed the blood of the unbelieving polytheists was transferred to shedding the blood of the unbelieving Jews. When the Jews rejected Muhammad's religion, rumors began to emerge of a Jewish military alliance with the polytheists of Mecca, inciting fear and anger among the Muslims of Medina. *Allah* then declared that the unbelieving Jews and the unbelieving polytheists were equally evil: "Thou shalt surely find the most violent of all men in enmity against the true believers (Muslims), to be the Jews and the idolaters" (Koran V (82)). Once the Jews and polytheists were joined together as evil equals, *Allah's* instructions of terror *jihad* against the unbelieving polytheists could reasonably be applied against the unbelieving Jews.

In 625 a *rumor* of an aborted effort by the Jews of the Benu al-Nadir Tribe to assassinate Muhammad set Muslim swords of *jihad* in motion. In response to the rumor, the whole al-Nadir tribe was confined and then deported from Medina. Homeless Muslims from Mecca settled into their vacant houses and farms. With paranoia running high, another *rumor* surfaced that the Jewish tribe of Benu Qurayza had agreed to a military conspiracy with the polytheists of Mecca to jointly attack the Muslims of Medina. Even though the rumor proved false, *Allah* ordered Muhammad to supervise the beheading of 600–900 male Jewish captives of military age. Wives were abducted and sold with their children to fund the purchase of horses and camels for future terror *jihads*.

In the year 628, the concept of terror subjugation (*dhimmitude*) first manifested itself in the religion of Islam. At that time, Muhammad attacked the Jews of Khaybar, who had refused to convert to Islam. They owned and cultivated some of the richest oases in the Hejaz. After several days of battle, the

Jewish warriors were so badly beaten that they bargained to trade their lives for political and religious subjugation. *That fear-filled offer identifies the introduction of terror subjugation by Islam.* After Muhammad beheaded the chief and took his wife as a concubine, he accepted the Jew's request that they subjugate to Islam and divide their income with Islam if he would spare their lives.

From his military expedition against the polytheists and Jews, Muhammad learned to know the fears that controlled the victims of subjugation. The concept of subjugation, *dhimmitude*, was gradually refined to expand Islam, showcase its supremacy, and enrich the followers as they fed on the assets and labors of the Jews. Approximately two years later, Muhammad subjugated the defenseless cities of Christian Tabuk and Christian Duma and simplified the payments of subjugation. Several months thereafter, *Allah* revealed to Muhammad a single text, Koran IX (29), that approved his terror war, *jihad*, and terror subjugation, *dhimmitude*, against Judaism and Christianity, until there was total and complete surrender.

> Fight against them who believe not in God, nor the last day, and forbid not that which God and his Apostle have forbidden, and profess not the true religion, (including) those unto whom the Scriptures have been delivered (Jews and Christians), until they pay tribute (*jizya*) by the right of subjection (willing submission), and they be reduced low (feeling subdued). (Koran IX (29))

In this text, the imperative "fight" is the primary command of *Allah*. It is clearly a ceaseless "fight." There is no cessation, it says, "until" Jews and Christians are subjugated, which is symbolized by paying the tribute (*jizya*). Terror *jihad* then is a constant for Islam. Jews and Christians that neighbored Islam were confronted and coerced to fight, die, convert, or be subjugated (*dhimmitude*). Many neighbors of Islam, village to village, continue to face the same form of terror behavior threat today.

According to Koran IX (29), Muslims must terror *jihad* "until…the right of subjection" (a willing submission). In other words, the defeated Jews or Christians must willingly covenant (*dhimma*) that they are an inferior people and are willing to live life as such in subjugation to the authority of Islam (*dhimmitude*). In the text, IX (29), the two major interdependent teachings for the promotion of Islam are terror *jihad* and terror *dhimmitude*. These two terror behaviors are indivisibly coupled together. The first command is to fight and defeat Christians and Jews. The second is to subjugate them to live in a state of *dhimmitude*, from which Islam can legally suck up their wealth, their purpose, their integrity, and their unbelief, thereby extolling the supremacy of Islam.

The Expansion of Terror Subjugation

In denial of Koran IX (29), Western advocates of Islam promote the falsehood that they endorse a special relationship with Christianity. But how does *Allah* view Christians? As Muhammad struggled but failed to lead the Jews to Islam, he also nurtured the need to convert Christians. The closest significant Christian settlement in Medina was several hundred miles distance. Nonetheless, Muhammad communicated with Christians and invited emissaries to dialogue with him. Muhammad's initial perception of Christians was appreciably better than that of the Jews. For example, in the same chapter that *Allah* declared Jews and polytheists as evil equals of unbelief, Christians were honored as friends: "Thou shalt surely find the most violent of men in enmity against the true believers, to be Jews and idolaters: And thou shalt surely find those among them to be the most inclinable to entertain friendship for the true believers (Muslims), who say, we are Christians. This cometh to pass because there are priests and monks among them; and because they are not elated with pride..." (Koran V(82)).

Such feelings of goodwill were initially applicable to Christians of monastic orders and in particular to the Christians of Abyssinia (Ethiopia) who had protected the followers of Muhammad when they fled the persecution of the polytheists of Mecca. Slowly but surely, however, *Allah* and Muhammad's rhetoric against Christians became increasingly hostile. As Christians rejected Islam and its prophet, *Allah* prohibited friendships with Christians: "Thereafter, *Allah* said, 'Let the Muslims seek the society and friendship of their own..." (Koran III (55)). *Allah's* command for Muslims to reject Christians and Jews and to form no meaningful friendships with them is clearly stated in the Koran: "O believers (Muslims), take not Jews and Christians for your friends and protectors. They are friends and protectors of each other...fear God if ye be true believers" (Koran V (53, 57)).

The rejection of Christians as friends and protectors closed any meaningful connections between Muslims and Christians as persons and institutions. The Koran's instructions to avoid dependent or personal relationships with Jews and Christians has never been abrogated by *Allah* in the Koran. Today, the isolation of first generation Muslim immigrants in Western society may seem to fit the normal behavior pattern of immigrant peoples. However, after several generations of such behavior, as per example in France and Germany, it may be better understood as a testimony to the authority of *Allah's* teachings of isolation. Similarly, when Western nations attempt to protect Muslims in political or natural disasters, as for example after a tsunami, they may soon experience deep suspicion, fear, *rumor*, and destabilizing forces set in motion by *imams* teaching Koran V(53, 57).

As Christians rejected the teachings of Islam, *Allah* rejected the creeds of Christianity. First, *Allah* charged that Christians had concealed the signs and revelations in the Bible (John 14–15) about the coming of Muhammad: "O ye who received the Scriptures, why do ye clothe truth with vanity, and knowingly hide the truth?" (Koran III(71), LXI (6)). Second, although Christians taught that "Christ Jesus" was crucified as the Son of God, *Allah* charged, "yet they slew him not, neither crucified him" (Koran IV (157). Third, Christians taught the deity of Jesus, the Christ of God, but *Allah* charged, "God hath not begotten issue; neither is there any other god with him" (Koran XXIII (91)). "They are surely infidels who say, verily God is Christ the son of Mary..." (Koran V (76)). Fourth, Christians taught God is Trinity, but *Allah* charged, "They are certainly infidels, who say, God is the third of three. For there is no God, beside one God" (Koran V (76)). For the crime of teaching and worshipping false "gods," *Allah* transformed the more committed Christians into "apes and swine" (Koran V (60)).

The Koran attacks the character of Christians, calling them liars (Koran III (61)), perverted transgressors (Koran III (110)), materialists (Koran III (187)), blasphemers (Koran V (19)), untrustworthy (Koran V (67, 73)), companions of hell (Koran V (89)), and unbelievers (Koran V (46)). Already in the early years of Medina (622–624), Christians, Jews and the polytheists were lumped together as "the worst of creatures," because they rejected the prophecy of Muhammad: "Verily, those who believe not, among those who have received the Scriptures (Jews and Christians), and among the idolaters, shall be cast into the fire of hell, to remain therein forever. These are the worst of creatures" (Koran XCVIII (6)).

Allah's dehumanization of Jews and Christians portrays them as legitimate objects of hate by Muslims who seek to be faithful to the injunctions of *Allah* in IX (29) to execute terror *jihad* and terror *dhimmitude*. That raises a serious question for the American media: Do such Muslims deserve to be called the radicals and extremists of Islam? Furthermore, *Allah* does not call a few Muslims to terror *jihad* against Jews and Christians. All Muslim men are required to participate in the ways of terror behavior, *jihad* and *dhimmitude* (Koran IX (36–45)). For us in the twenty-first century, the most important consideration of the text IX (29) is that its authority continues to endorse terror behavior against Jews and Christians into perpetuity. It was one of the final messages of *Allah* (631). Sadly enough, there is no abrogation of terror behavior, *jihad* or *dhimmitude*.

> Fight against them who believe not in God, nor the last day, and forbid that which God and his Apostle have forbidden, and profess not the true religion, (including) those unto whom the Scriptures have been delivered (Jews and Christians), until they pay tribute (*jizya*) by the right of subjection (willing submission), and they be reduced low (feeling subdued). (Koran IX (29))

Understanding Terror Subjugation

A key text to understanding terror war and terror subjugation as legitimate behavior in Islam is Koran IX (29). This is a text for Americans to know, to understand, and to memorize. In this text, *Allah* authorizes war toward and subjugation against all non-Muslim peoples, in particular the Jews and Christians. *Allah's* guidelines are no call to dialogue, discussion, or reason. They are a call to arms, to fight and to subjugate!

> Fight against them who believe not in God, nor the last day, and forbid not that which God and his Apostle have forbidden, and profess not the

true religion (including) those unto whom the Scriptures have been delivered (Jews and Christians), until they pay tribute (*jizya*) by the right of subjection (willing submission), and they be reduced low (feeling subdued). (Koran IX (29))

Western advocates of Islam deny the legitimacy of terror war (*jihad*) and terror subjugation (*dhimmitude*) against the Judeo-Christian world, in fact, they argue militant Islam is a myth. They explain the historical payment of tribute (*jizya*) to Islam as simply that of a "poll tax" for providing military protection to Jewish and Christian communities. That explanation misleads. Read the text.

In the context, it is clear that *jizya* was compulsory for Jews and Christians; *Jizya* symbolized the enforced submission of non-Muslim people to Islamic authority. Contrary to the propaganda of the Western advocates of Islam, it was not welcomed by Jews and Christians, but was the alternative to conversion or total destruction. It says, "Fight...until they pay *jizya*." *Jizya* was not paying a "poll tax" for military protection; it was a mark of subjugation. In Arabia, paying a tax was viewed as an act of subjugation. To pay a tax to the Muslim caliphate confirmed the submission of a Jew or Christian to *Allah* and Muhammad.[6] In contrast, in America a "poll tax" is a head tax often associated with voting and voting privilege. Use of the term "poll tax" to describe forced payments by Jews and Christians who were living in legal servitude to Islam is a serious corruption of the teachings of the Koran. Read the text.

Furthermore, the text says that Jews and Christians were to pay tribute (the *jizya*) by the "right of subjection." The word "right" means that it was a legitimate tribute because the Jews or Christians had officially and legally acknowledged defeat and the status of subjection. Subjection means, "to bring under control or dominion: SUBJUGATE" *(Merrian-Webster's Collegiate Dictionary)*. The word "subjugate" comes from the Latin, sub+jugum; literally it means, "under a yoke." Americans ought not confuse being under a yoke with freedom and tolerance. When we are under a yoke, we are in the company of the ox and the ass. In the context, it means that Jews and Christians become hands and feet in the service of the more powerful Islam. The people of Christian Tabuk were placed under the authority of Islam. That condition of servitude was radically different from payments for militia protection. In Islam one of the major purposes of Jewish and Christian subjugation was to honor the supremacy and authority of Islam.

The text, Koran IX (29), also says that Jews and Christians were not only to be in subjugation but in the right spirit of subjugation, in proper submission. They were to "pay the *jizya*" with a submissive heart. Submission means, "a legal agreement to submit to the decision of arbitrators: the state of being submissive, or compliant: an act of submitting to the authority or control of another; meekness" *(Merrian-Webster's Collegiate Dictionary)*. Therefore, submission in this context means to legally submit to the control of Islam. In addition, consider the participle (willing) as it is translated in IX (29) as "right." What does that mean? It means that *Allah* required Muslims to make subjective judgments about the willingness of the heart of the defeated Jewish and Christian victims. Was the victim sufficiently compliant, i.e., meek enough? Or were more coercive measures necessary? How "willing" a spirit is "willing" enough? How is this oppressive behavior in any way related to a voluntary poll tax for military protection?

The subjectivity of the circumstance increases when the text, IX (29), demands that the victim must experience smallness, lowness, and inferiority, i.e., feeling subdued. In practice it means that Muslim authorities must assess and analyze the genuine attitudes of a Jew or a Christian. When they conclude that the subjugated Jews or Christians adequately sense their inferiority, then the designated punishments or hardships for the victims may be reduced. The setting, then, is one in which the community of Islam, the adherents of the Koran, or simply a single Muslim man control not only the behavior of their victims but also are entrusted with the responsibility to investigate and control the inner attitudes of their victims.

The conquered unbelievers, Jews and Christians, had no freedom. They were legally inferiors to Muslims in the Islamic judicial system. As such, they were in servitude. Any rebellion or protest against their subjugation was an invitation to greater violence and degradation. In fact the Koran orders that any non-Muslim people who rebel or revolt "shall be slain, or crucified, or have their hands and their feet cut off on the opposite sides, or banished from the land' (Koran V (36)). Amazing! In her study of *dhimmitude,* Bat Ye'or describes the *dhimmitude* of Jews and Christians as a state inferior to that of a slave. The greater the degradation of the *dhimmis,* the greater was the exaltation of Islam. *Dhimmitude* was the showcase of Islamic victory. It was proof of Islamic supremacy.[7]

As we review the instructions of the Koran commanding the terror subjugation of Jews and Christians, Western advocates of Islam may confront us with the oft-quoted words of Muhammad, "Let there be no compulsion in religion." Wherever I travel in the world, I hear that quotation used by leaders of Islam as a denial of terrorism. But they certainly know that phrase came early in Muhammad's ministry, when he was endeavoring to convert Jews and Christians to Islam. Without a doubt, they know that those words of tolerance were abrogated by the message of Koran IX (29). They seem to enjoy the gullible reception of such distortions by Western Christians.

In the middle of the secular, agnostic state, does the Western world, does America, really begin to understand the seriousness of their offense against Islam, historically, when they failed to acknowledge Islam as the religion of truth and Muhammad as the fulfillment of prophesies in the Torah and the Gospel?

This issue is huge, and people unschooled in religion are vulnerable to missing the point. When Muslims insist that Christians profess Islam as the religion of truth (Koran X (29)), that is no superficial request. Such a profession (Koran III (64–71)) means that Christians must begin by rejecting God as he is known in the Bible, as he is known historically in the ecumenical creeds, and as he is known in Christian churches throughout the world today. Think about it: (1) Muhammad rejected God the Holy Spirit as the third person of the Trinity and he claimed himself to be the Counselor prophesied by Jesus in John 15:26; (2) he rejected Jesus as the Christ, the Son of God, saying "They are infidels, who say, verily God is Christ the son of Mary" (Koran V (19)); (3) he rejected God as Father, for God is not open to personal relationships with his creation and creatures.

In summary, Muhammad not only rejected the Triune God of Christianity, but the heart of the Gospel: "For God so loved the world that he gave his one and only Son, that whoever believes in him shall not perish but have eternal life" (John 3:16). In the religion of Islam, there is no atonement to enable a person to have a relationship with God, *Allah* is transcendent and thereby unknowable to human beings.[8]

Allah's condemnation encouraged Islam to shed the blood of Christians and Jews as if they were animals; inflict on them emotional, mental, and physical suffering; teach them their wrongs; offer them conversions; and prepare them to burn in eternal hell (*dhimmitude*). Often rumors of rebellion incited vicious bloodshed upon victims already under the yoke of Islam. For centuries, the yoke of servitude was on the shoulders of Jews and Christians (*dhimmi*) to promote the supremacy of the religion of Islam *(Islam uber alles)*. The murders, humiliations, and subjugations of the Jews and Christians are a regulated, programmed extermination of inferior peoples—not an Auschwitz, but a more comprehensive, protracted eradication in which Islam feeds on non-Muslim peoples' labors, assets, bodies, and persons.

Summary

The Koran is the official record of *Allah's* messages to Muhammad and his followers. Although those initial messages are dated between the years A.D. 610–632, they are easily understood today. In fact the Koran describes its messages as plain and clear for the ordinary, average person. Today the Koran is the ultimate authority in the religion of Islam. As such, America ought to have a major interest in understanding its teachings on the subject of terror behavior.

In the middle of confusion created by Western advocates of Islam who claim that terror behavior, *jihad* or *dhimmitude*, has no legitimate place in true Islam, it is of critical importance for American leaders themselves to investigate the Koran. Clearly, *Allah* granted Islam permission to terror *jihad* against its initial oppressors, the polytheists of Mecca. The Koran describes that terror behavior with violent imperatives such as "kill," "slaughter," and "slay" (Koran II (191)). Terror behavior is considered a legitimate response against any form of suppression that hinders Islam (Koran II (192)).

For America, it is important to see that terror *jihad* is a legitimate response by Islam against more than the anti-Islamic military behavior of Western governments. In Islam, *terror jihad is viewed as a legitimate defensive action against any non-Muslim peoples who suppress the exercise of a Muslim's faith.* That ought to be more than an attention getter for political and religious authorities of America. Obvious to all, the laws of America, which protect freedoms to suppress and offend sacred rites, are on a collision course with growing citadels of Muslims migrating into the United States. Obvious as well is that adherents of Islam hold their government accountable to promote socio-religious behavior, the sacred rites, the religious education of their children, and protection against offenses by unbelievers. How does the political leadership of America plan to deal with this clash of civilizations, which they are introducing to the United States?

We must acknowledge that terror behavior *jihad* and *dhimmitude* are modeled in the biographical traditions and are clearly ordered by the Koran. There is no abrogation of terror behavior toward non-Muslim peoples. We may desire the evidence to be otherwise, but the realities are incontrovertible. When followers of Islam perpetrate coercive terror behavior upon non-Muslim peoples of the world, they are honoring and behaving in accord with the ancient authorities of Islam.

As Americans assess terror war, *jihad*, and terror subjugation, *dhimmitude*, they must see that the subject of terror behavior in Islam is far more than a theoretical debate between fundamentalists of Islam and Western advocates of Islam. It is about millions and millions of non-Muslim victims, many of them Jews and Christians, who are allegedly trapped within a violent network of oppression in the Middle East, Far East, and Africa. Having reviewed the teachings of terror behavior in Islam, we must begin to focus on more than the teachings of the Koran and the life of Muhammad. We must visit and observe real people. If we journey into the heartland of Islam, behind the Crescent curtain, what will we witness as to the attitudes and behaviors of Islam toward Jews and Christians?

CHAPTER FOUR

Journeys into Neighborhoods of Islam
Kaduna, Nigeria

In my independent review of the ancient authorities of Islam, I observed that terror behavior is modeled by Muhammad in the biographical traditions and is clearly taught in specific texts of the Koran. That is not to say that the Koran is a textbook of terrorism, but it undeniably enjoins faithful followers of Islam to inflict coercive forms of terror violence upon non-Muslim peoples. Likewise, the biography of Muhammad is not the story of a lifelong terrorist, but it does portray a life that evolved step by step into practices of terror behavior: first against polytheists, then Jews, and finally Christians.

From my experiences with Western advocates of Islam, I expect them to protest the findings. But they really ought to publicly step forward to acknowledge these observations and deal with them. For progress in relationships between Islam and non-Muslim peoples, we need the facts, not posturing for the media with defensive whining and colorful accusations. Some Muslim scholars do seem to delight in a mischievous sort of dishonesty, for example, that militant Islam is a myth. But for many of us in America, there is really no light side to Islam. Outside of its best-known trait in the Western world, that of terror behavior, Islam also impedes the personal growth and development of its own followers by means of detailed legalistic regulations from Islamic holy law, the *sharia*. Muslims are prohibited from making many personal choices that would otherwise be opportunities of freedom for them to exercise and develop their spirituality, individuality, and humanity.

Having come to the completion of my review on terror behavior and terror teaching in the ancient authorities, I need to discover whether or not these instructions and models of terror behavior are adhered to today in the ordinary, average neighborhoods of Islam across the world. I plan to invite comments and testimonies from non-Muslim peoples who live near these cultural, religious, and political centers in the Islamic heartland. My goal is to discreetly maneuver my way into their company, deep inside the more hidden places of Islam. When non-Muslim peoples have the confidence and the courage to tell me of their experiences, I will listen. I propose to quietly tiptoe into neighborhoods where Muslims live their normal way of life behind the Crescent curtain. For this hide and seek venture, I begin in Nigeria, where I am familiar with the physical terrain and acquainted with the religious divide.

Nigeria is an extraordinary country in which to examine the state and condition of non-Muslim peoples who live in the cultural/religious/political neighborhoods of Islam. Nigeria is located in West Africa and has a population of approximately 135 million people. The northerners probably submitted to terror war, *jihad*, as early as the eleventh century, and thereafter, many of them converted to Islam. As proved to be the case in other areas of North Africa, tribal foot warriors were no match for the horses and camels of the Muslim cavalry.

In southern Nigeria, Christian missionaries arrived in the eighteenth and nineteenth centuries via the seaports of

Harcourt and Lagos. Today the vast majority of southern Nigerians are Christians. Currently the population of Nigeria is approximately 40 percent Christian and 40 percent Muslim. Most Muslims still live in the north, and most Christians still live in the south. In central Nigeria, the two religions cautiously intermix, but in recent years terror *jihad* has intermittently turned the region into a killing field.

With Nigeria selected as my first destination, plans were put in place, and I soon departed in the good company of my camera man, Doug, and brother, Sherwin. A few days prior to our departure, Doug received news that a bloody massacre of sixty to seventy Christians had occurred in one of our target search areas, Yelwa Plateau, in central Nigeria. According to the report, a small group of devout Christians from a Roman Catholic congregation had customarily assembled together at daybreak for early morning prayers to seek God's blessing on their business of the day. At 7:30 A.M., Monday, February 23, 2004, a Muslim mob firing guns and screaming "Allahu Akbar," suddenly attacked them. They locked the church doors, forced their victims into positions of submission, and then brutally beheaded many of them. Gasoline was poured over their bodies and set afire.

To receive that report several days before departure certainly raised our anxiety level. We had no political or corporate resources to execute a rescue if necessary. We were three vulnerable Americans. Certainly unsent. Possibly unwelcome. Our confidence was solely grounded in the purpose of our mission. For Sherwin and myself, conviction of purpose is a palpable reality. Our father viewed purposeless people with a deep sadness. His consistent message was that God gives a person life for a reason. Do not waste it!

Since 9/11, my brother and I shared the view that America urgently needs to gather an accurate understanding of terror behavior as it relates to Islam. Now we were actively engaged in that pursuit. As we completed the last leg of our flight to Nigeria. Sherwin recounted to Doug the details of a much earlier visit we had shared together with a young Iranian refugee named Ben. After the story, Sherwin discussed his concern for Americans who seem blind to victims of radical terror behavior within the Islamic world.

"Refugees like Ben are everywhere. How many of our leaders take the interest and the time to ask them why they fled their homelands? Non-Muslim peoples, flee Iran, Iraq, Egypt, Sudan, Somalia, Syria, Saudi Arabia, Pakistan, Afghanistan, and Indonesia—they are in America from all these states of Islam from around the world. Why is that? What was Ben's crime in Iran? As a Muslim, he believed the testimony of a *dhimmi,* a poor, suffering, Christian farmer of Armenian extraction. He converted to Christianity. For that conversion, he was charged as a criminal, imprisoned, ordered to recant, and threatened with execution! Believe it or not, Islam still practices its eleventh-century forms of inquisition. As congenial as Ben is, he tends to tell any interested passerby his amazing story of escape as a fugitive through Iran and Turkey to get to an American Consulate in Greece."[1]

Sherwin is right, victims of Islam walk by us every day on the streets of America as refugees, many of them indigenous Christians who escaped a life of *dhimmitude* in the Middle East and Africa. The list is long. Christian Sudanese refugees are especially noticeable. I find them young and remarkably friendly. They gladly share their experience and knowledge, just for the asking. But then there are also many fine-featured Muslin refugees who have fled the battlefields of vicious, mindless warlords of Somalia.

When in Dearborn, Michigan, I invited a young Muslim fellow, Muhammad, to visit me at Starbucks. He agreed and later showed up with his friend, Ali. They enthusiastically shared some of their experiences in America. As we parted company, I asked them, "Whatever made you guys immigrate to Dearborn?" You know what they both said? "Our fathers were afraid we'd get killed over there"[2] (Syria and Lebanon). Hard to imagine they came here to be safe, near Detroit. They did not come for money. They did not come for democracy. They did not come for freedom. The fathers came for the safety of their sons. They came from the Middle East to live next door to the murder capital of America so that their children could be safe.

By the time KLM (Dutch airline) staff prepared the cabin for arrival, night had already settled on the city of Lagos. Customs and immigration proved uneventful, and shortly we were curb-side searching for a ride. Soon a cabby for NACHA (Nigerian Airport Car Hire Association) Taxi, named Sufian hustled us off to the Sheraton Lagos Hotel and Towers. For the next day, I had scheduled to meet Somini Segupta, a contributor to *The New York Times.* On October 14, 2003, he wrote the front-page story on religions in Nigeria. His article was fascinating, but he cited similarities between Islam and Christianity that were ridiculously unreasonable, and I was curios to know his agenda. The fact that he stood me up increased my skepticism of his and other press releases from Nigeria.

That afternoon Sufian chauffeured us to the Lagos National Airport, where we purchased tickets to fly into the interior. As we returned, while waiting at a busy intersection, several young men leaped on our cab, shouting, banging the roof and windows, rocking and whipping us back and forth. Sufian knew them as young Muslim troublemakers. That night over supper we assured each other that Nigeria was clearly the right place to begin our exploration of terror behavior in Islam.

Our flight was a one-stop, then on to Jos. From my past, I remembered Jos as a small city of paradise with cool breezes on an elevated plateau. But more endearing than the climate was my memory of an experience there in the year 1968. In that whole calendar year, Jos was the only place that I was able, but once, to taste my favorite food: real ice cream. Shortly after arrival, our Hausa guide, Peter, met us at baggage claim. After formal introductions, we were whisked off to a guesthouse of HEKAN (*Hadaddiyar Ekklisisyar Kristi A Nigeria*), or in English, Church of Christ in Nigeria (COCIN).

That night we visited Mark, our adviser recently wounded in an auto collision, to finalize details for our journey north. He was alert, but frail. He introduced his associate, Luke, who had volunteered to arrange our visits with victims of Islamic terror behavior in the cities of Kaduna, Jos, and Kano while Mark was hospitalized. Luke's success in making key contacts for us in the north was in part due to his many relationships with church leaders committed to indigenous diaconal and pastoral ministries.

Luke was a gentleman. His smile radiated a kindness. "Welcome to Nigeria, brothers." He spoke slowly and deliberately, in sharp contrast to Peter, our young Hausa translator. Luke's excitement over our search project took me by surprise. He thanked us for coming and for our interest in the wounded. He told us that we were his fist visitors from the West who came to observe the life and experience of non-Muslim peoples within the Muslim neighborhoods of northern Nigeria.

He very pointedly, so as not to miss an item, stated his travel arrangements for us to date: "You requested a translator who speaks Hausa and English. You have one. You already met him, Peter. You need contacts with non-Muslim people who live in neighborhoods of Islamic culture, near and/or under Islamic authorities. That is arranged, and I included some Muslims as well. The visits are scheduled in Kaduna, several in Plateau, and then Kano. You asked that I arrange a van rental for travel. That too is cared for. My driver, Naga, is available if you wish, can I assist you in any other way?"[3]

Expressing our deepest appreciation, I wondered aloud with some hesitation, "There's one other issue, Luke. What is this that I hear about a 'widow's refugee camp?' Are these widows and children from the terror *jihads* in Plateau State? May we visit with them? Is it possible for you to work it out?"

Luke paused and wrinkled his forehead as if to correctly measure my question: "That is not easy. It worries me. The road is near impassable, very dangerous for you. We have reason to believe that foreign fighters now operate a *jihad* training camp in that vicinity. The road is safe for us at the moment. For you, I think not. It is far too dangerous."[4]

Shortly thereafter, we parted ways for the evening. Mark gave us a loaf of bread, bananas, and a small tin of instant coffee. For our evening meal, we opened a few cans of tuna and broke bread together in the old HEKAN guesthouse. We talked into the night about an aspect of terror *jihad* we had previously not considered, the plight of widows and orphans.

An Overview of Kaduna

Our journey on the road north was interrupted by numerous Nigerian army checkpoints. The purpose for the checkpoints seemed twofold: to block the arrival of terrorists to prop up *jihads* in the state of Plateau, and to apprehend terrorists escaping for greater safety in the Muslim north. With few exceptions, we witnessed drivers bribing (*dash*) soldiers at every location. Obviously, no terrorist needs training camp to learn how to get through Nigerian security. Corruption is a way of life among Nigerian officials. Sherwin and I both paid substantial bribes to smuggle videos of terror *jihad* out of country.

After five hours of stop and go travel, we arrived, checked in at a modest hotel, secured our room, and prepared for the coming days. Kaduna city is the capital of the state of Kaduna, a city of political intrigue. Even though it is located in northern Nigeria, the religious population is divided evenly between Christians and Muslims. When any one questions, *"Is Islam really a religion of tolerance and peace?"* or, *"What is it like to live next door to large populations of Muslims with political authority?"* Christians in Kaduna should have answers.

For many years while Nigeria was under British rule, terror behavior appears to have been suppressed. However, since Nigerian independence in 1960, the passing of two generations, and the arrival of the Muslim Brotherhood from Egypt and Sudan, terror *jihad* began to rock Kaduna. Terror *jihad* against the Christian community, which the Associated Press describes as "ethnic and secular riots," is a matter of record in the years 1980, 1982, 1984, 1987, 1990, 1991, 1992, 1994, 1995, 1997, 1998, 2000, 2001, 2002, 2003, and 2004.

To prepare ourselves for a better understanding of Islamic terrorism and the price paid by its victims, we took a brief overview tour of some of the devastation perpetrated against Christian facilities in recent years. As we traveled, the fact that the terror behavior targeted Christians became very clear. Christian symbols, crosses and churches, within the neighborhoods of Muslim majorities seemed special objects of anger. We photographed the ruins of churches, parsonages, educational facilities, an activity center, and guesthouses.

We viewed churches that were repeatedly torched in 1987, 1992, 2000, 2002, and 2003. An NKST *(Nongo Kristu Sudan Tiv)* church sanctuary, which had served several hundred worshipers, was now nothing more than broken walls and cement floor. The sanctuary was destroyed in 1987 by angry Muslims objecting to an open-air worship by Christian evangelists at the campus of the Kaduna State College of Education. Regardless of the destruction and threats of future terror, NKST had courageously rebuilt. However, in 2002 when the sanctuary was again razed, along with the parsonage and guesthouses, NKST leaders encouraged their people to go elsewhere. The second attack was generated by Islamic rage related to a local newspaper report on the Miss World contest of November 2002.

That year, the Miss World contest was taking place in Kaduna. A local newspaper published an article that questioned how much Muhammad would probably have paid for a Miss World candidate to be one of his wives. Charging the newspaper with blasphemy, Muslims burned the newspaper office to the ground. They then turned on Christians. Almost every church in the northern section of Kaduna, with a 90 percent Muslim majority, was destroyed. Out of fear, the Miss World contestants moved to London, but the victims, the Christian families, were unable to escape. According to a local clergyman, Bishop Josiah, the Muslim leaders instigated the violence to rid the community of illicit dress and blasphemy, both of which violate Islamic holy law. He stated emphatically that *sharia* law has no legitimate place within the Nigerian democracy. Church leaders from across Kaduna agree with the Bishop and told us that no matter what the rumor or the excuse, Islam attempts to terrify Christians, destroy their churches, and to coerce their withdrawal from the northern sections of the city (and northern Nigeria).

We viewed the ruins of several HEKAN churches. The church on Gure Street was burned three times. According to our guide, no one was killed. The pastor and family fled. Everything that burns was set afire. Even the pastor's motorcycle was torched. Its useless, charred frame still stands erect where the former parsonage door once hung. As Islam threatens and brutalizes its Christian neighbors, the victims move away from the Muslim neighborhoods. The pastor and his people relocated in Kaduna South. They return on weekends to worship, but no longer mix among the Muslims of the North. Concurrently, Muslims who lived in the south have moved to the North, afraid that if and when another terror attack comes, Christians may retaliate.

Another Church of Christ, a mile distant, was set aflame four times, in 1987, 1992, 2000, and 2002. The whole church building is now a fort, constructed completely from cement. In 1992 three pastors of the church were slaughtered. Most of the members fled their homes, but they still come to prayer meetings, bible studies, and Sunday worship.

An unbelievable sight, located near the soccer field of the Nazarene Christian School, is the three-story tall, empty shell of the YMCA building. In November 2002, the beds and game tables had been burned, the unsecured tools and appliances looted, and the secured machinery smashed and destroyed. Since 1969, the YMCA, a community-building project sponsored by Europeans, was an interactive play area for Muslim and Christian youth. Next to the YMCA are the burnt remains of a technical training school. German manufacturers, like Siemens, had donated the machinery. Although the Europeans supported the training school financially, the faculty and student body was a mix of Muslims and Christians. It will eventually be rebuilt, but this time among the Christians in Kaduna South. The YMCA, however, must be rebuilt on the same location according to its original charter. Still standing adjacent to the YMCA skeleton is the Nazarene Christian School. Presently 80 percent of its student-body is Muslim children.

Through the debris and devastation of the previous years, we viewed major financial losses to the local churches. Obviously, because of our connection with Mark and Luke, the majority of the sacked and burned churches we observed were HEKAN, (*Hadaddiyar Ekklisiyar Kristi A Nigeria*). Although few have said so, the financial losses mean agonizing hardship to HEKAN headquarters and serious discouragement to its membership. An associate pastor at the HEKAN headquarters, Reverend Marki, described the situation:

"We have a serious problem in this country today. Islam conquered northern Nigeria by *jihad* and they are heirs of *jihad*. We are the victims, the Church of Christ in Nigeria (COCIN), in the crises of 1987, 1992, 2000, 2002, and 2004.

Jihad has seriously affected the Church of Christ. We have lost members, properties, children, wives, and buildings which were sometimes attacked three, or four, and even five times.

"The united Church of Christ in Nigeria (COCIN) is an indigenous church, organized in 1961, without any foreign missions or missionaries, or foreign support like the Anglican and the Roman Catholic churches. We are blocked at every turn by Islam—for employment, for admission to government schools, positions in the government—all are efforts to make us leave these areas to the sole jurisdiction of Islam. We struggle to gather money to construct our churches, and then they burn them down again. Islam receives fighters coming from Sudan. The army and the police, they at times fail us. It is a painful thing. Even when the Federal army is called for our defense, Muslim soldiers sometimes desert to join the *jihad*."[5]

Our last stop was a HEKAN church in Gillian. The church was attacked in 2000 and again in 2002. The pastor said that in the 2002 attacks the Muslims collected the wooden church pews and set them afire in the middle of the sanctuary, but "the roof refused to catch fire." So, repairs were, "thankfully," limited to re-painting, replacing of musical instruments, and the purchase of new pews. As we walked through the church annex, we learned some extremely distressing information.

While we stood in a dark, narrow hallway, the pastor explained, "Several church members were killed as they rushed through here to escape the armed Muslims in the 2000 *jihad*." He paused at the choir room and quietly opened the door. "This is where we lost ten of our smallest children. They ran here for safety. They locked the door for protection. All of them died from burns and suffocation."[6] Obviously, the burning of the church annex, the killing of adults and children, make a spectacular point of conquest for Islam—for them possibly a proof that *Allah* is the true God and that Christians live under his curse.

Today most church members come from distant places to worship and participate in the programs of discipleship and Sunday school. They say, "We remain as witnesses for the Lord. 'He came to set the captives free!'" I admired these courageous Christians, but do they really have a choice? How could these suffering people possibly raise funds to construct another church facility in the safe area of Kaduna South. And for how long will Kaduna South be a safe place?

Visits with the Wounded

After our tour, we visited together with elderly Nigerians, for-mer residents of Kaduna North. The first introduced herself as Mary Jeames. Mary's smile did not mask her anxiety. Her hands were rough, calloused, and scarred from manual labor. Although the terrifying experience she shared was seventeen months past (November 2002), she told it with passion. When the "Miss World terror" began in Kaduna, she was away attend-ing a funeral. When she arrived home, she was completely sur-prised by the *jihad* taking place against Kaduna Christians. She faced what she described as her "night of horror." Houses were burning. Bodies were in the streets. She offered the shelter of her house to a fleeing woman with a small child.

Torches of the mob-like activity lit the street. As she watched the brutality, she heard voices calling her house "a house of evil." She prayed and went inside to hide. Her house was next.

She heard, "Throw fire into this house...a Christian infi-del." She and the woman with a child ran out the back door and climbed over the fence to escape.

She said, "I saw three bodies on the street...they poured petrol and burned them."[7] She joined other Christians who were watching their homes burn. To defend themselves, they resorted to throwing stones at their attackers, who then fled.

The police arrived at 3 A.M. and arrested the now homeless people for refusing to comply with government curfew.

Mary's house was newly built. She had moved there five months before the *jihad*. As I listened, I learned that she was a careful planner, thrifty, and money-wise. To get through the season, she held in storage and traded off and on as many as thirty bags of maize and three bags of rice. Now she found herself with nothing. The church provided her food and clothes.

Joseph Gyang is soft spoken, an elderly man, his dress clean and simple. At the time of the violent attacks, he was earning his living as a security guard for a local business. He rented his house from a Muslim landlord. In his story, he made it very clear that his house was not burned. He said that the attackers knew it was Muslim owned. But on February 22, 2000, the terror makers did break in and steal most of his possessions. He introduced an itemized list of his losses, each item with its estimated value (Appendix A). He set his total loss at N68,500.00

I asked Joseph, "Why do you think they attacked you?"

Without hesitation, he explained the events of the day: "Muslims attacked Christians who were marching to the Government House to protest against Islamic *sharia* law." Joseph was not part of the march, but he complained with deep emotion about the issues of *sharia* in Kaduna State. "It has no place in Kaduna State, or our Nigerian democracy."[8]

Joen Alamba joined us. He witnessed the killing of many Christians in the Rimi area. He ran and hid in his office for two days. His family was spared, and they did not burn his house. Like Joseph Gyang, he rented from a Muslim landlord. Joen, too, thought the whole issue centered on the insistence by Muslim leaders that Kaduna State implement Islamic *sharia* law in place of the current legal system of Common Law adopted from the British.

"But Joen," I said, "American newspapers consistently explain these attacks as 'ethnic and sectarian fighting.' They do not mention marches and efforts to implement Islamic *sharia* law within the democratic nation of Nigeria" (e.g. *The Wall Street Journal*, May 12, 2004, p1).

As if hit by a stick, his response was immediate: "It's Muslims only that start this evil, and it's rooted in *sharia*." The issue was not open for discussion. "We have lived together in peace for a hundred years under Common Law, before this *sharia*—even before the white people came we had traditional law to govern us. We do not need Islamic *sharia* law. The politicians said that *sharia* would not affect us as non-Muslim people. Then tell me why they are stoning Christians in Zaria after making *sharia* law the law over there?"[9]

Later we visited with Mshenil Ssjmbia Wimi. He made the point that in early February 2000, Islam had a formal demonstration at the Government House demanding Islamic *sharia* law in Kaduna:

"Nobody interfered with them. No Christian tried to stone them. But, when we went to the Government House that day, we were attacked. We retreated. We fled. We couldn't believe it. Many of us were killed. They burned shops and churches. An Arabian School (*a madrasa*) is close to my house. They destroyed my house. They did not set it afire. They were afraid to burn the school. They used clubs and axes. Everything was ruined. We lost it all. My wife and children ran away. For several days I could not find them. Eventually we found each other at our church on Sunday."[10]

Laitu Jonahtam was a strong but elderly woman with no formal education. She told the story this way: "We Christians go out to rally. They gather at the Baptist church, pray, and then march to the Government House. The Muslims start to throw stones. They want their own law, Islamic *sharia law*. So, the leaders took us back to church. I saw dead bodies around me, and I was glad to go back to the church. They killed an Ibo boy in front of me, even though police are there. It did not matter. They attacked the police station. They shouted, 'Allah is great.' I could not go home for three days. I had no food for three days, and I was scared to go to the market. They came into my house and stole my bags of rice. I had nothing to eat."[11]

Bishop Yacuba of the Christian Association of Nigeria recounted his experiences with the terror behavior of Islam. "As the Christian Association, we gathered to see the Governor about Islamic *sharia* law. We did not want *sharia*. Things behind it ban us from worshipping our God. We marched to the Government House, not happy against *sharia* law. We reached there but cannot see the Governor. While there, our Christian people are being attacked by the Muslims, true, so many people being killed that day. I was wearing my clergy collar and people told me to take it off.

"Buildings were burning, many dead people on the road. Christians did not react, not prepared. They did not know it was gong to happen. It was a peaceful demonstration. When told our people were being killed, and our churches burned, some of our youth reacted with violence as well. A sad time in Kaduna, all over. Our government tried to stop the killing and burning, really tried.

"This started February 2000 and in May again, worse than first. We were in the Government House. While meeting a *jihad* started. I was chosen to go out and see what was happening. My own church was in flames. That day we lost our pastor and chairman of that church, and seven other members were killed. We experienced a lot of our churches burned, in the first and the second *jihads*. Two or our churches suffered burning three times by Muslims. They looted the church properties and took our possessions. Because of the confusion, they could loot. Last year November 2002 with the Miss World contest, our whole church was pulled down. Muslims surrounded it."[12]

Sherwin interrupted, "Why did they attack your church, Bishop? It was the newspaper that printed the story about Muhammad."

The bishop answered, "The church was near the newspaper office, surrounded by Muslims. Then they attacked our church too. It is in the heart of town. But why burn our churches because of this Miss World? I do not know. Why is it that Miss World is related to the church? With any little problem, it is the church that is attacked."[13]

A Visit with Martha Toon

Late one evening, we had the opportunity to visit with a board member of the YMCA, Martha Toon. At that point in our visits, Islamic *sharia* law had become a front and center issue of conflict from place to place, so I asked Martha, "So much of the violence obviously centers around Islamic holy law (*sharia*). Enlighten us, Martha—what is your experience with Islamic *sharia* law? How did it affect you and your community life?"

Martha responded guardedly, "I want to talk at two levels: my personal level and my organizational level as a board member of the YMCA of Kaduna. The first crisis of 2000 affected me more than the second one. It took everyone unaware. I brought the children to school at 9 A.M. At that time, there was a peaceful demonstration to protest *sharia*—Christians were carrying palm branches as a symbol of peace and shouting, 'No *sharia* in Kaduna State.' Muslims organized and began to throw stones at the demonstrators. At 10 A.M. I sent my driver to get my children at school. He barely succeeded and took them home. I was unable to get home, and I didn't know whether or not my driver had succeeded. I was in Sabo three days. I tried to go back to my family earlier, but it was too dangerous. The army did not allow me.

"Soldiers helped on the third day. Luckily, the children were safe. I never went back to my house. It is not safe for Christians. All of them left and relocated in a short period of time. I lost many Muslim associates on the social level. Youth in the YMCA were killed. The first days of attack were my personal experience. In that period, they did not burn down the YMCA Center.

"The second experience was while I was at work. They started burning churches. A lady wrote an opinion in the newspaper about the Miss World contest—wondering what Muhammad would give for one of these women to be his wife. It was called blasphemy. They burned the newspaper house, Christian churches, and then the YMCA, which had cost about thirty million Nigerian nairas (three hundred thousand U.S. dollars). They also razed the neighboring vocational training center and looted its contents. The day it happened, our youth were having a function. Many jumped out of the building; some died. Other YMCA youth were killed in other places."[14]

"How did they get killed?" I asked.

"Muslims came to their houses with cutlasses, machetes, and guns. Others were fleeing and ran into the Muslim militia. When the crisis was happening, some younger Christians countered them and killed them. In the second attack. I was mistaken for a Muslim. Christian brothers nearly killed me in my car. I tried to convince them. 'I'm a Christian from Sabo,' a business area of the Nigerian National Oil Company. They retaliated against the Muslims by attacking a mosque in Sabo. I tried to pass through to get to the Christian area. They threw stones at me. I shouted. 'I'm one of you !' They told me to recite the Lord's Prayer. Then they let me drive away in my damaged car.

"Both the Vocational Training Center and the YMCA are completely ruined. The training center will be re-located in the Christian area, Kaduna South. Since the 2002 crisis, the state government tried to compensate some of what people lost. The highest amount of compensation was granted to the YMCA, 1.7 million nairas. But the loss was far greater. An evangelical youth ministry from Wittenberg also gave 1.9 million nairas to rebuild with a new hostel. The total rebuilding cost will be about one hundred million nairas (one million US. dollars)."[14]

Then I asked Toon, "What do the Muslims seem to be thinking?"

"It seems that Muslims want to build a mosque there, but our charter says that we must remain in this location. We must bring in Muslim and Christian youth to teach them love and respect for each other. We kept the primary school for two hundred children. Eighty percent of them are Muslim. We also have Muslim teachers to demonstrate our desire to share with them.

"However, Muslims, many Muslims, three weeks ago came and attacked the YMCA center again. They claim it is a *sharia* area. They need to locate a prayer center there, so *sharia* says the Christian facility must go. These Islamic *sharia* laws seem to give them permission to destroy our churches and Christian facilities if they are within a certain distance of a mosque or prayer center. We asked for help from the government to set a committee. We visited the police commissioner. We visited Muslim leaders—to allow peace to reign at the organization level. But we only heard, 'we need to talk more.'"

"What is your view? Will you be able to work through the Islamic *sharia* law issue?"

"This *sharia* issue, we never expected this. In 1996 I attended school and worked here. We didn't know the difference between a Muslim and a Christian. As a businesswoman, I do a lot of things with Muslims. It was a big surprise—all of a sudden this relationship was broken, like this right now." She snapped her fingers. "I do not know about the future."

"I think we will find our way out of this by discovering the foolishness of what we are doing…breaking up Nigeria. But is that the desire of the Muslim leaders? Many communities are torn apart. People in authority, we the leaders, we must find a way to resolve the conflict. It's give and take at the moment. The push is against Christians. It's been very political. For us, it is now self defense."

"Interesting that you mention that you didn't even know whether a person was a Muslim or Christian... when you were young. Why all of a sudden a surprise? From where did the *sharia* business come?"

"Religiously, for Muslims, they have greater contacts with outside countries. That has influenced the way they think. Other Muslim groups came in the 1970s. The Muslim Brotherhood came in the '70s, also groups from Iran, Afghanistan, and Egypt. Our Nigerian Muslims have learned what other followers of Islam are doing religiously.

"I think from a sociological perspective, it is troublesome to Muslims that Christians are going to school more. The *madrasas* (schools) of Islam do not seem to educate them for life and work. They teach the Koran. Some graduates only beg in the streets as urchins. Christians share more in success. Always Christians are trying to go to school.

"So two things seen to influence Islam—out of country contacts and Christians have a greater education—so the Muslims feel vulnerable. The third factor is political. Political leaders have used religion to control people. Muslims are planning this kind of thing. The military ruled the country for a long time after our independence. They used religion and they used tribes to manipulate the people. That manipulation increased the crisis. The policy of *sharia* was deliberately put in the constitution by the military in 1978, 1979, but *sharia* was never legally adopted by our democratic government." [14]

Protest Against Sharia Law—A Justification For Terror Jihad

Martha Toon articulates several significant factors which contribute to re-occurring terror *jihad* in Kaduna North. The influence from other Islamic countries certainly disturbed the restive posture existing between the religion of Islam and

Christianity. Her claim, "We didn't know the difference between a Muslim or a Christina," as recent as 1966, indicates that a radical transition had developed between then and now. Some of that, as she says, is due to foreign influence. The Muslim Brotherhood from Egypt and Sudan has certainly demonstrated its commitment to the basic tenets of terror behavior in Islam. The terror models of Muhammad and terror teachings of the Koran had obviously lain dormant in Nigeria for a long stretch of time, as in other Islamic regions that had been occupied by the British, French, Spanish, and Dutch militaries.

Along with foreign influences of terror behavior, Toon also mentions that Christians are better educated than Muslims. She sees the *madrasas*, theological schools of Islam, as a negative Muslim education because they fail to educate students to function effectively in the contemporary world. Toon could also have added that the foreign sponsored *madrasas* contribute to the emergence of terror behavior in Nigeria because they teach the basic principles of the Koran. In spite of all of the conflict, Toon, like may other Nigerian Christians, still calls Muslims "brothers" and continues to think of them as they behaved in years past when Nigeria was under British rule.

The foreign influence of the Muslim Brotherhood and the teaching of the *madrasas* coordinate with each other to exacerbate what Martha Toon calls, "the crisis of *sharia*." Throughout our visits in Kaduna, Christians cited Islamic *sharia* law as the critical issue. Muslims, as well, pointed to *sharia* as the "touch point" of violence.

When we visited with the director of educational services at the Bureau of Religious Affairs on Islamic Matters in Kaduna, Habib Umar Mahmud, put it this way: "Christians were being agitated by *sharia*." The president for the Islamic voice of Justice in Kaduna, Kabiru Buhari Saleh, supported Mahmud's point of view and called it political, saying, "Protesting against *sharia* is mostly a scapegoat for Christians against Islam." Then he added, "Christians fear it will keep them from proselytiz-ing." [15]

After my visit with these learned men, I had a more accurate understanding of what was happening in Kaduna. According to Islam, a *fatwa* for terror war (*jihad*) can only be issued in defense. So in the Muslim mind, what was the justification for the burning and killing of Christians? Clearly it was the Christians' protest against Muslim efforts to implement and apply *sharia*. That also raises the question as to whether the Kaduna Christians, and America for that matter, really under-stand Islam and the place of *sharia* in Islam. Do they under-stand that devout Muslims view *sharia* as the greatest achieve-ment of Islam? It is more than law. For many of them, it is a way of life. It is holy law. *Sharia* is a practical reconstruction of the words of God (*Allah*) as they were expressed in the life of Muhammad and recorded in the Koran. *Sharia* is a legal mas-terpiece from centuries of sacred labor by Muslim scholars that defines life in every significant detail for followers of Islam.

When Christians protest the implementation and applica-tion of Islamic *sharia* law, it is viewed as a momentous insult to Islam and to the God of Islam. So should the Kaduna Christians, should America, should Europe embrace *sharia*? Why do the Christians of Kaduna reject Islamic holy law? Clearly, the answer is precisely because Islamic holy law is built on the teachings of the Koran and the models of Muhammad. That means that *sharia* is constructed with all the hate, the prejudice, and the bigotry that *Allah* expressed against the polytheists, Jews and Christians. *Allah* calls Muslims to terror-ize and legally subjugate Jews and Christians as inferior peo-ples (Koran IX (29)), "the worst of creatures" Koran XCVIII (6)), and so may *sharia*. It is no wonder that Nigerian Christians agitate and protest against the efforts of Islam to officially institutionalize *sharia* law within the state of Kaduna and the nation of Nigeria.

From my interviews, it is apparent that the Christian community of Kaduna does not fully grasp the negatives of Islamic *sharia* law. For them, it seems that their fear of *sharia* is more of a tacit knowing. They sense that something is very wrong with Islamic *sharia* because of its angry and destructive adherents. Many non-Muslim peoples of Kaduna do not "know" the nature of *sharia* law or the roots of *sharia* law anymore than many non-Muslim Americans.

A point, for example, that seems unclear to many Christians in Kaduna (and many of us non-Muslim peoples from around the world) is that there appear to be significant distinctions of "code" made in Islamic holy law. Penal Code *sharia* had been in place in northern Nigeria since 1976. Penal Code supposedly governs personal matters in the lives of Muslims. The current controversy, however, really involves attempts by Islam to implement Criminal Code *sharia*. Criminal Code governs external matters in the lives of Muslims. Criminal Code *sharia*, then, is actually an alternative legal system to the current Nigerian legal system of Common Law. Within Criminal Code *sharia*, there are no guaranteed freedoms such as we have in American democracy with the Bill of Rights. In fact, to the contrary, in that *sharia* must be faithful to the word and will of *Allah*, it must define Jews and Christians as inferior creatures and implement regulations to control and expose that inferiority.

When we visited with Habib Umar Mahmud, a Muslim educator in Kaduna State, I asked him why many Muslim leaders insisted on Criminal Code *sharia* law. He answered, "In my experience, the need for *sharia* was an outcry of the Muslim community against crimes. We need Criminal Code *sharia* law. It is enshrined in the constitution as of 1979, not before. It was not part of the legal system under British colonization. That was Common Law. That is the legacy of the British. However, Penal Code *sharia* law, the personal laws of the Muslims, 'was' permitted, but that is incomplete. Criminal Code *sharia* law must be included. Penal Code *sharia* law deals with civil aspects of personal lives. It is incomplete when it does not embrace Criminal Code *sharia* law. Criminal is connected to civil. Now there is a wave of crime. There is a need for conviction on the part of Muslims. They cannot get along without Criminal Code *sharia* law."[16]

Habib presents a very simple, practical argument that Muslims need the Criminal Code for "conviction." In the West, the argument fails many of us because we tend to view conviction as personal, a power **within** us; but in Islam, the comprehensive legal system, *sharia*, controls decisions for most every aspect of life, and thus "conviction" for a Muslim is communal, viewed as a power from **without**, i.e., from the law and the enforcement of the law. Habib later argued that Criminal Code *sharia* law is a "religious right" guaranteed in the Nigerian Constitution. According to Christian leaders, that opinion is rejected is Section 262 of the 1999 Constitution.

In order to bring peace between the residents of Kaduna, the Executive Governor, AHL Ahmed Mohammed Makarfi, appointed an "Eleven Plus Eleven Committee for Peace, 11+11." The eleven Christian members of the committee and the eleven Muslim members of the committee signed "The Kaduna Peace Declaration of Religious Leaders," dated August 22, 2002 (Appendix B). The introduction to the document reads as follows:

> In the name of God, who is Almighty, merciful and compassionate, we who have gathered as Muslim and Christian religious leaders, from Kaduna State pray for peace in our State and declare our commitment of ending the violence and bloodshed, which has marred our recent history.

According to our faiths, killing innocent lives in the name of God is desecration of His Holy Name, and defames religions in the world. The violence that has occurred in Kaduna State is an evil that must be opposed by all people of good faith. We seek to live together as neighbors, respecting the integrity of each other's historical and religious heritage. We call upon all to oppose incitement, hatred, and the misrepresentation of one another.[17]

One of the major considerations of the "11+11 Committee for Peace" is the conflict over Islamic *sharia* law. The Kaduna State Muslim community submitted a position paper concerning the application of the *sharia* legal system on Muslims (Appendix D). *In its document the Islamic community makes it clear that sharia law is absolutely necessary for a Muslim to be a Muslim.* The Christian members of the "11+11 Committee" also submitted a position paper regarding the effect of *sharia* law on the non-Muslim, Christian population (Appendix E). *In their document the Christians concluded that the application of Criminal Code sharia in Kaduna State must not be permitted.* They write, "The bottom line, which is absolutely non-negotiable, is that the *status quo* should remain." Both position papers name specific aspects of Criminal Code *sharia* law that would apply to northern Nigeria and are viewed as positives by the Muslim communities and negatives by the Christian community.

The position paper of the Muslim community (Appendix D) specified that (1) Friday be a work free day like Saturday and Sunday; (2) *Haddi* lashing (whipping) be a legal form of punishment for Muslims for the sin of adultery, defamation of character, for injurious falsehood, for drunkenness in public places, and for the drinking of alcohol; (3) *Sharia* law regulates all decisions on a Muslim marriage (a female is 50 percent of the value of a male); (4) *Sharia* law govern "any questions regarding the validity of a dissolution of Islamic law marriages or the guardianship of an infant" (5) a *wakf*, gift, will, or succession where the endower, donor, testator, or deceased person is Muslim can only be inherited by Muslims; (6) where all parities of the proceeding are Muslims, the case must be determined in accordance with Islamic laws.[18]

The position paper of the Christian members of the "11+11 Committee" (Appendix C), specifies that (1) Criminal Code *sharia* law is incompatible with other legal systems and only exists in Islamic states with Islamic governments, such as Iran and Saudi Arabia; (2) Christians cannot inherit from their Muslim parents because they are Christian, the parents and children have no voice. A Christian wife married to a Muslim husband has no inheritance and is subjected to Criminal Code *sharia* law; (3) it would produce two conflicting judicial systems. Common Law and *Sharia* law create opportunities for injustice and anarchy in cases between Muslims and Christians; (4) Criminal Code *sharia* law curtails freedom of religion because it honors *jihad* as appropriate legal action against Christians; (5) Criminal code *sharia* law forbids the propagation of any religion other than Islam as in Saudi Arabia and Iran; (6) under Criminal Code *sharia* law Christians may not hold a position that exercises any authority over a Muslim.[19]

The disagreement between the Muslim and Christian members of the "11+11 Committee" remains at an impasse. Since the signing of the Kaduna Peace Declaration of Religious Leaders on August 22, 2002, no significant resolutions have been obtained. In fact, two months after signing the agreement, the streets erupted into an explosive terror *jihad* led by Muslims of Kaduna North, once again burning Christian churches, Christian houses, and Christians on the streets. According to some sources, the underlying justification for the terror *jihad* was once again that Christians rejected the implementation and application of *sharia*.

Obviously the view of brotherhood between Muslim and Christians, which existed during the British occupation, has collapsed. The damages to Christian properties in Kaduna North have been severe; the financial losses disheartening. By far the most disturbing outcome is the killing of people, defenseless, often helpless people. Reliable numbers are not available. Witnesses of corpses in the streets and the killing of Christians outside their homes and churches tell a story of a tragic death toll, hundreds and hundreds of people. One can only imagine the horrors as men, women, and children suffered, suffocated, and burned. How many others have been murdered?

As Americans, our interests are often in the body counts, and we tend to lose sight of the long-term ramifications of the poverty which ensues when a husband/father is killed in African cultures. The widows and children have no aid to dependent children, no food stamps, no Medicaid, no disability insurance, no social security, no pensions, and no life insurance. The husband/father is all of these rolled up into one: the papa. The papa is the security of life. When he is killed, how vulnerable become his woman and his children? The church may stand as a shield of security, but many of the churches are indigenous (no foreign assistance) and suffering from hideous financial blows from terror *jihad*, and that over and over again. Without the church, what are the options for these widows and children? There is the extended family, but they live together. They too are wounded. For their livelihood, are they forced to submit to men of Islam as they did in the days of Muhammad? We may also wonder about the elderly whom we met, like Mary, Joseph, and Joen. As Americans, we are not apt to think of the subsequent effects of looting the aged. The clothes, furniture, and bags of maize and rice are all essential to life. They serve as food, a place to sleep, warmth for the body, and even as barter for medicines at the pharmacy. Suddenly the simple future is stripped away. The houses burned or razed mean homelessness. Afraid, what frightened souls dare return to the property of their former dwelling? The devastation and dehumanization are not from an earthquake or windstorm, but from those faithful to "divine guidance" in the religion of Islam.

Terror behavior in Kaduna showed no signs of spontaneous riots by hysterical mobs. The personal accounts we hear indicate that the terror behaviors were deliberate and controlled. The terror behavior was planned and had religious justifications and rational objectives.

In our visit, three persons testified that their homes were not burned because they were rentals, owned by Muslims. In two of those cases, attackers in the middle of the bedlam ordered which places were legitimate targets. That is not mob behavior. In another situation, Mshenil's house was razed to the ground by clubs and axes because the attackers feared burning the *madrasa* next door. That is not riotous behavior. Christians' homes, shops, and institutions were sacked and destroyed.

Furthermore, if there were spontaneous, mob-like behaviors of young Muslims, then it seems appropriate that the spiritual leaders, the *imams*, of the mosques at which they pray, should seek to restore the honor of Islam by punishing these young offenders for their inappropriate behavior, not by cutting off hands or heads, but forcing them to make restitution to the aggrieved parties—the homeless, the widows, and the orphans. Want peace? That would lead to peace. That would grind terror behavior to a halt in Kaduna North. Return the stolen goods. But that does not happen. No one is punished by the spiritual leaders of Islam or by the Muslim leaders of the state government. Why?

Islam offered no compensation of any amount to anybody, not even to the YMCA. What does that say about the character of true Islam off-camera in the heartland? In fact, a board member of the YMCA thought that Islam wanted the property of the YMCA for a mosque, which sounds like a supremacy issue. A mosque in a Muslim neighborhood is usually built higher than a church or synagogue to demonstrate the superiority of Islam. In that regard, the towering YMCA building was probably a long-term irritation to some of the faithful followers of Islam.

In the religion of Islam, there appear to be serious, sacred, legal grounds of terror *jihad* against the Christians of Kaduna. Islam may now be using as a central issue Christian opposition to the implementation and application of Islamic *sharia* laws. This is no small matter. Islam insists "that a Muslim cannot observe and practice his/her religion effectively without the *Sharia* legal system in place" (Appendix D. p. 6). The Islamic spiritual leaders of Kaduna say the implementation of the holy law of Islam, *sharia* law, is "a religious obligation" and "compulsory for Muslims." The necessity of *sharia* can be put no clearer.

If the holy law of Islam is absolutely necessary for a Muslim to be a Muslim, as is stated in the position paper of the Kaduna Muslim Community, then terror *jihad* against the Christian objectors is for them justifiable; not radical, but simply an honest, legal ruling by Islam. This is obviously an issue that needs greater assessment by Americans as they evaluate Islam. It should be at center stage. What the Nigerian Muslims are stating is not some novel idea. It is deeply rooted in the ancient authorities, the history, and the culture of Islam.

The strategic objective of this terror *jihad* against Christians in Kaduna and elsewhere in Nigeria appears to be an effort to coerce and to wear down resistance by Christians to Criminal Code *sharia* law. That comports with the purpose of terror behavior as defined in Koran IX (29) by the phrases, "willing submission" and "feel themselves subdued." The purpose of terror behavior in Islam is to "fight" the enemy; to weaken his will, to cripple his finances, to damage his life-view, to change his faith, to demonstrate the supremacy of *Allah*, and to force those who resist Islam to flee so that the territory may be reconstituted as the *dar al-Islam*, the redeemed land of *Allah*. We have observed the state and condition of living as non-Muslim (Christian) neighbors to Islam in Kaduna North. The terror behavior of Kaduna is a drastic change from the days of British rule, when people could not tell the difference between a Christian and Muslim. That does not mean that all Muslims today practice terrorism in Kaduna, or for that matter, in Nigeria, but it does reveal that the models of terror *jihad* in the ancient authorities are still exalted as divine guidance for faithful Muslims to emulate.

Even if only a small number of Muslims perpetrate terror violence, where is the Muslim opposition? If it exists, and I think it does, it is obviously weak and cowardly. I cannot help but ask, how many non-violent Muslims are intimidated by *the models of Muhammad and instructions of the holy Koran and therefore* **acquiesce to the violence with passive support and silence?**

All Muslims are trapped by the theology of terror behavior, cognitively or otherwise. They live in fear of death and hell should they transgress the will of *Allah*. That is a powerful force for any spiritual persons, especially in the realm of a legalistic religion. Do Muslims need to escape this system of abusive control as much as non-Muslims need to escape from its violent consequences? How do we deal with these issues? Certainly the answer is not to surrender to terror behavior or the threats of terror behavior. We must not trade cartoon restrictions for peace. We must not trade Criminal Code *sharia* law for peace. If that is correct, Americans probably ought to stop walking in that direction. That pathway toward peace will ultimately demand that we trade away our freedoms for Islamic holy law. Personally, that is more than I will pay. Peace under *sharia* is not peace for non-Muslim peoples anywhere in the world. In such a case, peace is not the answer.

For the sake of Muslims and non-Muslim peoples, Americans need to stop the public disgrace of repeating the lie that Islam is a religion of peace and tolerance. Instead, they need to examine the teachings and behaviors of Islam for themselves, especially terror *jihad* and *dhimmitude*. They must expose the violence and abuse from the historical records and from current on-the-ground actual events, like those presently taking place in Nigeria. They cannot afford to lie and deny. At this moment in history, Americans have one way to deal with Islam, and that is with as many of the facts as they can place on the table. They need to understand Islam. The need to share among each other, as much as possible, the realities of terror behavior within the religion of Islam. They need to begin now.

State Secretary of the Christian Association of Nigeria

In our final visit in Kaduna, we were privileged to share time with the State Secretary of Christian Association of Nigeria, Reverend Joseph Hayab. His is a member of the "11+11 Committee." More than skeptical of the peace dialogue, I asked Hayab, "What do you think: doesn't it appear you're going to lose in this conflict?"

He answered, "If we lose, we will all lose. We are called to live without a sword. I teach what the Bible teaches. I'm not a cheek for everyone to slap, but I will not preach violence. That is to betray us. I preach peace. Do I just say it because of the situation or my convictions? I will shine even if they kill me today. A Christian witness is not killing for killing, nor fire for fire. After each crisis, some Muslims always turn to Christianity. After every crisis, we sit down and worship God, brothers. If they come to my house to shoot me, when it comes to religious violence, I will preach against it."[20]

Sherwin objected, "Every person has a right to defend his family, no?"

Hayab continued, "Or course if it comes to that, but more important, Christians need to stick with the peace program and not run."[20] He testified that in every occasion of terror behavior, Muslims have converted to Christianity. As Hayab was listing his goals for the "11+11 Committee," our driver, Naga, persisted that for our safety, "The van is running and we need to go now." We said our "God Bless" to these very amazing people.

The concept of dialogue with Islam about Islamic holy law seems foolhardy. In Islam, *sharia* is the will of *Allah* for Kaduna, Nigeria, and the whole world. Nothing is more important to committed leaders of Islam that the reality of *total and complete sharia worldwide,* subjugation of the land of the unbelievers, *dar al harb,* and the rule of *Allah* everywhere, a total *dar al Islam.* By way of principle, Islam cannot negotiate *sharia for it is the will of Allah.* Divine revelation is non-negotiable. For the faithful of Islam, the concept of negotiating peaceful relationships with unbelievers through bi-partisan concessions must appear immoral. Clearly in any negotiations with Islam, America (the "Christian West") will make concessions of its freedoms, not Islam. Is that the price of peace?

CHAPTER FIVE

Journeys into Neighborhoods of Islam
Plateau, Kano, Nigeria

On the evening of our return to Plateau State, we visited together with a lifelong resident, Ms. Rebecca. She served for many years as a secretary to a Christian world relief agency. In the course of our visit, we shared views on the possible purpose of terror *jihad* in Plateau State. For Sherwin and myself, it was 9/11, *déjà vu*, destruction and execution. Once again we sat in the seats of the powerless. More painful to us was the political and religious silence from America.

After dinner, Rebecca told us of her experiences as a victim of the first terror *jihad* in Jos, September 7, 2001. At the time, she was still living at her mother's house. Her immediate neighbors were Muslims, and the relationship was friendly. On the week of the terror attack, however, she and he mother heard loud arguments. She explained, "There was a real conflict between them and several Muslim guests who a had recently arrived."[1] Days later, terror *jihad* was launched against the Christians of Jos.

She said, "My mother and I escaped by climbing a small hill behind our house." As they hid, perched near the top, they could view the violence below. She added, "The most terrible thing I remember is that as we hid behind some bushes, a small, elderly man came hurrying down the path toward our house. They caught him, he pleaded for his life." She repeated the phrase as if caught in a trance: "He pleaded for his life." She closed her eyes and covered her face is if to spare her from visualizing that memory over again. She continued, "His pleas meant nothing. They cut off his hands. Then as if to joke with him, they put his cut off hands in his pockets."[2] We were speechless.

A Visit with Reverend Adaki

The following day, we arranged as short visit with a distinguished, soft-spoken gentleman who was obviously still in trauma, Reverend S. Adaki. Only four weeks previous, his village had suffered a sever terror attack. All seventeen churches in Yelwa were destroyed.

"Have you ever before had any experience like this one?" I asked.

"No," he answered, "but I remember a Muslim celebration earlier, on November 8, 2003. I think it was a 'Sela Celebration,' the birthday of Muhammad. They killed three of our men who were selling cows in the market place. Fulani Muslims claimed the cows were stolen. Nothing happened after that until Tuesday."[3] He paused. His hands were shaking nervously. We offered him a drink of water and encouraged him to take a rest.

Soon he continued, "Later, on Sunday, February 22, 2004, there was much shooting of guns in our town. It lasted through the night."

Sherwin questioned him, "Who were they shooting? Animals? People?"

"They were firing into the sky to celebrate. I complained to the police, and on the next day, Monday, nothing happened. Then on Tuesday, the 24th, some of our people went to church for prayers as usual before they were off to work. That is when the attack came."

I looked at Doug and he at me. Both of us were remembering the report of the Roman Catholic congregation.

Reverend Adaki continued, "They fenced us in. They blocked all the roads out of the city. By 7:30 A.M. they were shooting people, burning places, churches and houses."[4]

Reverend Adaki told us that thirty-nine of his members were killed inside the church that morning and that others were shot and killed as they attempted to flee. Another source later informed us that over fifty Christians were slaughtered inside his church, a Church of Christ in Nigeria (COCIN). He also remembered a phone call made by a woman inside the church that described the butchering of men and women. She was begging, "Help us! Fire is everywhere. Our people are being slaughtered."

A Jos newspaper reported that forty-eight charred corpses were picked up in this church. They had been shot, "macheteed" many times, doused with gasoline, and set aflame as human torches. Some families that could identify the remains of their loved ones took them to arrange funeral services. A security team collected what remained of the corpses and bones and buried them in a mass grave. They said they did not want the COCIN leadership to see what they had seen—"a horrendous sight."[5]

Reverend Adaki spoke with deep emotion: "The churches of Yelwa were all burned to the ground. Many Christians were killed, others injured. Christian homes were burned, razed and looted. Little children caught in the rampage watched their parents struggle in the agony of violent death."[6]

According to newspaper reporter Yiljap Abraham, top security officers were at a loss as to how communities of peace-loving people would have accepted Muslim mercenaries, even housed and fed them, without reporting them to the governing authorities. They were also pained by the refusal of the Muslim villagers to give them any vital intelligence.

I asked Adaki, "How many attackers were there?"

The Reverend struggled for composure, then said, "There were as many as two thousand. Many of them carried machetes (cutlasses). They had many guns. They were shouting praises to *Allah*."[7]

"So why did they do this to the Christians of Yelwa?"

By now the reverend was exhausted, but he insisted on answering. Holding his right fingers in his left hand as if to count, he tried to explain: "First, because they want Muslims to be the only religion in this country. Second, they want to weaken Christians in Plateau State and make them flee. Third, Christians are not happy to have *sharia* law. In (Islamic) *sharia* law Muslims who convert to Christianity are executed. I know at least five Muslims from Yelwa who have become Christians this past year. Muslims are also converting to Christianity in other places of Plateau."

Soon after, we said our farewells to the reverend. His parting words to us were special: "Thank God Almighty for bringing you people. May the Lord bless you."[8]

Yelwa is no longer a city with a religious mix; all homeowners are now Muslims. Yelwa is redeemed (*dar al-Islam*). The Christians have fled or are dead. In Jos, a local lawyer, who wished to remain anonymous, said that the government knows "the architects of terror," but has refused to arrest them. Not one perpetrator of the terror *jihad* has been arrested and prosecuted since the violence began in Plateau State in 2001.

A Visit with Ezekiel

The next day, Ezekiel, a local Christian businessman, invited us to his office to provide an opportunity for personal interviews with victims from the devastation by terror *jihad* against their villages during the previous weeks. As they shared pictures and films, Ezekiel provided translation of the mostly Hausa commentary.

From pictures taken at the Yelwa Hospital, we saw stubs, but no hands; heads but no ears, and wounds recklessly carved by machetes. Benjamin told how hundreds and hundreds of Christian people, elderly and children, fled in mass down the roads and through the fields on lories (trucks), motorcycles, and bicycles. Others ran and walked with their children. He described how young Christian men were gathering together to resist the mercenaries of Islam with clubs, bows, and arrows.

In the village of Bolgani, houses were torched. Lories, autos, and motorcycles were soaked in petrol and set ablaze. Even the "shelling machines" for corn and rice were set aflame and rendered useless. The chief of Bolgani village said, "Over two thousand Muslim men had attacked his village. They threw Molotov cocktails into our houses and onto our roofs."[9] Ezekiel carefully showed us pictures of charred remains of human bodies.

From Karkashi village, Paul spoke of more burned bodies, houses, and churches. Refugees were fleeing everywhere. The chairman of the Roman Catholic Church said they were attacked by hundreds of Muslim invaders, as many as two thousand. They knew no reason for such an attack. People were slaughtered in churches while attackers shouted, "God is Great!" Federal soldiers were brought in to restore order, but some Muslim soldiers joined the terror *jihad*, going door to door asking names. When a person answered with a Christian name, he was executed.

Benjamin told of his visit to the Shendam Hospital. A young victim, named Matthias, told how Federal soldiers belonging to the Islamic faith forced him to kneel. Then they shot him twice and left him for dead. Other victims of Federal soldiers were also brought to the hospital. We had heard and seen enough.

That night I recorded my deep admiration for a very special people and my profound grief with the lack of news coverage of terror *jihad* in Nigeria by the American media. I began to realize that the "global village" is more a political perception than a reality.

A Eulogy of the Falling Trees

If a tree fell in the forest with no one to hear it fall, did it make a sound? That distant question of my college youth mysteriously visits me tonight as I rest among the dead. If a tree falls in the forest with no one to hear it fall, does it make a sound? Tacitly, the answer nags me, until I finally hear aloud, "It makes no sound." The falling tree makes no sound when no ear can hear the fall. With a fresh scent of terror behavior, I see the bleeding of the silent falling trees.

The trees of Nigeria are gorgeous ebony, king's ebony too. These are trees of smiling faces, bright eyes, white teeth, and proud shoulders. Their heights are average. Their branches are embracing. Their lives are gentle. These Trees love life, very simple life. They happily walk for water, dig the earth for yams, and devotedly nurture their young.

The trees of Nigeria are falling. Alas, these kindliest, loveliest, simplest trees of the human forest are fast falling. So, I ask, "Why fall there, friend Tree? Is it of sickness or disease?"

Tree timidly replies, "No, not me."

I ask again, for I wish to know, "Help me to understand, oh gentle Tree. Why fall, the cursed AIDS, maybe?"

With sounds of sorrow, Tree answers me, "No, not AIDS, thank God, for medicines are few."

But my friend Tree, what is your pain to fall?""

Then Tree, in grief, cries aghast, "It is the bloody axe."

These falling trees of Nigeria make no sound. In the early morning of February 24, 2004, the bloody axe felled one hundred thirty-five trees in the village of Wase. Now the trees are gone, with only ash and trash of former homes, churches, and shops to witness their fall. A survivor tells of the event with wet eyes, tears dripping down his face of pain. He is a soft-spoken gentleman of education, sixty years in age, still in shock. His beloved trees fell hard that day, but made no sounds in the Forests of the World.

These falling trees of Nigeria made no sound. In the region of Yelwa, eighty trees humbly bowed in a stark and simple Roman church saying their early morning prayers to bless the day. They too were felled, suddenly and brutally gone. The cruel axe severed their branches from their trunks. Lying in that beheaded form, matched kerosene sent their bleeding pieces smoking into the skies. But these falling trees made no sound in the Forests of the World.

These dedicated falling trees of Nigeria make no sound. Systematically felled in February and March of 2004, the simple villagers were unprepared and no real resistance was made. For years past, they had grown into the comfort of safety that comes from kindly neighbors, but then from afar the strange enemy's holy axe suddenly did fall. From village to village in the state of Plateau, thousands were felled. Now the fallen trees are gone, but the places they fell are still easily found for those who question and care. Begin in the village of Bolgani and Karkashi and then simply follow the ashes or view the pictures with me. These falling trees of Nigeria, though great in number, they made no sound in the Forests of the World.

These innocent, falling trees of Nigeria make no sound. At the break of dawn, on the edge of town, they see the holy aggressors' axe. Stunned, they freeze in defenseless panic while another holy attack begins. Papa trees fall and the madness comes—to run to the field, to ride the bike, to hide in the hedge—a collage of choices for frantic minds. The tragic and the bizarre blur each other. Fresh widow and orphan flee, no Papa Tree. The roof smokes, kerosene leaks down the walls, flames burn the beds, and the yam for the evening meal. Havoc, fear, and flight all mix into each other. No other help, no police, no fire truck, no 911, no social security, only Papa Tree—and now no more Papa Tree.

THESE FALLING TREES MAKE NO SOUND IN THE FORESTS OF THE WORLD

Why do Americans hear little to nothing of this vicious policy of violence? Is it geography, race, possibly religion? We have done this before, not so proudly, with the holocaust of the Jews in Germany. Are we looking the other way again? Where are the voices of churches of the West on this matter? Certainly leaders of American churches have ties to Nigerian churches. Are they terrorized perhaps for the safety of their staff? Why is there no firestorm? Why the eerie silence? Is this racism, ignorance, cowardice, or possibly wisdom I am unable to understand? How are we to understand the silence to the violence? Is it possible that the Western press is a victim of religious prejudice? Is an explanation, possibly, that Muslim advisers staff the German and French sites of the Associated Press through which they receive Muslim reports from the terror killing fields? If so, is this political correctness gone awry? Would the Associated Press publish a bishop's investigation of an archbishop as independent, objective reporting?

Today we praise the non-violent resistance of the greats, Reverend Martin Luther King and Mahatma Gandhi. If the press and religion had been as silent for them as they are for the victims of terror behavior in Nigeria, who would know their names? How can non-violent resistance succeed with no public support from the free press and the agents of righteousness? Why are no American demonstrators protesting the violence of Islam against the black Christians of northern Nigeria and the black Muslims of Darfur?

Why, after as many as ten years of terror behavior against black African Christians in Nigeria, has there been no significant investigation published by non-Muslim Western reporters? Or did I miss reports by CBS, CNN, BBC, and the *New York Times?* Is this a repeat of our failure to address the atrocities in Sudan throughout the '80s and '90s?

When the press consistently dismisses the terror behavior of Islam in Nigeria, as "ethnic and sectarian conflicts," is that from ignorance or is it that with intent of malice? These are not issues of tribes. Christians and Muslims are in many cases from the same tribes. Christians are found in almost every tribe, as are Muslims. A Hausa attacking a Hausa is not an ethnic or tribal conflict. These are outrageous, murderous acts of terror behavior, perpetrated by Islam to redeem the land of the unbelievers to *dar al-Islam* and to coerce the implementation of Criminal Code *sharia* law. Why is this tragedy hidden from the West? How can that silence possibly enlighten those of us from the West who wish to evaluate terror behavior in the religion of Islam?

Another question: how many times can the press say "sectarian conflict" without somebody asking, "What do they mean by sectarian?" I understand a "sectarian conflict" as an accurate description of the fighting between the Sunni and Shia in Iraq. But in Nigeria, the conflict is not between the sects of Islam. The Muslims perpetrating terror behavior belong to no radical schismatic Islamic sect. They simply execute instructions of their sheiks that draw from the ancient authorities of Islam (A.D. 610–632). The Christian victims are not sectarian. They profess the Apostles' Creed (circa A.D. 200). The issue of "sectarian conflict" by the American press incorrectly implies to readers that the conflict is merely between religious fanatics.

This is no "sectarian conflict," so why does the press call it that? Faithful followers of the religion of Islam, in their minds justifiably so (Christian suppression of *sharia* law as a suppression of faith), are attacking the followers of the religion of Christianity. This is not about sects. It is about religions. It is about Islam attempting to fulfill its mission to impose the divine will of *Allah*, the Islamic *sharia* law, worldwide and its main obstruction is Christianity, not the Untied Stated armed forces.

Oppression in Kano

Back in 1967, on my fist visit to Kano, I was captured by two remarkable sights: pyramids of bagged groundnuts (peanuts) that stood as tall as any Kano building, and an outdoor gathering of thousands of Muslim men in a coordinated performance of Friday prayers. On this visit, I saw neither. Clearly the population of Kano had grown. Kano residents think the numbers are somewhere between 650–750 thousand. As for religion in Kano, everyone seems to agree that 95 percent are Muslim and 5 percent other. With those percentages, Kano serves as an ideal neighborhood in which to explore the behavior and the tolerance of Islam.

A Visit with Ishaku

Shortly after our arrival, we met several local non-Muslim residents at a partially constructed church building in the Christian ghetto. A northwesterly breeze at times rattled the patched tin roof, occasionally interrupting our conversations. At first, we were introduced to Ishaku Doli, a graduate student in economics from Bayero University Kano. Ishaku was impressive in stature, in credentials, and in her self-confident demeanor. She was excited for our interest, curios to know our objectives, and convinced that God would use us to achieve his ultimate purposes. She introduced herself with a Christian testimony:

"I count myself privileged to be a Christian. I was raised in a Christian family and taught Christian ethics, but that doesn't make me a Christian. I saw the need to invite Jesus Christ into my life as Lord and Savior in 1970 when I was in primary school. I was baptized by middle school. In whatever circumstance I find myself, I am first and foremost a Christian. All out to please God is my philosophy."[10]

Ishaku is a lifelong resident of Kano and went on to compare her early years of education in the 1960s and 1970s to that of the children today. She said, "I started my education in a mission school, but eventually my parents transferred me to a public school. In those days there was no need to go to a special school to realize your potential. Today, my children go to private schools because of changes in the public schools. I'm reluctant to send them to public schools for several reasons—government instruction leaves much to be desired with its incantations of Islam. Children are forced into Islam. If they resist, they are bullied and intimidated. Since my experience, things have gone from bad to worse. Right now my children are in secondary school, and they live at home in these their formative years so that I can monitor their development. After their first college degree, they may live elsewhere. My primary concern is to lead our children so that God meets them."[11]

"Ishaku, we do not face issues that you face with Islam. Do you feel religious pressure at Bayero University?" I asked.

"Constantly I am reminded that I constitute a small minority, but I can live with that," she said. At a young age, I appreciated comparative religions. 'Why am I a Christian, not a Muslim? Is there anything that makes it better than the other?' I studied the Bible and relationship to God. I went beyond that, 'Why am I not a Muslim?' I also studied the Koran.

"The contrast is that in Christianity, God is reaching out to man. In Islam man is trying to reach God. In Christianity, we find exclusive expressions by the Lord Jesus about himself as the key to our relationship to God. 'I am the door, the good shepherd, the way, the truth, the life—not in Islam. Islam states commandments by God, but in Islam a man has no relationship with God—only in Christianity, only in the Bible. This keeps us standing! God's grace is sufficient—over and over again.

"In spite of all of Islam's challenge to us, Christianity is still on the move, waxing stronger in Nigeria. Once you profess to be a Christian, you have no reasons to fear. Even your adversary respects you. This is my experience. A story is told about a rich man in this town whose accountant was a Christian until the day he thought he'd please his master and become a Muslim. Only then his master let him go, saying, 'Since you've become a Muslim, I cannot trust you.' Some of them know that our God is the true God. Some people come to Christianity by reading the teachings of the Koran."[12]

"Really, Ishaku, I haven't heard of that before," I replied.

"Islam fears real Christian faith. Christianity, in the eyes of Islam, is its greatest threat. You do not fear something that is weaker than you are. They dread Christians coming close to them because contact with Christians make them lose their identity as the superior people. We are the light of the world. We are the salt of the earth. What are they more afraid of? They push Christianity away. That is our experience.

"Back to your question about feeling pressure. Bayero became a full-fledged University in 1978. As such, provisions were made for places of worship on the campus. In Nigeria that means financial allocations for a church and for a mosque. But the Muslims have refused to allow the church. There is no church building on the Bayero campus. In 1979, Christian students were encouraged to come together for worship. They were very few then and were allowed to use the lecture theatre for worship. They requested other off-campus Christians to worship with them, like nurses from the hospital. The little church kept growing. Then the University prohibited off-campus Christians from joining. That did not stop them. They kept growing. Every Sunday, Christian students of Bayero meet at the lecture theatre at the University. Now they have three worships, two in English and one in Hausa, 7:00 A.M 8:45 AM., and 10:30 AM. The Hausa worship is full to capacity, and they need more space, but they still have no building.

"So what did Islam do to them as the church grew? Persecution! In 1987 and 1990, Muslim students attacked them at worship. They threw stones at them. Even if we build a church now, it's going to be torn down. So why do they attack Christians? To stop us from believing! To stop us from living the Christian life in their presence! They fear a real faith because it makes them look small. But the more they try to stops us, the more we grow, just like the New Testament. Some of the national newspapers blamed the Christians for the attacks in 1987 and 1990, but the Bible tells us to 'live peaceably with all men.' Some of the Muslim students that witnessed the attacks later became Christians themselves—a sad but wonderful statement of fact.[13]

I replied, "Ishaku, I'm sure that the testimonies and conversations of those Muslims were never published by those newspapers. But answer this: can Christian professors speak of their convictions when they teach your classes?"

She answered, "Yes, at the university, whatever you are convinced of, it is a place for the impartation of that knowledge. 'Be wise as a serpent and harmless as a dove.' It requires wisdom. What makes you an authority is what you believe to be true. Christian professors were accused in the early 1980s by an international newspaper of teaching Christian views. They were at that time mostly Christian instructors in the economics department, a light shining brightly. Since that time, 1985, there is an unwritten code; no Christian professor should be admitted to the university and no Christian on staff should be promoted. Some Christian professors with a Ph.D. have taught for twenty-five years and are still classified as lecturers."[14]

I asked, "So why are they still here? Why not move to a more comfortable environment?"

She answered, "They say it is their calling as Christians. Their students know that they are different. They are Christians. They have the Spirit of God with them. They teach not to earn a living, but to glorify the Lord. As a minority, in the situation of darkness, they are called to be the light and to teach us to be the light."[15]

I said, "So I wonder Ishaku, how does this work? Do they make life miserable for these Christian instructors and for you as Christian students?"

"The heart of the challenge is that we must live peaceably with all men, with all humility. Normally we have harmonious working relationships between Christians and Muslims alike. Our relationship is one of understanding and respect as long as it does not come to religion. Then we are opposite of each other. The Holy Spirit regenerates Christians from within, even to love the enemy. I find that true in my day-to-day experience.

"Muslims live by the moral law, *sharia*. The spirit of *sharia* is harsh and often used as an instrument of oppression—a tooth for a tooth, an eye for an eye, or a life for a life. That is Muslim behavior everywhere in the world. When do we see to the contrary? There is no grace of God. All this noise about Islamic *sharia* law, people are unable to live by the law. They are always working for justification. *Sharia* can only be used as an instrument of prohibition and punishment.

"In Kano, I am rejected because I am a Christian. My children are not accepted in this place. It is an unwritten code. 'No Christian should be admitted to the University.' That is true of students as well as faculty. So Christians must work harder even though they are not promoted. Since 1985 no Christian instructors have been recruited at the university, only Muslims."[16]

"So, Ishaku, at the university there is an unwritten code not to recruit and not to promote Christians in the faculty. I assume it is unwritten because, after all, Nigeria is by it constitution a democracy with clearly specified freedoms. I also understand it is an unwritten code for administrators and teachers in the primary and secondary schools 'to bully,' as you said, non-Muslim students to learn and practice the relation of Isalm. Are there any other experiences that you wish to address?"

"I have two issues close to my heart. First, the West tried to serve this part of the world with radio and other instruments of media to disseminate information and education. This is presently not serving the Christian community. The BBC, even the Voice of America, has a caliber of people employed who do a great disservice in describing real events. They employ all Muslims. They control the media. The way they pass information is to further incite people to violence. They spread lies and set Nigeria on fire. Muslim journalists use the media to misinform the West. The West does not understand the source of its information, which is of course to their detriment.

"The second area is about Christian students' ministry in the rural areas. This has been very successful around Kano. But Muslims are using government policy to frustrate those efforts. As soon as a village is interested in Christianity, they cut off the means of water, electricity, education, and other resources. They see that this mission has long-term significance. They want to stop it. The rural areas surrounding Kano are converting to Christianity and in the future will challenge the Muslim residents of Kano. That is why in the last election Islamic *sharia* law became the main issue. Islam wants to forbid evangelism by Christians. *Sharia* law is used as an instrument of political oppression."[17]

Donven Maden joined our discussion at that point. She is also a graduate student in the economics department at Bayero University Kano. She presently serves on the University Chapel Committee and has been actively involved with the students in planting churches in the rural areas. Their first ministry was in the village of Yatopa. They built a small church with financial assistance from churches in Plateau State.

She explained, "After a few months, Muslims were sent in the darkness to destroy the building. At the time the pastor's wife was in the church. She was killed. The village rebuilt the church and warned the Muslims that they were prepared to shed blood to resist them.

"Islam does not allow us to establish a church. That is a regulation of *sharia* law. If we do, they try to destroy it. Their objective is to wreck and ruin our efforts to spread the Christian faith. Islam is a cultic movement. It sheds blood like it has demonic spirits. Muhammad intoxicated his men with a paradise. The only sure way they can get to paradise is to die in *jihad*. In the villages around Kano, the people who retain their tribal religions see Islam as a fighting people. So they refuse Islam. They see clearly that Christianity is about love and life hereafter and that Christians are a people of peace."[18]

I asked. "Donven, anything more you wish to tell us about Islam in Kano?"

"If you are a Christian, you are denied admission to the schools. You must change your name to a Muslim name. That is true through the whole educational system in the north, primary to university. Education has been especially important to Christians, and that policy puts them at the crossroads, to reject or affirm their faith. The Central Educational Committee rejects Christian names, even those with very high scores. Scholarships to school in Britain are only given to Muslims. That was not true before 1976."[19]

Eventually we parted ways with these special women. They again thanked us for our interest and seemed heartened by a visit from brothers from the West. While we were packing our materials, one of the local pastors, Nelson, came by and invited us to visit a few sights of interest in Kano. We were soon on our way.

The only city comparable to Kano, in my experience, is Khartoum. Streets are filthy dirty. Traffic lights are often inoperable. Police direct traffic, but movement is mostly by push and shove. A small walled city stands at the heart of Kano and reminded me of "bin Laden's Mosque" in Khartoum, an intelligence center for Islamic operations. A tour of the center would have proved interesting, but all of our efforts to meet Muslim leaders in Kano were rejected.

As we passed a school, Nelson told us about how the former schools of Christian missions from the West were taken over by the government and organized as public schools: "The agreement with the mission boards was that free education would be provided to all the children of Nigeria. That has not happened. The Muslim politicians have changed the names of the schools so as to honor Islam. Now the public schools are also used to educate children in the sacred rites of Islam. If our young Christian girls attend these public schools, they must wear Muslim dress and offer Muslim prayers.

"Violence against non-Muslim people in Kano State is common. In Kazura, two months ago, they burned down thirteen churches because a Muslim accused a Christian girl of insulting the prophet. Four children were burned to death. No one hears of these atrocities because there is no free press here, everything is under Muslim control."[20]

"In a sense, Nelson, you live with our 9/11 every day." I concluded.

"We experienced your 9/11, he said. You didn't know that, I guess. On 9-13-01, the Muslims of Kano celebrated the attacks against New York and Washington. They burned U.S. flags in our streets. In support, they burned Christian churches and Christians' houses. Some Muslims now have received sophisticated weapons via Sudan so that they can kill many people at a time. In the middle of all the trouble, we find ourselves with no place to bury our Christian dead."[21]

"That seems unbelievable. You have no place to bury your dead?" I asked.

"No, our cemetery is full for years," he replied. "That is a fact. The Muslim officials of Kano will not allow us to purchase land to use as a cemetery for Christians. Recently, an elderly woman arrived here to escape *jihad* in Yelwa. She died. We were forced to ship her body out of Kano State back to Plateau State for burial."[22]

Curious, I asked if we could visit the Christian cemetery.

Soon our van pulled up to the entryway of the old and only Christian cemetery in Kano. Several Muslims were seated in the middle of the driveway, casually playing at a board game. Our driver blew the horn and they dispersed. Once in the cemetery, Nelson showed us the method by which they now bury corpses alongside and on top of other corpses. Headstones are no longer an option.

He explained, "This is the only Christian cemetery in Kano, and it is full. To bury a Christian in a Muslim cemetery is, of course, forbidden as an abomination to Islam. So you need to convert to Islam to get buried."

As we walked the perimeter, I noticed broken walls and well-beaten paths. According to Nelson, it served as a thoroughfare for foot traffic during the busy hours of the day. In one corner of the cemetery, I saw a man urinating. As we walked, I also noticed places where others had defecated. Nelson pointed in the direction of his former residence, now a relic of smoke and ashes.

"They burned my house to celebrate your 9/11. We escaped over the wall,"[23] he said.

I was adjusting to burned-out houses and churches, but here I found a new dimension of intolerance: the refusal to grant a permit to buy space to bury the dead. Here was indisputable evidence. No one makes this up. It is mean and ugly. It is here for the whole world to come and see. But then, who would publish that story to the world?

To me the purpose of this intolerance seemed clear. Death and burial is significant in every world religion. The god of a religion who is unable to provide his people with a burial place for their dead would appear to many as not much of a god, if a god at all. The purpose of the practice to block an official place of burial is probably to portray the weakness of the God of Christianity. The other acts of intolerance in Kano do the same—a god who is unable to provide education for his children, promotions for his workers, security for his families, places of worship for his believers, and in the end no place for the burial of his dead—certainly does not represent a credible divinity in the world of Islam. These acts of intolerance by Islam remain shielded from the rest of the world, but for all of the local Muslims (and Christians) they serve as a testimony to the reign of *Allah* and replicate the behavior of terror subjugation (*dhimmitude*)

A Visit with Simon

The next day a gregarious fellow by the name of Simon came by for a visit. His smile showed a set of perfect white teeth. As he sat on his chair, he seemed eager to share his opinions and experiences as part of the 5 percent minority in Kano. His bright-orange shirt enhanced his dark facial features, while the ceiling light from our room bounced off his shining forehead, exaggerating his very distinct widow's peak.

He knew the purpose of our visit and our interest in him as a non-Muslim, a Christian living in an Islamic culture. "We want to know what it's like," I said. "In America we are taught that Islam, except for its radical fundamentalists, is a very tolerant and peaceful religion. So here we are in Kano to evaluate the reality of that claim, where the politics and culture is 95 percent Islam. So what is your experience, Simon?"

Simon had a resonating baritone voice and spoke with confidence. "It is not easy living among Muslims in Kano. We are relegated to almost nothing."[24]

"Explain yourself, Simon," I prompted.

"Well, for example, Islam controls all the local media. They respect nobody else. They have the power. Even though the constitution of Nigeria demands that religious television programming be equally available, they cut off Christian programs when Sunday morning comes. The television screen is blank. African Independent Television is seen in Lagos and elsewhere, but it is turned off in Kano."[25]

"So Simon, you're telling me that when African Independent Television broadcasts Christian worship or other educational programs, the Muslim authorities run interference in the receptors?" I asked.

"Exactly! It's not an official policy, of course; then we could pursue the issue legally. We have a divided nation—45 percent Muslin and 45 percent Christian—so the constitution was drafted to protect the religious freedoms of each. But we have no freedoms and there is no tolerance. There are Islamic programs all the time, but nobody else, no respect for persons or the constitution. When Islam has the numbers and the power, then it has no tolerance, no honor, and no freedom. That is the dark side of Islam. Muhammad was very tolerant of the Jews until he had the military force.

"The idea of tolerance by Islam is propaganda. As an example, Muslims burned my church to the ground because they decided to build a mosque west of the church. When they prostrated toward Mecca for their prayers, they saw the church. To them that was an abomination, so they burned it down.

"Violence against Christians is a way of life here. You never know when they will strike. I remember the violence of Islam in 1991, the so called 'Bunke riots.' Bunke was an evangelist who was invited by the churches of Kano to lead an evangelistic crusade. The Muslims went on a rampage. I saw thirty dead bodies. One pregnant woman had her baby cut from her body while she was alive. They killed the whole family.

When BBC reported the terror *jihad,* they called it the 'Bunke riots,' October 15, 1991. But they were not riots. They were brutal acts of oppression. They killed and burned Christians and churches. Christians, the victims, were reported as the aggressors. The BBC news coverage is by Muslims. Only Muslims work for BBC; check for yourself. I do not think the people in Europe know what they are doing here. How could they? For many years the Voice of America did the same."[26]

Yakuba joined us. He is a pharmacist and member of the Hausa tribe. "I was working with the hospital before I resigned in 1985," he told us. "I backed away from them to be free. They know you are a Christian, so there is no promotion. You remain in the system, but you don't go anywhere. That's part of the Muslim practice to make you abandon Christianity, especially for a 'Hausa man' like me. If in my youth I had not converted to Christianity, there would be no delay in my promotion,. I could be a commissioner. My classmates are commissioners. If I had gone back to Islam, I would be a commissioner. My parents are Muslim, but sent me to a Christian school for a better education."[27]

A Visit with Farouk

That evening Farouk Isah Yahaya visited us at our hotel. Farouk was a young man, twenty years of age, who had converted to Christianity. His father was an *emir,* and a teacher of the Koran, who received his Ph.D. from Oxford. Farouk told of his experience as a Muslim boy. His father had many wives. Farouk had twenty-three brothers and sisters. We were curios as to how he was taught to view non-Muslims, especially Christians.

"Anyone that is not a Muslim is a pagan. We were taught that Christians are planning to kill Muslims."[28] Farouk's words concurred with the Muslim spirit that had recently ignited controversy in northern Nigeria over a polio vaccine. The vaccine was rejected by Muslim scholars because they believed that the vaccine from the West contained "anti-fertility agents" to make Muslim male semen infertile ("Sharia panel faults report on polio vaccine").[29]

"I grew up as a Muslim," Farouk said. "I was taught how to destroy Christians. As a child I was not permitted to have a Christian friend. Every Christian is an agent of Satan. If I kill a Christian, it is not I that do the killing, but *Allah. Allah* takes pleasure in killing Christians. My people in Islam are uneducated and brain-washed. They believe all of these things. The little money they save is used to go to Mecca. It is required in the religion of Islam."[30]

Farouk also shared how his Muslim family lived together, very independent of his father, except for possibly a short time on an occasional evening. At the close of our visit, he told us that the church was still suspicious of him. They thought he might be a spy for Islam. They accepted him, but cautiously. They watched him with "a careful eye."

A Painful Journey Home

Early the next day, long before the call to Friday prayers, we were driving south to Plateau State. As we discussed the state of non-Muslim people in neighborhoods of Islam, we shared the very consistent, often irrefutable testimonies about terror subjugation in Islam. The behavior is so brutal and so blatant. Even though the abusive behaviors are from "an unwritten code," many of them conform to the official practice of *dhimmitude*, which marginalizes and enforces an inferior status on Jews and Christians.

Examples of *dhimmitude* are the consistent practice of no permit for building or repairing a church; no permit for the purchase of land for a cemetery; restricted admissions without

Muslim names to primary and secondary schools, colleges, and universities; the compulsory practice for all students to perform Muslim prayers and study the Koran, no scholarships for non-Muslim students, no non-Muslim political authority, and non employment or promotion of Christian teachers or professor within the educational systems.

The acts of abasement, intolerance, and violence in Kano are consistent with testimonies of the Christians in the states of Kaduna and Plateau. The abusive acts of intolerance portray a tragic similarity to the legally coded practices of *dhimmitude* by Islam throughout the centuries. For example, the refusal to grant building permits to churches is consistent with the behavior of Islam toward Christians throughout the Middle East since the year A.D. 640. not only has the restriction to build new churches been its practice, but the razing of hundreds of churches in northern Nigeria, burning and looting them, is also consistent with the terror behavior of Islam.

In her studies of ancient documents on the practice of *dhimmitude*, Western scholar Bat Ye'or uncovered frequent violations of Jewish synagogues and Christian churches. Worship centers were razed and set afire for the alleged crime that *dhimmis* had exceeded their rights, failing to comply with their inferior status as prescribed by regulations of their subjugation.[31] Their hearts were not "right" enough, "subdued" enough, or "lowly" enough (Koran IX(29)).

The refusal of Muslims to grant Christians a permit to purchase land for a cemetery also has similarities to *dhimmis* under the regulations of *sharia*. Christians and Jews were not permitted to lament aloud at a funeral or in a cemetery. If a Muslim onlooker reported inappropriate wailing, the cemetery could be closed or destroyed. In some Muslim traditions, the inferior status of non-Muslim peoples was extended into eternity. On the Day of Judgment, *Allah* would sentence to hell a Jew or Christian as atonement for the sins of a Muslim.[32]

Farewell

On the final evening of our Nigerian tour, we visited our new friends as best we could. With heavy hearts we said our good-byes and the next day began our long journey home.

As we flew from airport to airport, three serious issues kept surfacing in our discussions. First, we were deeply impressed with the Christian people of northern Nigeria. They seemed to understand that their commitment could cost them their opportunities of financial success, their possessions, their homes, their children, and possibly their lives. Nonetheless, they took their stand. They have not run. For myself as a Christian, I am very proud to belong with these people. They have a place to stand. They are standing. I wish to stand with them.

Second, we were absolutely amazed that the religion of Islam is able to portray itself in the West as a religion of peace and tolerance. The lie is so egregious. The evidence in Nigeria is so unbelievably overwhelming. In these hidden neighborhoods of the heartland of Islam, there is no debate about who did the violence. The razed buildings are there. The practice of regulating and demonstrating the inferior status of Christians within the government and schools, even cemeteries, can easily be documented by anyone.

Third, we were deeply troubled by the silence of the Western press and Western churches. We could understand the practice of the press. It is a free press. But where are the voices of Western church leaders? They could have long ago gathered an understanding of terror behavior in Islam. Tragically, many Western church leaders failed to take a public stand in defense of the massacred Sudanese Christians of the 1980s and 1990s. Millions were killed. Millions were displaced. Nigeria may be in the early stages of a comparable tragedy. Why the bloody silence from many of the Western "agents of righteousness?"

As I assess my journeys into the Islamic neighborhoods of Nigeria, the evidence does clearly indict Islam for acts of terror behavior (terrorism) against its Christian neighbors. Before my visit, I had the slight hope that maybe Islam had evolved and abandoned the oppressive behaviors from its past. Even while in Nigeria, I did not want to accept the testimonies of brutal, bigoted acts of violence, and the devastation that I was witnessing. The world is such a better place when we believe that Islam is a religion of peace and tolerance. Who does not wish to believe our politicians and pastors? Who does not wish to trust the American media as a solid anchor from which one can gather an accurate worldview?

However, we took the time to explore the life of Muhammad and the teachings of the Koran, unlike many pastors, politicians, and journalists. There we saw the clear models and the specific instructions for terror behavior, *jihad* and *dhimmitude. The idea that Islam may still revere those words and models of terror in the twenty-first century is probably unbelievable to most of us as Americans. How can any of us bring ourselves to believe that a religion that controls the minds of 20 to 25 percent of the world population promotes **a sacred terror behavior program** against its non-member neighbors?* The thought is just too terrifying. As I analyze my reactions to the Nigerian experience, I begin to wonder whether my initial urge to deny the reality of terror violence in Islam is problematic for other people, politicians and media giants included?

When I returned from Nigeria, I sent a message to a close friend who is a chief administrator for a significant world relief organization Africa and Asia. I shared what I had witnessed. In response, he contacted his legal department in northern Nigeria. Within hours, my report was confirmed. At that point, I was shocked that as a qualified, active administrator in a very successful organization was actually unaware of these terror tragedies. He spoke several languages, travels the world, has had primary residences for twenty-five years in South American and African countries, and earned his Ph.D. in England. Yet he appeared totally oblivious to the active terror behavior by Islam within his own province. I wonder now if he is also trapped in a hope against hope denial?

Out of concern for Nigerian victims, I forwarded a descriptive article to my denominational magazine. Within three days, the article was turned down. The editor's response was, "We will investigate the situation in Nigeria by use of our own staff." Whether he did or not, I don't know. I do know I never saw a published report. He promoted dialogue with Islam, but to me dialogue is more than gestures of inclusiveness. It must involve honest discussions of real subjects, like the terror behaviors in Nigeria, *jihad* and *dhimmitude*. Is the editor in denial also?

Sherwin and I witnessed the devastation. We listened to the wounded, their personal accounts of oppression, persecution, and subjugation. *Do the terror tragedies that Sherwin and I witnessed in northern Nigeria not exist, perhaps, because we as people have a need for them not to exist? Is it possible that we are so weary of conflict disrupting our personal lives, personal happiness, and personal goals that we refuse to see them? Is it possible that the greatest terror of all, for us as people of the West, is the reality that Islam is a religion of terrorism? Is our greatest refuge from that reality to cover our eyes?*

For me the most distressing aspect of witnessing terror *jihad* and aspects of *dhimmitude* in democratic Nigeria, other than the victims themselves, was the conformity of that behavior to the acts of Muhammad in the Jewish villages of Arabia and to the instructions of the Koran, "Fight against them who believe not in God...profess not the true religion (even) those unto whom the Scriptures have been delivered...until...they be reduced low" (Koran IX (29)). These actions of terror behavior in

Nigeria, *from the official eyes of Islam,* could legitimately be practiced in the defense of Islam, for the Christians of northern Nigeria had publicly and deliberately refused to accept the implementation and application of Islamic *sharia* law in their neighborhoods. The Christians saw Islamic *sharia* laws as a threat to their religious freedom and human dignity. Some saw those laws as salutes to the supremacy of Islam, which would in turn marginalize their status to that of an inferior people, *dhimmis* (Appendix C). Can we see that?

In Kano we listened to testimonies of victims who live within a 95 percent Islamic neighborhood, which imposes the affects of an unofficial *dhimmitude* on the less than 5 percent Christian minority. Churches are burned. Christians are stoned. No permits are granted to construct new church buildings. No permits are granted to purchase land for Christians to bury their dead. A process of Islamization is active in order to force Christian children into Islam. For example, in some state-sponsored schools, Christian children are required to change religion and/or to change Christian names to Muslim names in order to qualify for official student registration. In other public schools, Christian children must study from curriculums established by the Koran and must participate in sacred rites of Islam. In educational and political systems, Christian professionals are unable to receive promotions because Islam (Islamic *sharia* law) forbids them to fill positions that hold authority over a Muslim. These oppressive behaviors conform to those of terror subjugation, *dhimmitude,* but, absurdly, they are taking place within a democratic nation with a constitution that prescribes and protects individual freedoms.

That is not to say that these Muslim leaders with whom we visited are monsters. They are not crazy radicals. We dialogued together. They willingly shared their convictions for the need of *sharia* law in Nigeria. They explained the necessity for the implementation and application of Islamic *sharia* law for the life of a Muslim. In the course of our visits, we had no reason to doubt their sincerity. When they attempt to impose Islamic *sharia* law upon a community, they believe they are doing the will of *Allah* and acting for the good of humanity. They and others like them may at times rouse a rabble crowd and lead them, or point the masses in what they call "the divine direction," but in their hearts they believe Islamic *sharia* law is vital for the whole human race to enable all of humanity to live in obedience to the will of the holy Creator. Life in Islam is primarily about obedience, not freedom.

Unlike twenty-first century Americans, many Muslims, like Habib Umar Mahmud, seem to view freedom as dangerous, as an opportunity to disobey. Think about it. What experiences of freedom exist for Muslims in Islam? Islamic *sharia* law is the religious tool most desired by *imams* to make Muslims good Muslims. It controls their lives. It governs their behaviors. It forbids many personal choices. Islam is a closed, controlled culture. In that sense, Islam functions as a cult as much as a religion. Even meaningful contact with the outside world (Jews and Christians) are restricted and often forbidden by Muhammad and the Koran.

As we review terror behavior by followers of Islam in Nigeria, we see faithful followers walking in obedience. Why do we need to keep distorting that reality in the West by describing the faithful as wild extremists and radicals? Is that part of our need for a hope against hope denial of the realities of terrorism in Islam? These dear Muslim people are not initially our enemies by their personal choices, nor by their reactions to our so-called "crusader behaviors," but rather they are our enemies by divine instruction. They adhere to the traditions of Muhammad and the teachings of the Koran. They need Islamic *sharia* law, as Habib put it, "for conviction." In addition, we as Christians and Jews are correctly viewed as the major obstruction to the advancement of their faith at the time of Muhammad and today.

Even worse in the history and the teachings of Islam, Christianity is seen as the great threat to their final goal to govern the whole world by Islamic *sharia* law. Why does that fail to get traction in the mind of the West and in our so-called dialogues with Islam?

Can Muslims be any different than they are? How can the devout Muslims of Nigeria sympathize with the Christian widows and orphans who are victims of their terror *jihad* making? How can they weep for animals, for slain pigs as it were? The infallible Koran has taught them that the Christians and Jews after all are *kafirun*, "the worst of creatures" (Koran XCVIII (6)). Those teachings, sadly enough, have not mysteriously evaporated with the past. Muslims are not evil people by choice. They are not stupid. They hold offices of great prestige in the culture and civilization of Islam. Unwittingly, however, Muslims seem trapped inside the self-perpetrating legal controls of Islamic *sharia* law, which provides them no exits.

What if we, like them, were born to Muslim parents in northern Nigeria or Saudi Arabia? By birth we would then also be trapped within the religion of Islam. As faithful Muslims, we too would be inclined toward terror behavior of our religious culture, supported by our ancient authorities. How then would it be correct for Western sympathizers for Islam and Western proponents of Islam to look at us and classify us as radical fanatics instead of faithful believers in true Islam? How would it be legitimate for them to say that we do not belong to true Islam? Work with me here. How rational, how defensible, an argument is that?

Nigeria may well be in the early stages of a religious civil war. Both Christians and Muslims have divine orders to bring their religious message to the whole of Nigeria. The Muslim north is using the traditional methods of terror *jihad* and *dhimmitude* to take control of central and northern Nigeria. In addition, according to numerous sources, Islam is interestingly buying

Christians in the north and the south by paying off their debts, or by simply paying cash of approximately two thousand Nigerian nairas per convert. Muhammad modeled that practice (*dawa*) when he conquered Mecca and purchased the conversions of his former enemies by payments in camels and the release of valuable hostages, as for example with Sufyan and Khalid.

On the other hand, Christians, mostly evangelicals, are using the traditional tools of evangelism to successfully convert Muslims in central and northern Nigeria. An amazing achievement when we realize that a Muslim's conversion to Christianity may well cost him his relationship with his family and possibly his life! Of course the methods and outcomes differ radically from each other. Christians are instructed to bring the message by word and example (Matthew 28:19, 20), not by violence of the sword (Koran IX (29)). As per outcomes, Islam imposes a closed and controlled form of life for Muslims and non-Muslim peoples to increase faith and obedience by use of law and strict punishments. In contrast, Christianity sponsors something of an open life of freedom for Christians and non-Christians to make personal choices to obey or disobey.

I suspect that if a civil war does eventually break out, it will be described to the West in forms of denial, such as, "It is a war for oil," "a war for the Union," "a war for democracy," or "a war for freedom." All of those descriptions will be small pieces of reality, but they will only confuse and misinform the West if they are stripped from the religious factor. In the greater reality, if civil war in Nigeria is reported in the Western media, it will probably be covered as ineptly then as it is being covered at present. If the war, by some weird stratagem, is related to religions by the Western media, it will probably be portrayed as a justifiable Islamic *jihad*, faithful to the Islamic creed that *jihad is only on defense. The argument will be that Christians forced Islam into terror jihad by blocking the implementation and application of Islamic sharia law, a necessity for every true Muslim.*

Islam will accuse Christians of suppressing the sacred rites of Islam. Western sympathizers of Islam and Western proponents of Islam will blame Nigerian Christians for the narrow-minded approach to the necessity of Islamic *sharia* law for a Muslim to be a good Muslim. The argument will spin that Islamic *sharia* law is very similar to the Ten Commandments for Christians and Jews and that the suppression of Islamic *sharia* law is an act of religious bigotry and fanaticism led by Zionists and right wing evangelical Christians. Sadly for all the so-called dialogue, who in the West knows the difference between the Ten Commandments and Islamic *sharia* law? One percent of college students?

CHAPTER SIX

Journeys into Neighborhoods of Islam
Sudan

After my experiences in Nigeria, I was eager to visit the African nation of Sudan. On this particular journey, I was especially interested to learn more about Islamic holy law. Did Islamic holy law play a significant role in the fifty years of war in Sudan between the followers of Islam in the north and the Christians in the south, as it did in conflicts of Kaduna, Nigeria? Of course I was also interested in again pursuing whether the attitudes and behaviors of Islam during the war and postwar periods reflected terror behavior, *jihad* and *dhimmitude*, as it is modeled and taught in the ancient authorities of Islam.

I knew that a visit to Sudan was far more complex than a visit to Nigeria. For starters the United States had broken diplomatic relations with Sudan, so just the ordinarily simple task of obtaining a visa to Sudan would be no cakewalk. My only personal connection with Sudan was my Sudanese friend, James Khan, who had recently returned from Darfur. He had used the nation of Chad for a backdoor entry, with rebel troops escorting him and others into the Western Darfur region. Since he lives near Pasadena, only an hour drive from my home in Palm Springs, we were soon able to arrange a get-together.

James was scarcely recognizable at first glance. He must have lost twenty-five pounds, and he was no heavyweight to begin with. "You look like a scarecrow, Jimmy," I said. "What in the world happened to you?"

"Well, Marvin, when in Darfur, you share what you have," he replied. "Even though I was out-of-country only five weeks, I lost a ton. It didn't help any that I got deathly sick with diarrhea. For several days I needed my old friend, Thomas, to help me drink a glass of water. Thank the Lord! I was carrying some Imodium. But I'm getting better."[1]

"So what was your mission in Darfur?" I asked.

He said, "I went for several reasons. As you know, the conflict is described as Muslim against Muslim. But there are also Sudanese Christians in Darfur who escaped from the Civil War by fleeing to Chad and then were forced back across the border into Darfur. So I was asked to check on their condition. In addition my church is trying to get a line on the charges of genocide. Who is responsible? It seems Arab Islam of the north is the major sponsor of the killing and destruction committed mostly by the Janjaweed militia. According to my contacts, they are well armed, well disciplined, and often commit atrocities against the civilian population. They rape and abduct the young women. They burn villages and loot anything they think is of value, much like they did against us in the south for fifty years. I suspect that some Saudi princes are providing funds to purchase them advanced weapons just as they did against us when we threatened them in the Nuba Mountains and the Blue Nile in the 1990s.

"Personally, I am also trying to get a grip on the cause for this genocide. As I told you before, Khartoum Arabs used Africans to initially fight against Christians in regions of the south. Now it is their turn to die, but why? Some have explained it as a conflict between the farmers and the nomads. The Arab nomads wish to graze their cattle, and the African farmers wish to fence their cattle and grow crops. There is probably some truth in that explanation. But as I told you before, I always thought the war in Darfur was a racial issue. In my experience and knowledge, the only use Arabs have had for Africans for thousands of years is to make slaves. Go see how many 'free Africans' you can find in neighboring Egypt. They treated me like an animal. Displaced African Sudanese are killed, abused, and forced to return to the oppression of Sudan. But after my recent visit to Darfur, I am beginning to believe that the genocide is about more than racism."[2]

"What do you mean by that, James?" I asked.

"I find that difficult to explain without some context," he continued, "so, let me simply say what I think may be happening in Darfur. I think the genocide may well be a *jihad* for a cleansing or purification of Islam in Africa. Now why do I think that way? The Islamic leader of Sudan for the past thirty years is Hasan al-Turabi. He is a devout member of the Muslim Brotherhood and a strong adherent of Wahhabism out of Saudi Arabia. Turabi was a major religious, political force behind the establishment of Sudan as an Islamic state. He was the personal push behind President Numeiri's declaration in September 1983 that Islamic *sharia* law is the law of all Sudan, the north and the south. I think he is still a force to reckon with. But Turabi is not Sudanese. He is not an African. He is not an Arab African.

He is an Egyptian, evicted from Egypt by President Nasser as a member of the Muslim Brotherhood. That means he does not think like a Sudanese Muslim. He does not believe like a Sudanese Muslim. As a member of the Muslim Brotherhood, he is committed to the restoration of Islam as it was at the time of Prophet Muhammad. He rejects the Jews and the Christians, but he also rejects 'folk Islam' as a corrupt form of true Islam.

'Folk Islam' was the Islam of Sudan before our independence from Egypt and Britain in 1956.

'Folk Islam' is a merging and a mixing of the religion of Islam with African tribal religions. In a way, Islam was co-opted by the 'witch doctors' of our tribal religions. They became the holy men of Islam. When we pray as Christians, we often pray in the name of Jesus. When many of these Sudanese Muslims pray, they pray through their ancestors. Followers of 'folk Islam' in regions of the Sudan practice communication with their dead and claim to perform miracles. It is very powerful and influential.

"Initially, when Turabi came to power, he joined hands with 'folk Islam,' but it seems to have been only for the purpose of political power. He used the African Sudanese Muslims to fight the African Sudanese animists and Christians. Now that most of the southern power is in ruins and many non-Muslim Africans are injured and displaced, the *jihad* appears to have turned against the 'unclean' African Muslims of Darfur.

"I am uncertain as to the origins and present make-up of the Janjaweed militia used by Khartoum to attack Darfur. They fight in the name of orthodox Islam, and I think the soldiers are adherents of orthodox Islam. I remember when the so-called elitist army of Arab Muslims was put in place, called the Peoples Defense Force (PDF), to defend the Islamic state of Sudan, when the south was putting extreme pressure on government forces in the Blue Nile and was moving closer to Khartoum. I think the Janjaweed could be the equal of the People Defense Force or some combination of sorts. Whatever militias are used by Islam, I am beginning to believe that the genocide in Darfur is another creation of Turabi's evil mind to purify Islam."[3]

"That is a new take on Darfur for me, James," I said. "Life with you is always interesting. When do we get to go together to Darfur? More important for the moment, do you have any suggestions for my current situation? I need a visa and in-country contacts in order to arrange visits with Christians from the south."

"Marvin, you will never get to Darfur by way of a visa from the Sudanese government," he replied. "Even diplomats from the United Nations and the United States have difficulty visiting Darfur. So if you want to go with me, we go through Chad. But from our telephone conversation, it sounded like you want to know more about Islamic *sharia* law and its affects on the displaced people from the south. I think you should visit with Jacob Deng from Des Moines. At the moment, he is most in touch with the dispersed people of southern Sudan, more than I am. He can help you with a visa. A good opportunity for contact is a Prayer and Fast Day scheduled in Des Moines on the third Sunday of March. I think you will meet a number of Christian Sudanese refugees."[4]

"As I arrange my visit, do you have any suggestions for reading materials?" I asked.

"I recommend that you go on-line. I am always surprised what I find. Otherwise I can think of two books you will find generally helpful. For me both of them are well done. One is by a Christian author, Isaiah Dau. I think he wrote it for his doctoral degree, *Suffering and God: Theological Reflections on the War in Sudan*. The other book is a more recent, well-documented study of the life of Hasan al-Turabi as the Islamic leader of Sudan, *Revolutionary Sudan*. I can't remember the name of the author."[5]

As James and I shared and compared information and opinions on Nigeria and Sudan, we struggled together with other questions. *Was the cleansing of Sudan a preparation for the cleansing of Africa? What was the real purpose of the twenty-six training camps established by bin Laden and his Afghani fighters in the Khartoum region of Sudan? What happened to the tens of thousands of African children kidnapped by Muslim forces in Sudan? Are they future fighters and future suicide bombers for Isalm? If so, where are they and where will they strike?*

As we said our goodbyes, James gave me a video of Christian children fenced inside an Islamic "religion-training" camp. He added, "The man I hired to photograph these children is now in hiding, a *fatwa* was issued for his execution."[6] As I was driving home, I thought of the radical subjugation that Islam had imposed on James and the indigenous peoples of southern Sudan, now scattered as refugees across Sudan, Africa, and the world.

The Journey

In March 2004, at a Prayer and Fast Day in the city of Des Moines, I shared my day with Christian refugees from Dinka, Nuer, and other tribes of Sudan. A friend from Iowa, Gary Hortsman, and I were the only non-refugee Americans present. Each Sudanese speaker inspired me (with the assistance of translators). Each message was a challenge for Christian "brothers and sisters" to move on with life and remain faithful to God's calling. Frankly I had expected some anger, threats, blame, and talk of retaliation, but similar to my experience with Nigerian Christians, I kept hearing hope and praise. Amazing.

At afternoon break-time, I shared my needs with Jacob Deng. He seemed thrilled at my plans to visit Sudan, not many other Americans were making that journey. He readily agreed to share contacts and to assist in the creation of a working schedule for my visits into southern Sudan. At the close of the day, we shook hands in a common interest to uncover and record the behavior of Islam toward non-Muslim peoples in Sudan. Although I had visited a delightful and worthy people that day, I knew I was a long way from entering Sudan. In the days that followed, I received warnings from the U.S. State Department not to travel to Sudan. They could not protect me. I dismissed the warning as routine. How can the United States government protect an American inside an Islamic culture anywhere? We cannot do that in Iraq with one hundred and thirty thousand American soldiers. Could we do that in the United States?

Deng told me to e-mail the Sudanese government to request a visa, which proved very unwise for a long list of reasons. Sudanese officials responded with instruction that I needed to purchase a dated roundtrip ticket in order to apply for a visa. I purchased my tickets and made application. I was then rejected. I lost the cost of my ticket and had no visa. I worked that routine twice. I lost twice.

Frustrated, I called Deng. He gave me a personal contact in Sudan by the name of Phillip. When Phillip knew my source was Jacob Deng, he seemed prepared to work with me. He recorded the information pertinent to visa application, instructed me to fill out another visa application form and mail it, along with my passport, plus three hundred dollars to an address in Washington, D.C. then he told me to wait and he would call me within a week or so. Sure enough, ten days later, Phillip was on the phone: "We have the right connections in place. You will have your visa shortly. Look forward to your visit." Later at the Khartoum Hilton, I would learn from a staff member of Secretary of State Colin Powell how impossible it was to obtain Sudanese visas for U.S. officials.

In July I was off to Sudan, but alone. Most of my friends thought I had gone over the edge on this one. Because of short notice, my flight plans proved ridiculous. I flew Los Angeles, Minneapolis, Cincinnati, Amsterdam, Nairobi, and Khartoum. By the time I reached Amsterdam, I was into serious sleep deprivation. Flying economy never helps. Afraid I might miss my next flight, I refused to close my eyes. I walked. I ate. I walked. I ate. Eight hours passed. By departure time, my body clock was so confused that I sat wide-eyed through the darkness of my seven-hour flight to Nairobi.

At 6 A.M. we landed, and I faced a ten-hour layover. Again desperate for sleep, I paid the fees for a Kenya visa. Once outside the airport, I hailed a taxi into Nairobi. As I checked in at the Meridian Hotel. I confirmed at the front desk a wake-up call for 1:00 P.M. to allow ample time to catch my next flight.

At 12:59 P.M. I awakened to looked at the clock. I showered, shaved, packed my bag, and paid my bill. My wake-up call never happened. On my taxi ride to the airport, the sky was clear and the sun shone brightly. As I chatted with the cabbie, Fredrick, a herd of giraffes came running through the fields parallel to the taxi...a breathtaking sight. I thought, *what a splendid way for a friendly nation to greet and entertain its visitors. Thank you, Kenya, for sharing your wildlife!*

Customs, immigration, and a walk to in-transit travel went quickly. At the departure gate, I visited with a Kenyan who resided in Ventura, California, and I almost missed my flight to Khartoum. A set of security screens blocked my vision of the plane and the doorway to the boarding access ramp. Having heard or seen nothing, I felt uneasy and asked a Kenya Airline stewardess when we were boarding.

"I think everyone is onboard." She said.

"Not me," I said, as I ran toward security. "I must get myself a watch." As everyone who travels Africa knows, at that stage there is no longer any room in the overhead compartments for carry-on baggage, which posed another problem.

When I sat down, they closed the door. Next to me was a gentleman named Tom, who I discovered was a Christian missionary in Khartoum. I am sure he did not volunteer that information to everyone who sat near him. He told me that in eight years time he had three converts from Islam to Christianity. He was at the time returning from a holiday break in France. Since I was curious as to how he viewed the French situation with Islam, I asked. Without hesitation, he said, "I think France is on its last fling as a Western nation. Its Muslim population may be as high as twenty percent. Just the Muslim birthrate will bury the French way of life in three, four decades. Unlike French birth control, Muslims are real 'baby makers.'"[1] Tom appeared bright, articulate, and strong; a gentleman with whom I wished to stay in touch. I got his name, address, and telephone number.

Since Nigerian soldiers detained me at customs in Lagos during the Biafran War, my anxiety always runs high every time I enter a port of customs, and it was very high at Khartoum. As the last person in line to check through from my flight, I was able to catch the attention of a valet standing in the bag claim area. From a distance I pointed to my bag on the conveyor belt. He grabbed it and eventually the others. By the time my paperwork cleared, most Sudanese had left the terminal. Now things would get serious.

My mind was spinning. What would Sudanese customs do? How effective was the "underground" in Sudan? Was there really an "underground?" Our U.S. State Department warned all travelers not to carry recorders, cameras, and film into Sudan. They would be confiscated. I ignored them. One suitcase was filled with technological materials for Phillip. Another huge bag was filled with clothing for the displaced and homeless. As I walked across the terminal with my valet, a very tall, well-dressed gentleman stepped up on my left side, put his hand on my shoulder and asked, "Dr. Marvin?"

"That's me," I said.

He continued forward at a brisk pace to speak with the custom agents. Then he was gone. Now came the moment of truth. As I looked into the eyes of the agents, I was greeted with smiles. My bags were immediately green-tagged, and I was never asked one question. As I walked toward the exit, I noticed Tom sweating through an interrogation; but I had an adrenaline rush. I wanted to shout, "There is an underground!" and leap into the sky.

When I pushed my way through the terminal door, I was greeted by a blast of hot desert air. I stepped forward into the darkness, searching and hoping to find my new Sudanese contacts. Suddenly they surprised me, jumping from the bushes and shouting in chorus. "Welcome to Sudan." They embraced me like and old friend. I was deeply pleased.

Phillip, my personal contact, referred by Jacob Deng, was eager to visit and discuss plans. Soon we were driving to the Khartoum Hilton in a very special entourage created in my honor. One car led, another took up the rear. The car in which my bags and I were packed was safely tucked in between. The mystery of how these displaced peoples secured three cars together at the same time in the territory of Khartoum still baffles me.

Hotel registration was no formality. Front desk personnel were pushed aside, and I faced a second port of "official" immigration. My passport with visa was withheld. I objected, "My passport has never been taken from me in any other country of the world." I was ignored.

It was explained, "If your records are in proper and correct order, your passport will be returned in three days. You are not to venture beyond the Khartoum city limits during your stay in Sudan. If you violate that order, you will be incarcerated."[8]

That was a serious blow to my travel plans to visit southern regions of Sudan for the coming weeks. What to do now? How did they know my plans?

As I closed my eyes that night, I tried to visualize the new faces that greeted me at the airport. I thought of how their families had cultivated, pastured, and hunted the rich lands of southern Sudan, possibly for millenniums. Now many of them were outcasts in their own land, the Sudan, "the land of the blacks." Strangers had stolen their heritage. Many of them fresh widows and orphans, fled the Muslim forces, scattering across the desert wastelands. Tens of thousands of the children were kidnapped and missing. How many of them were captured and imprisoned in Islamic "religion-training camps?" How many were sold into slavery?

The next day while Phillip was working to re-arrange my schedule, his right hand man, Benjamin, joined me at the hotel. Curious, I asked, "Why are all the women wearing headscarves a the Hilton?"

"Why do you ask?" he responded. "Do you ever see women in Saudi Arabia who are not wearing headscarves? Sudan was declared an Islamic state, governed by Islamic *sharia* law."[9]

"But my understanding, Benjamin, is that presently Islamic *sharia* law is 'frozen,'" I stated.

"That is true, Marvin, but that does not change the Islamic culture, politics, and military. Islam still intimidates and bullies non-Muslim people. See the women serving here in the restaurant? Watch them and compare them to the women seated at the tables."[10]

"All of them are wearing headscarves." I answered.

"Yes, Marvin, but the servers are Christians. Look at them. They smile at you, interact with you, look you in the eye. They are wearing headscarves, but they are not Muslims. They do what they must do to work here. The women being served at the table do not look at you that way. They look down. They look away. In Islam, eye contact with a man is inappropriate. It is against the law. The freezing of Islamic *sharia* law is mostly political talk, Islam is the boss in Sudan."[11]

"Ben, do you see the woman with the gold colored jacket to her waist standing near the door? No matter where I go in the hotel, she seems to show up."

"Welcome to Sudan, Marvin. She is probably with Sudanese intelligence and you are her latest surveillance assignment. I doubt she will follow us from the hotel, but we will see. I thought that since you have a vacant schedule today, we could view the city together."[12]

As we stepped from the lobby, a doorman showed us to a taxi. Several miles from the Hilton, we passed two large church buildings, one Coptic, the other Anglican. Both were constructed when Great Britain was the political authority in Sudan. Far more striking than the churches was a mosque nearby. I noticed a large number of Mercedes automobiles in its parking lot. So I asked Ben. "What mosque is that?" he waved me off, motioning toward the Arab taxi driver.

Several miles later, in a dirty, dusty part of town, we stopped by an internet café and began walking. As we were looking at shoes in a storefront window, Ben said, "It is called, 'the bin Laden Mosque.' It is known as the central intelligence operation. Bin Laden first came because of his interest in the success of Turabi, when Sudan was declared an Islamic state with *sharia* law. After bin Laden's victory over the Russian military, he returned to Sudan with men from his Afghani militia (*mujahideen*). Bin Laden and Turabi became close friends, both deeply religious and both lovers of Arabian horses."[12]

"Why would bin Laden put his intelligence center in a mosque?" I asked.

"I think he probably constructed the mosque, so that could be a reason. But Islam is that way. No parts of Islam are separated from other parts of Islam. Islam not only worships one God, but Islam is one. The mosque, the worship , the politics, the education, the law, the police, and the military—they all work together as the community (*umma*). Western people struggle with that idea because they legally separate religion from life."[13]

"I understand that bin Laden established twenty-six terrorist (militia) training camps in Sudan. What do you think is his purpose?"

"I suppose it is easy to jump to conclusions on that. Obviously Sudan is a close neighbor to the birthplace of Islam. Look at our borders with Eritrea, Egypt, Libya, and Chad. They are strong nations of Islam. So in that sense it is natural that Islamic militia are found n in our area. But I have been told that the Islamic Council of London has approved plans for Islamizing the whole African continent. When you study a map of Africa, it becomes crystal clear that for the Islamic countries of the north, southern Sudan is the strategic gateway into what is left of this rich, black continent."[14]

After a two-block walk, we flagged another taxi. "Why another taxi?" I asked.

"Mostly because of you, Marvin. I do not know if we are being followed. Intelligence was very concerned about you last night. How do they know you?"[15]

"They do not know me, Ben."

"I think you may be sruprised. Have you communicated with them?"[16]

"Yes, but I have security."

"Well, Marvin, I think we may all be surprised at the skills and techniques of Sudanese and bin Laden intelligence."[17]

As we rode the streets of Khartoum, I began to think of the problems I had with my computer since my contacts with Sudan immigration via the internet. My paranoia worked overtime. What did they know?

Ben got my attention: "Tomorrow morning I plan to take you to the women's prison for a 10 A.M. program. After that I think John Tang will be coming in on the bus from Malakal. He escaped his Muslim slave master and is still fragile emotionally."[18]

When Ben dropped me back at the Hilton, my first sight as I entered the lobby was a heavy-set woman wearing a headscarf with a gold colored jacket to her waist. Suddenly a British soccer team burst into the lobby. The next day the Brits were scheduled to play the Sudanese. That evening I visited with several of the British players. We shared opinions on Islam and the Iraqi war. As I left them, one of the players gave me his card and encouraged me to call his cell phone in case of trouble.

The next morning, I was off to the women's prison of Khartoum. Chaplin Thomas led me on a brief walk through the compound, and then we took our seats together in an outdoor pavilion. More then two hundred women prisoners gathered to join in Christian worship sponsored by the Presbyterian Church of the Sudan (Appendix E).

Our host honored us by providing "backless" benches for our comfort, which in my experience is typical African hospitality. The prisoners, on the other hand, sat together on the floor, an exceedingly colorful throng, dressed in the brightest greens, reds, yellows, and blues. The prison attendants, mostly women, stood together dressed uniformly, wearing white tops, turquoise skirts, and pure white headscarves. Several Arab women observed from a distance. As I waited for the service to begin, I snapped several pictures, but a police officer warned me that cameras were forbidden within the prison area. I put my camera away.

In normal Presbyterian style the center of the worship was the sermon, on this occasion presented by Mrs. Mary Kur Deng. Her biblical texts were carefully chosen so as to touch the thinking and feelings of the scattered, displaced, homeless, and now imprisoned, refugees.

> But this is a people plundered and looted, all of them trapped in pits or hidden away in prison. They have become plunder, with no one to rescue them; they have been made loot, with no one to say, 'Send them back.' (Isaiah 42:22)

After connecting with the downtrodden, she noted with emphasis the New Testament words, "This is the verdict: Light has come into the world, but men love darkness instead of light because their deeds are evil" (John 3:19). The message was obvious, at least to me, that these women prisoners were victims of the darkness, but in the darkness they had an obligation to live as the light.

"Thomas," I said, "it seems to me that almost all of these women prisoners are Christians. Why are they in prison?"

He explained, "Well, first of all, 80 percent are Christians, but technically they are not in prison because they are Christians. The laws of Islam convicted them of an actual crime. As women they had no real defense in court because a woman's testimony under Islamic *sharia* law is valued as only 50 percent that of a man, plus they are Christian, so their testimony is viewed as unreliable. If a Muslim man says a woman is guilty, she is as good as convicted."[19]

"So where is compassion and tolerance for these poor souls, Thomas?" I asked.

"You are looking at it," he answered. "Remember that most of these are displaced Christian women from the south. They have no resources. They have no clothing but what they wear. They have little to no food. Many of them are widows. Some of them still have small children and find feeding and caring for them extremely difficult. Small amounts of money trickle in from American and European churches, but that is it. Islam has blocked all non-Muslim relief assistance, no real foreign support for these women. Islam has closed those doors, political and religious.

"President Bashir and the NIF (National Islamic Front) did successfully close down 'Operation Lifeline Sudan' some years ago. Today Christian agencies that wish to assist displaced Christians and other non-Muslim peoples are prohibited from entering Sudan. Any world relief supplies, including those from church organizations, can only be distributed through Islamic centers. That also applies to UNICEF. Christian relief agencies were being dismantled as early as the mid 1960s. Of course the problem with the Islamic centers is the denial of goods and services to non-Muslim peoples. The only way for them to receive support from an Islamic center is to convert."[20]

"So, how does that relate to these women prisoners?" I asked

"Well, what do these Christian women do to stay alive, for money, food, and medicine? They will not convert to Islam. They will not prostitute to Muslim men. But there is a skill that they still can use, but it has become illegal under Islamic *sharia* law. They know how to make wine. So they make it and then they sell it on the black market to the Muslim men of Khartoum. Some Muslim men like wine. If Sudanese intelligence identifies and arrests them for alcohol consumption, then they seek mercy by revealing their sources. That is the story of many of these women prisoners. Convicted for the crime of winemaking. Of course they are unable to pay any fines, so they serve time in prison. It is just one of the many terrible tragedies from Islam forcing its religious authority on all the people."[21]

The women prisoners generally appeared healthy to me. Most of them were described as "displaced persons." That means that the houses and the farms that they used to live in are burned, destroyed, or in some cases occupied by the enemy. It is known as 'booty' in Islam, a legal right to the possessions of the enemy. Making wine is in some cases the only alternative these women have to that of converting to Islam to obtain the basic necessities for life. Formerly, organizations like Bread for the World, Menonite Central Committee, Church World Services, and UNICEF provided assistance to victims of disasters both natural and man-made. Relief by such agencies is prohibited in Sudan, as it is in many other Islamic nations. The goods, foods, and medicines are received by Islamic organizations and then distributed by Islamic centers to promote allegiance among the Muslim population and conversions from among the non-Muslim population.

As I was leaving the prison, a woman rushed toward me. She said, "My name is Kate, and I am here from Britain to visit these women. I noticed you taking pictures. Will you please mail me a few copies? Here is my address." I agreed, but later lost her address. So much for my good intentions. Kate was troubled that the women were incarcerated for the simple crime of winemaking.

A Visit with John

Early the next morning, I decided to check out Ben's suspicion that I was under surveillance of the woman wearing a gold-colored jacket to her waist. I went to the e-mail center. After several minutes, I stepped away from the computer to the door. She was standing in the hallway. Later, at breakfast, she sat at a table across the room. She was always there.

While awaiting Ben's arrival, I noticed that most people in the lobby and adjoining coffee shop were Middle Eastern, but that there were also a good number of Chinese, dressed in traditional Western-style suits and ties. The "surveillance woman" was also on the job. When Ben arrived, I was out the door. We traveled five to six miles in the city, paid the cabby, walked several blocks, and caught another cab. At our next stop, we walked ten to fifteen minutes along a paved road and then into a back alley. Ben knocked at the door of a small, broken-down shelter. Once inside I met John and his Uncle Nathan, who had been waiting patiently. John was a young member of the Nuer tribe and preferred to speak his tribal language. Uncle Nathan translated, and Ben assisted when necessary.

Whenever John smiled, he lifted his hands to cover his very boyish face. His uncle Nathan appeared weary. His eyes were jaundiced. Viewing the two, I was overwhelmed by a sense of extreme pity. Briefly, I was unable to speak. Embarrassed, I wiped the tears from my face. The two beleaguered faces had momentarily captured the immense tragedy of the southern Sudanese—millions dead, millions disabled, millions homeless, tens of thousands imprisoned, and tens of thousands enslaved.

I said, "John, I understand that you escaped from your salve master. Tell me how it happened. How did you become a slave?"

He answered, "I was captured by the Muslim soldiers, and later they sold me to my Muslim master. He would not allow me to use my Christian name. 'From now onward, your name is Abdullah Muhammad.'"[22]

"What were you doing when you were captured," I asked.

He replied, "I was eleven years old and was trying to earn some money, so I often went into the forest, near the river. When cattlemen came to cross the river, I would give them a hand in making the cattle cross over. Usually they would give me some coins. While I waited for the cattlemen to come, I fished for the evening meal."[23]

"Did your father think you were safe doing that kind of work in the forest?" I asked.

"My father was killed in the war and my mother is blind. She is now unable to do much work. That is why I tried to catch fish when I was not chasing cattle. The other boys working with me that day lost both of their parents. The soldiers took all four of us, tied our hands, blindfolded us, and threw us on their camels."[24]

"How did you know that these were Muslim soldiers, John?"

"I knew that immediately because I saw them earlier in the village going to the mosque. "When they came, I was very afraid. What were they going to do? They had guns. I knew other boys had been captured and taken away. Sometimes the boys were returned for ransom, but mostly they were sold to the people of the north. They had no parents. They had no money. A short time prior, a friend of mine was captured, but he escaped to tell the police. The police arrested the soldiers, but the next day the solders gave money to the police and were set free. The police were Muslims, too."[25]

"Where did they take you?""

"They took me to Keila, a Muslim village. I do not know how many days was the journey because I did not know night and day from the blindfold. Sometimes they stopped to drink water, but mostly the camels were running. I think they were afraid someone was following them. In Keila, they told the people that we were escaped slaves that they had captured. 'If they run, bring them back.' I did not understand them, but one of my friends understood some Arabic.

"The journey was exhausting for us on the camels. We were carried for a long, long time. It was always night. We could not see. The camels were always moving. I did not eat for several days, but I was not hungry for food."[26]

"So what did your master make you do?" I asked.

"As a slave I was to watch the cattle. I was still in Sudan, but very far away from my home. Every day I needed to watch the cattle or I would be sold. I stayed there. The man in charge of all the cattle was a former Christian who had also been a slave. He converted to Islam and was granted his freedom. He was kind to me. I stayed by Muhammad one year. I did not try to escape. I was threatened that if I run away, then they will catch me and cut my Achilles tendon."[27]

"Did you understand what the threat meant?" I asked.

"I did, because I saw them do it to Hammed. He tried to escape. He wanted me to go with him. When they caught him, they brought him back. They made him build a *tugul* house (a house of mud and sticks) for him to stay in by himself. Then they made me watch as they cut his Achilles tendon. They gave him an injection to numb the area. Then they cut him with a sharp knife. After that he cannot run. It is very hard to walk, even when it heals. He cripples now. He needs to use a donkey to help him watch the cattle and the sheep" *[material in parenthesis mine].*

"Uncle Nathan, how common a practice was it to catch young boys and make them slaves?" I asked.

"It was a common occurrence. It was easy money. It is legitimate trade for Islam. In *jihad*, the enemy women and children are part of the booty. Muslim officials had no care for the orphan African kids. Usually they would capture boys between seven and twelve. They raided the villages in southern Sudan, took the orphan children, and then sold them in the north to Muslim nomads, or to whomever paid the most *dinars*. There are still many slaves in Sudan, but there are few Muslims who are slaves. When you convert to Islam, you are set free. That is part of the Islamization practice taking place in Sudan."[28]

"As a young slave, John, how did you keep your faith?"

"I did not speak Arabic. I refused. They tried to teach me. They tried to teach me the prayers. I kept speaking my language. They did not understand me. When they prayed, I joined them. I bowed with them toward Mecca, but I prayed the Lord's Prayer. Sometimes, I said the Apostles' Creed. I learned the Apostles' Creed in catechism from my church. After a while they asked me. 'Who is this Pontius Pilate?' I told them I was praying in my language. They tried to force me to pray Muslim prayers five times each day, but I did the Lord's Prayer and the Apostles' Creed. I would kneel and then sit up. I believed God would keep me safe because I am always praying. I never stopped."[29]

"Didn't you feel desperately lonely?"

John's response became deeply emotional. At first he choked, but then became very talkative. He said, "My Nuer language kept me separate and alone. They tried to get me to learn Arabic and become a Muslim. My safety was to hide. My language helped me hide. One day when I was caring for the sheep, my master hid a sheep. He said, "You lost one of my sheep. I will beat you. Where is my sheep? I will beat you unless you say, *"Ilaha illa Allah, Muhammad rasul Allah"* (There is no

God but *Allah.* Muhammad is the messenger of God). He went to get a stick to beat me, but while he was gone, the sheep he had hidden returned. He became very angry and threw down the stick and said. 'He has a devil. I tried to beat him and something stopped me.' I feel God was protecting me."[30]

"Did you have anyone to talk to?"

"No."

"Did you cry at night?"

As if I touched a nerve, John became anxiously energetic. He said, "I cried very quietly so that they could not hear me. I thought my master was making a plan to beat me and destroy my manhood. One morning he was going to the mosque at 5:00 A.M. He found me praying and crying in my bed. I tried to tell him with sign language that I had a dream. He said. 'You have a devil.'

"My master tried to beat me, but his father tried to protect me. 'Keep him happy and he will accept our religion.' Then I was told that if I would go to an Islamic school to learn Islam, they would send me back to my home with a wife and cattle to teach my people in the ways of Islam. In the meanwhile, we kept moving from place to place."[31]

"Did your master ever beat you?"

"One day while I was watching the cattle, a terrible storm came. I lost the cattle and I became lost in the forest. That night in a dream I saw my mother calling me. 'Come to where I am.' I was lost in the forest for two days. I ate from the gum trees to feed my hunger. A man found me and asked if I was Abdullah and lost from the storm. He put me on a camel and brought me back to my master. I was afraid they would cut my Achilles tendon. But I think they could see that I had been lost and was exhausted. They killed a lamb to celebrate my return. My master said, 'You were lost because you have a devil in your mind.'

"After that I told them that I love them. I meant it like the Bible says, 'Love your neighbor as yourself.' They were happy.

They thought that I had accepted them. 'You are one of the family.' In the meanwhile, I was trying to learn Arabic because the other boys use Arabic to blame me for any troubles, and I could not understand and defend myself. My master and his father made me go with them to the mosque. But I kept having this dream that I was in the church and people were praying with me. That is when I began to make plans to escape. I decided I wanted to die or escape. I was not going to live the life of a salve. I knew a train ran from the city of El Fula, so I thought I could ride to my homeland."[32]

"So what did you do, John?"

"One day I ran into the forest. I heard it was a three-day walk to the city. During the day, I walked in the bush, and at night, I slept in the trees."[33]

"Why did you sleep in the trees? Weren't you afraid to fall out?"

"No, the trees are very big. I was afraid at night from the bears that they would come and eat me. On the third day, a man saw me, and I ran away, but I was very tired and I fell. The grass was very tall and it covered me. The man could not see me. I must have passed out. Later I awoke and discovered that I was very near Fula. In the city I went to the police. I could speak enough Arabic to ask for a place to stay and how to get some money. They told me to go into town. One man gave me a bowl of soup. I acted like a Muslim so the Arabs ignored me. For two years I worked and tried to save money to ride the train. Twice my money was stolen.

"I talked to an African man. He told me that the train went to Khartoum and that almost every Sudan tribe had some people in Khartoum because of the war. If I went to Khartoum, I could find somebody from my tribe so that they could help me find my mother. I asked him about tickets for the train. He said 'The poor people ride on the top of the cars. If you ride on the top, they will not charge you money, but if the police catch you, they will put you in jail.'"[34]

"Were you afraid of being caught?

"I was tired. I wanted to go home. The next evening I climbed the steps to the top of the railroad car. I took off my shirt and pants so that they could not be seen blowing in the wind. At night I was very cold and during the day very hot. In the daylight we would stop in cities. I would rest and find water to drink. The police captured people riding on top of the car in front of me, but they did not trouble me. In Kosti I got off the train and began to walk, I met a man from my tribe who knew of my mother. He told me she had fled and was living in America."[35]

"After all your experiences, how do you feel about life now?"

He hesitated. Once again his hands covered his face. After a long pause, he said, "I do not know, I am confused. I keep thinking that I did something bad. God is angry with me. But I do not know. Do I have a devil in my mind?"[36]

Uncle Nathan was facing me. I saw the tears in his eyes as he said, "When I get money together, we will go to the American Embassy in Cairo to try to get John a visa to the United States so that he can be with his mother."

I tried to assure John that he was well of mind, that God was with him, and that he had accomplished an amazing feat by his escape. I prayed with them, nephew and uncle, for peace, confidence, and assurance. I prayed for the way to America. A I stepped back into the alley, I knew I needed to go back to the hotel. I needed to be alone. I needed time to measure the dimensions of human depravity. I ordered dinner to my room that night and ate alone. I could not bear the presence of the woman in the gold jacket to her waist.

I kept thinking about John. How much damage had they done to him, physically and mentally? I thought of the short videotape passed to me by James Khan. I visualized the "brain-washing" of children in the "religious-training camp." Then I thought of all the other lost boys of Sudan.

I remembered the reports to the United Nations by Bishop Gassi of El Obeid, Sudan, who reported that in the Nubian tribe alone, twenty thousand children were sold into slavery. The United Nations' special reporter stated that women and children were deported for slavery and forced labor from Southern Kordofan and the Nuba Mountains. I also thought of the "religious-training camps." I wondered what, if any, connections the "religious-training camps" had with the bin Laden terrorist training camps.

I thought of the history of slavery in Islam. Initially, when my interest in Islam was perked by the 9/11 terror attacks, I turned to history. I always figured I knew a person best by what he did, not by what he said. So I purchased a copy of *Middle Eastern History* by Bernard Lewis.

I learned that slavery was always an active part of Middle Eastern civilization, before Islam and since Islam until the present day. Slaves became a uniquely significant part of the Islamic fighting machine, as early at the mid-ninth century. With my increased awareness of young Christian Sudanese boys forced into slavery, I thought of *devshirme* in Islam—how the Sultan of the Ottoman Empire conscripted young boys, took them from their Christian parents, and force trained them to become soldiers in the Islamic military forces. The conscripted boys from the Christian peoples of "Eastern Europe were known as the *Janissaries.*

In the fourteenth to the seventeenth centuries, the Ottomans, the military power of Islam during those centuries, conscripted Christian boys from the conquered territories of Romania, Macedonia, Bulgaria, Hungary, Serbia, Bosnia, and the Ukraine. Muslim solders entered the churches and ordered the clergy to turn over baptismal records for boys of appropriate ages, six to twelve. Those boys were rounded up and marched off into military training camps to be indoctrinated with Islam and trained in the skills of the Islamic military.

During those four centuries, the Janissaries became the strongest fighting force of Islam. In fact they conquered Constantinople and defeated many other armies of Christian Europe.[37]

That night I did not sleep much. I kept thinking of John, the missing boys, the "religious-training camps," and the "terrorist training camps" in Sudan. What am I to make of it? Tens of thousands of boys were torn from their families for four centuries and now again in Sudan for two decades, for what? Slavery? What kind of slavery? House slaves? Agricultural slaves. Industrial slaves? Military slaves? Suicide bombers?

CHAPTER SEVEN

Journeys into Neighborhoods of Islam
Sudan
A Visit with Tsol

The next day, Phillip joined me in place of Ben and we did "the taxi routine." Phil, as he preferred to be called, was in no way as serious as Ben. He laughed heartily and saw humor in the strangest of things. I also noticed that his walks were considerably shorter. As we were approaching a very dilapidated apartment building, Tsol stepped out from an alley to greet us. He was thin and tall. His English pronunciation was at times difficult to understand, obviously effects from his tribal language and the influence of the Brits. I thanked him for coming to Khartoum and reimbursed his travel expense.

Tsol shared how his life and the lives of his people changed in September 1983, when President Numeiri declared *sharia* as law for the whole of Sudan. That was when the war between the north and the south re-ignited into what became known as the Sudan Civil War. When the Dinka Tribe rejected *sharia*, the *fatwa* of *jihad* was issued and the *murahileen* (the Muslim army) was sent into Tsol's hometown area of Bentiu, a land rich with oil. The *jihad* was justified, as a defensive action for blasphemy, and simultaneously the oil holdings became legitimate booty.

"Did you enlist to fight?" I asked.

"I did not join the army. I was in school. My older brother joined to fight against the 'September laws' (*sharia*). The fighting was severe in our area. We escaped to a refugee camp near Kosti. Many widows and orphans accompanied us for protection from the soldiers. There were many orphaned children.

"In Kosti the Muslim government established public schools for our children. At first they attended, but when the tribal elders discovered that the children were learning from the Koran, they chose to construct their own school and asked me to be the teacher.

"War makes for strange things. One day I was a student, and the next day I was a teacher."

When the new school began, most of the Dinka children joined. Six moths later, Tsol was arrested. Intelligence agents forced him and many other young men to walk two hundred sixty-two kilometers to Khartoum. In Khartoum he was imprisoned.

"They put me in a very small room with one hundred other men for thirteen days," he explained. "They tortured us. We were like animals in a pen. The room was so crowded that we were unable to sit down."[1]

I could only imagine the ghastly filth from perspiration, urination, and defecation from one hundred men. They could not rest. They organized and took turns standing and sitting. At night, intelligence officials would call, "Tsol, do you know why you are here?" They did that every night. When he was finally getting sleep, he would hear his name, and then the same question was repeated, over and over again, through the time of darkness.

Tsol went on: "Next, they took us to the main prison, and they isolated me in solitary. No one was allowed to talk to me for one year. Nobody knew where I was. During that year, I was able to get a message to the African custodians of the prison. I told them who I was and where I was from. When they were off duty, they made contacts with my family. When my family finally came, they were allowed fifteen minute visits once per month."[2]

"How did you get out, Tsol?"

"I could be released anytime. That was the whole point of the question, "Tsol, do you know why you are here?" If I converted to Islam, I would be released. That was why I was arrested. They came to me. They told me. 'We want your people to convert to Islam, so we are taking away their leader.' After seventeen months, they released me with a permit that allowed me to travel to Kosti. But I had to remain there and was forbidden to teach. When I arrived back in Kosti, I saw that the three Islamic schools had collapsed, and I began my life again. I went back to teaching. We had four teachers on staff."[3]

"Why did they allow you to go?" I asked.

"After seventeen months in prison, they released me because they knew I was not accepting Islam. I cannot be a Muslim. I know Islam. I read the Koran. I cannot lie. I cannot do it. I reject Islam. It is not a religion. Islam is about force and war. Life is made so difficult that people finally give up. Islam does anything to make you a Muslim from threats to gifts. They will buy you a Muslim girl if you will join Islam. They made life a disaster for Dinka people. Sudan intelligence officers made an offer that if I taught in an Islamic school, they would give me a wife, a house, money, and a good position. I knew the other option was punishment, prison, fines, beatings, and torture."[4]

"How do you feel about Islam today?"

"The world must not be looking carefully at Islam in Sudan. It seems the world acts cowardly, not willing to confront evils used to coerce people to convert to the ways of Islam. Islam lies! Islam fights! It is not going away! It is not going to stop! Every time leaders of the world say that peace has come to Sudan. The hardship is past. What do they mean? What is better in Sudan?

Darfur is the new killing field of Africans. Soon, it will return to Kordofan and Jongli. Sudan is not free. Am I free? Are people in America free like me? America went to Iraq, why not Sudan?

"Even Muslims are not free, especially not Muslims who retain aspects of the tribal religions. I read Arabic. I read the Koran. How can a human being accept that as a religion? It s about getting money, other peoples' money; getting women, other peoples' women; getting houses and farms, other peoples' houses and farms. Islam is covetousness. Islam is my enemy. Islam is the enemy of Sudan. Islam has made Sudan a land of the devils. Islam is the enemy of the world.

"In 1998, they put me back in prison. They tortured and threatened to kill me."[5]

"Why?"

"Because I was teaching again. I was telling people not to be Muslim. I escaped prison through the help of friends. Now I am an outlaw in my own country. Ask your American friends to come and live with us under Islamic holy law. Why are they such silly people? Why do they believe our oppressors?"[6]

Phillip said that it was time to move along. We had another visit scheduled. I thanked Tsol for coming and blessed him. As we rode to our next visit, I tried to recall any publications that had addressed the details of torture chambers and methods of tortures executed by followers of Islam.

A Visit with Raphael

Phillip noticed a van tailing our taxi, so he asked to be dropped near the Internet Café. We drank coffee and shared an oddly shaped green bread roll. Phillip eyed the van from the door and decided we better exit by the alley. A fifteen-minute walk brought us to a large house with stucco siding located in a very shoddy district. Raphael was waiting patiently as he sat on a sofa in the corner of a room filled with a variety of African artistry, from carvings to tapestries. The room was noticeably cooler than the café, obviously from a contraption of water and a fan used for cooling, similar to a swamp cooler back home.

Raphael was well dressed. He wore a shirt of gray and white stripes with matching gray pants. He smiled, but maintained a serious composure. My interest was soon focused on his disfigured hands and missing fingers. Six of his eight fingers and/or finger tips were missing. To me, this man's appearance radiated "loving-kindness." If halos were discernable, Raphael's would be as bright as the sun. He spoke limited English, so Phil served as translator. I greeted Raphael and thanked him for his willingness to take the bus to Khartoum. He was more than gracious for the opportunity and expressed a genuine pride in sharing his experience.

Raphael came from the Nuba Mountains. He belonged to the Kurango tribe. Most of his tribe remained faithful to the tribal religion. In his early teenage years, Christian missionaries had trekked the region of the Kurango, but only a few members of the tribe converted. Several years later, Islam directed young Muslims to work with the children of the Kurango tribe to convert them to Islam. The tribe was greatly distressed, but no conversions took place and no mosque was built. Raphael remains one of the few who converted to Christianity

"One day when the fighting was fierce in the Nuba Mountains, I was hiking through the forest on my way home. Suddenly I was surprised and captured by Muslim soldiers. They charged me with the crimes of rebellion and blasphemy. They said, 'You are a rebel and a Christian.' I told them that I was no rebel, but I was a Christian. The leader said that all Christians are rebels. I told them, 'I am no rebel. I am a Christian.' I was beaten thoroughly. They tied my hands and legs. They crucified me. But I survived, and the next morning, they cut me down."[7]

"Why did they crucify you? What was the crime? What did they want you to do?"

"The soldiers insisted that I was an enemy. I was a Christian. I must confess that I am a rebel and convert to Islam."[8] As Raphael told me of his experience, I thought of the instructions I had read in the Koran: "The punishment of those who wage war against God (*Allah*) and his Apostle... is execution, or crucifixion, or the cutting off of hands and feet from opposite sides, or exile from the land: that is their disgrace in this world, and a heavy punishment is theirs in the Hereafter" (Koran V (36)).

"Did you know that crucifixion is a punishment for waging war against Islam?"

"No, but they told me I should join Islam and join the prophet. I told them I would not forsake Jesus. When the darkness was coming, they heated charcoal. Into the charcoal they put a hand-iron they had looted from raids on our village. The iron was red hot. It sizzled. Then they tied my hands to the surface of their army tank, behind the gunnery. They took the iron and ironed my hands. Destroying my fingers. I did not remember after that. In the night when I awakened, my hands were still tied to the tank.

"That morning they told me to convert to the true religion. I was enraged. I told them that Islam was not a religion, but an army of evil demons. My fingers were cooked, numb, and oozing blood. They pulled off my clothes and forced me to kneel. They rammed red hot peppers up my rectum. When I awakened, I was sweating in agony. They must have thrown me from the tank into the forest. When I gained consciousness, I was unable to use my hands to loosen the ties round my arms and legs. I knew I needed to get free before nightfall. The wild animals would smell me. I called for help, but no one came."[9]

"So how did you get free, Raphael?"

"An elderly man from my tribe found me and cared for me. When I was able to make the journey, he took me to a hospital in Medani. I was at the hospital for eight months. I healed, but lost the use of my hands." He held them for me to see. "I still feel pain in my chest from the beatings and torture."

"How old were you when this happened?" I asked.

"I was twenty-five years. After my experience of suffering, I knew that I needed to stop Islam. I went to a two-year school in Gedaref. After graduation I became an evangelist in the Church of Christ in Sudan. I still serve the Lord." He smiled with that serious smile.

"Were you able to get any aid from the Islamic centers?"

"No, they told me that I had been in a war zone so they could not help me."[10]

In the serious face of Raphael, I saw confidence and conviction. He had been "crucified with Christ." His fingers were burned off and hot peppers stuffed up his rectum. Now he viewed his experience as a divine calling to become an evangelist, and so he was, with a twenty dollar per month income. He married a war widow and has a family of nine. He regrets his inability to finance his children's education, but refuses to allow his children to learn in a curriculum governed by the Koran. Whenever time permits, he teaches his two oldest children, who in turn teach their younger siblings. Here is a man convinced in his heart that he and Jesus will overcome.

Initially, the government allowed Raphael to build a *tugul* house for himself and his family. After three years, government intelligence informed him that the land he had purchased was not legally surveyed, so they bulldozed his home. Raphael is again among the homeless. With Christian and Western relief organizations forbidden in Sudan, assistance is limited through the Islamic centers.

With my goodbyes, I provided Raphael what financial support I could. My friend Dale from Michigan gave me dollars to dispense at my discretion. My heart was torn. My Western customs seemed completely awkward and inappropriate. I simply took those broken hands and held them. "Thank you, Raphael.

Thank you, God." The smile on his serious face and his broken hands are an eternal memory of my journey into Sudan.

Why the War? Why the Terror Behavior?

As I focus on victims in Sudan, I understand that Western sympathizers and Western advocates of Islam will try to dismiss Raphael, Tsol, and John as the tragic consequences of war. Supporters of Islam will make references to the tragic suffering and death of Muslims in the Iraqi and Afghani wars. But that concern, as serious as it may be, is another issue, and it only serves as a distraction from the purpose of my journey into the heartland of Islam.

The purpose of my journey is to uncover the cause of the terrifying war between the Muslim north and the Christian south. To simply dismiss the victims of southern Sudan with the subject of the Iraqi war and the currently popular rhetoric of "peace not war," as if all war is without justification, is inexcusable and defies human reason. *When any ideology deliberately designs and executes a strategy of injustice to strip people of their basic human rights and freedoms, do the victimized peoples have no responsible, reasonable, and justifiable right to self-defense?* The victims of southern Sudan, and now western Darfur, demand more honor than that of a simple dismissal camouflaged by introducing other points of concern. The world has a moral obligation to identify the criminals of these crimes as much as they once did with the war crimes of the Nazis.

John was eleven years of age when captured by the Muslim soldiers and sold as a slave. His father had been killed and his mother blinded. The policy of selling children into slavery in the twentieth and twenty-first centuries should be front-page news. Why does America only review American history of slavery? In Islam, the capture of enemies, men, women, and children and selling them into slavery has been commonplace throughout the centuries. It was an intricate part of the Islamic economy. Selling enemy captives was a significant aspect of war booty. Muhammad sold captives into slavery to finance his *jihads*. It is important for Americans as they pursue an understanding of terror behavior in Islam to publicly acknowledge that those models of Muhammad are still replicated in the twenty-first century, and need to be publicly condemned.

Tsol was abducted, tortured, and imprisoned because he took a leadership role in the teaching of refugee children from his Dinka tribe. By teaching, he rescued the fatherless, the orphaned, and the minds of small children that the Muslim state was attempting to steal. First the Islamic government threatened the freedom of these children by use of *sharia* to control their behaviors, and then they executed a strategy to use the Koran to impound their minds.

Tsol was tortured and imprisoned. Today he is not honored as a hero in the West. Nobody knows his name, a blasphemer, a victim of Islamic *jihad*. Why do Americans respond to those acts of evil aggression by excusing the religion that perpetrates violent acts against the innocents? It is happening. We address the abuses of American soldiers in Abu Ghraib, a miniscule incident by comparison. Why do we not address the torture of Tsol?

In the case of Raphael, Muslim soldiers tortured him mercilessly, but for what? Conversion. Was Raphael a victim of war *per se,* or a religious war? Am I to say war is war and ignore the horrifying correspondence between Raphael's torture and the tortures taught by the Koran V (36) and VIII (12)? Western advocates of Islam can argue that these were random acts by undisciplined soldiers at war. That may hold some legitimacy, but the soldiers were not punished. Islam made no apology. Islam granted no assistance to Raphael. Islam dismissed him as a man guilty of living in the territory of war, his home (*dar al-harb*). Soldiers of Islam crucified him, burned off his fingers with an iron. There was no peace-loving tolerance to assist him.

I need to ask: How does Islam explain the correlation between the instructions of the Koran and the behavior of the soldiers? The crucifixion of Raphael was but one of many crucifixions of Christians in Sudan. James Khan witnessed the disfigurement and crucifixions of two Sudanese friends by Somali Muslims in a United Nation's refugee compound in Kenya. Why must I agree to ignore these violent religious behaviors with the over-simplification that war is war? These are legitimate issues for review. These are fair questions for any dialogue with Islam or about Islam. More importantly, what was the cause of the war in Sudan? What kept Sudan from peace throughout all the years? Think about it.

Sudan has been at war, or in a state of war, for the past fifty years. The initial division of the war was primarily between the north and the south. The more recent fight in Darfur has creat- ed still another division, that between the northeast (Arab) and the west (African), both mostly Muslim. The population of the north is about twenty million Muslims, Arab and African. The south numbers about ten million Africans, animist and Christian.

The war between the north and the south began when Great Britain granted Sudan its independence in 1956. Several factors contributed to the initial conflict, called the Anyanya War:

(1). For centuries, the northerners were known in the south as the raiders and traders of slaves.

(2). Probably the most significant factor was the failure of British authorities to invest and develop southern Sudan. James Khan stated, "We were valued as half human. Only four years of formal education were granted to the southern Sudanese, half that of the north. We were even forbidden to watch the British drive a motor vehicle per chance we too should learn how to drive."

(3). When Sudanese independence was declared, Britain established the north (and Egypt) to rule the south (an acknowledgement of the supremacy of Islam?). In the newly organized government, the southern Sudanese had no meaningful political representation.

When the north exercised political authority over the south, the south resisted. Many small, poorly armed, independent tribal militias fought off the north to protect their freedoms and their very right of existence. Most of the south eventually joined together in a resistance called the SLM (Southern Liberation Movement). Through seventeen years of war, the south resisted northern domination. In 1972, successful defensive efforts by the south brought the north to sign the Addis Ababa Peace Accord, sponsored by Emperor Haile Selassie of Ethiopia. The agreement lasted ten years.

However, *in September 1983, the cause of the civil war between the north and south **was abundantly clear**. President Numeiri cancelled the Peace Accord and imposed Islamic sharia law on the whole nation.* Even before the north imposed Islamic holy law, southern dissatisfaction was growing because the north had failed to implement promises linked to the Addis Ababa Peace Accord. In distrust, the south had organized the SPLM (Sudan Peoples' Liberation Movement) and the SPLA (Sudan Peoples' Liberation Army) in May of 1983 in preparation for any other northern mischief. When the north broke covenant and imposed *sharia*, the SPLA, under the leadership of Colonel John Garang, was prepared for battle.

When Numeiri declared *sharia* the law of all Sudan, it was a blatant expression of aggressive hostile behavior by Islam toward its non-Muslim neighbors. It was visible to the whole world. Severe punishments (*jihad*) were imposed on Muslims and Christians alike, e.g. cutting off a hand and the opposite foot. Although the religious leaders of Islam, Hasan al-Turabi and Ghazi Salahuddin Atabani, stated that Islamic *sharia* law was only applicable to Muslims and would not prohibit non-Muslim peoples from equal rights and duties, the south knew otherwise. The bigoted behavior of Islam toward the Copts of

Egypt and the former Nubian Kingdom of Sudan were no secrets in southern Sudan.

Under the leadership of John Garang, the SPLA won victories in the Nuba Mountains and Blue Nile. Anxiety began to grow in the Muslim north. In the elections of 1986, Sadiq al-Madhi became the new President, but the south continued to advance. Fear and the loss of young Arab men deeply affected the Muslims of Khartoum. The new Prime Minister began serious negotiations with the south (SPLM), promising to "freeze" (cancel the effects of) Islamic holy law.

The religious leaders of Islam, Turabi and Atabani, feared for the loss of their politico-religious gains of Islam and instigated a coup d'etat. On June 30, 1989, Colonel Bashir, a devout adherent to Turabi, became the president. Bashir immediately declared Sudan an Islamic state, and the war against the south became an official Islamic *jihad*. Islamic holy law was reaffirmed as the law of Sudan. Shortly after the coup d'etat... al-Taburi and his cohorts began a widespread use of the media, press and television, to persuade the Sudanese people that the new leadership of Colonel Bashir was committed to orthodox Islam...and that the real conflict in Sudan was between the sacred and the blasphemous, Arab Islam and Western Christians.[11]

Northern resistance to the southern surge was strengthened through the financial support of the Islamic nations, including some wealthy Saudi princes. The soldiers of the north (*murahileen*) were supplied with automatic weapons that brought massive devastation, destruction, and death to the south and changed the momentum of the war. According to reports from the World Bank, on behalf of Sudan, Iran compensated China and North Korea for not only guns, but as many as twenty advanced assault aircraft.[12]

The war in Sudan reveals Islam as a religion still faithful to bigoted acts of terror behavior violence against its non-Muslim neighbors. Islam (Sudan, Saudi Arabia, Iran, Iraq, and Libya) fought the non-Muslim south, viewed as Western Christians (Christian mission converts), to open the way for expansion throughout the African continent. Soldiers of Islam destroyed villages, farms, homes, schools, businesses, and churches in southern Sudan. Islam wounded and killed millions of non-Muslim Africans, soldiers of Islam displaced (made homeless) millions of non-Muslim Africans and provided them no assistance unless they honored Islam as their own religion. Independent Sudan is a story of war, not just any war, but a war [Koran VIII (12), (60); IX (29)] to impose *sharia* law.

Since Islam moved from the killing fields of the south to the killing fields of Darfur, our Western world continues to gawk at its obscene behaviors of terror. *We dialogue*. James Khan suggested that the genocide in Darfur is an effort by the Islamic leadership of Sudan to purify Islam from 'folk Islam.' Interestingly, the behavior of Islam against black Africans in Darfur (after years) proceeds without serious intervention. By the way, where are the Black Muslims of America on this issue of Darfur?

Why No Peace Accord?

Through all these years of bloody conflicts, what was it that stood in the way of meaningful peace between the north and the south? It was Islamic holy law. Before the coup d'etat of June 30, 1989, the President of Sudan (the north) was in agreement to cancel *sharia* in Sudan. That in fact appears to be the reason of the coup—to replace al-Mahdi with Colonel Bashir. The very idea of canceling *sharia* was an abomination to al-Turabi.

Consistently *sharia* obstructed any formal peace between the north and south. Of course Western sympathizers and Western advocates of Islam will disagree. But the record is clear. Dialogue was once again the cover used by Islam to appear conciliatory to the West, but at the same time maintain the killing fields of the south.

The first official peace negotiations were convened in *Addis Ababa* on August 18–20, 1989, several weeks after the June 30 Coup d'etat. At the first day of talks, Justin Yac Arop presented the issue of the south. He stated that the real problem, the issue at the heart of the war, was the intentions of one religion to dominate another religion. He raised the point that the presentation of the Khartoum government completely ignored the critical factor of Islamic *sharia* law. He pressed the north with the question as to what were their attitudes toward these laws?"[13]

The issue of Islamic *sharia* law as the major division between the north and the south went unanswered. The next day, Dr. Lam Akol from the southern delegation raised the same issue, that the peace program of the north had overlooked the canceling of *sharia* laws. Having received no substantial response to his point, Akol stated the discussion was stupid, that the south did not want an Islamic state but a secular state. The answer to Akol was that Sudan permits the ruling majority the right to implement *sharia*.[14]

Clearly Islam understands democracy as a system in which a Muslim majority means that Muslims have the authority to impose their values on the state. To many Americans, that was shockingly the case in Iraq when the newly formed government declared *sharia* the foundation of all future legislation. At the Addis Ababa negotiations, the Sudanese government argued that the south could exclude itself from any regulations of a religious nature. Better instructed than the American leaders on *sharia* in Iraq, the SPLM knew full well that *sharia's* endorsement of Muslim supremacy meant by its very nature that a non-Muslim peoples were downgraded to that of inferiors.

Think about it. *Sharia* forbids the construction of new churches. That means that Christians living in states with a majority of Muslims are forbidden to build a new church.

Sharia forbids the production, distribution, and consumption of alcoholic beverages. That means that non-Muslim people living in states with a majority of Muslims are forbidden to make or drink alcohol. *Sharia* forbids a non-Muslim to hold authority over a Muslim. That means that a non-Muslim person cannot hold any national positions, e.g. education, finances, politics, and economics.

The second official negotiation for peace took place in Nairobi, December 1–4, 1989. What was the obstruction to peace? President Jimmy Carter offered to lead the two sides toward a lasting peace. Carter came with the idea that the north, the NSRC, must simply cancel Islamic holy law. The leader of the Islamic delegation summarized Carter's approach. He thought President Carter neither saw, nor was he prepared to understand, the rationale of the Khartoum government. Carter seemed oblivious to the teachings of Islam with regard to the 1983 legislation regarding *sharia*. Neither did he understand the trauma it would be for Islam to forfeit Sudan back to a land of unbelief (*dar al-harb*) once it had been redeemed into the *dar al-Islam*. Carter seemed blind to the impediments of canceling or freezing those legislations in the context of the Islamic agenda for worldwide redemption.[15] The participation by our former president is an embarrassment of naïve political and religious leadership in America at the highest levels. After all the efforts by the southern delegation to cancel Islamic holy law, the Sudanese government refused.

Third, in the peace talks of Abuja (May 26–June 4, 1992), the problem of peace remained the application of Islamic *sharia* law. The leader of the north (Khartoum) maintained the right of the democratic majority to implement and apply *sharia*. But how many holy laws that protect the religion of Islam conflict with the religious freedoms of non-Muslim peoples? Simply consider, for example, the religious prohibitions of Islam: no production, distribution, or consumption of alcohol – no production consumption of pork – no inheritance of a Muslim to a non-Muslim child; no non-Muslim authority over a Muslim, no tax on a Muslim who has a mosque within his business or home, and no authority of a non-Muslim testimony in court against a Muslim.

The point is that Islamic law was not constructed to promote equality and equal rights, but for exactly the opposite purpose. It was designed to promote and protect followers of Islam as privileged people. It was used to define and enforce the inferior status of non-Muslim peoples. Such behavior is not unique to Islam, but comparable to practices of the Greeks with the Barbarians and to the Jews with the Gentiles. As a matter of fact, what government does not design its laws and regulations to favor its own people?

Two factors, however, make Islamic holy law unique. The first factor is that to Muslims, *sharia* was constructed from the words of God (*Allah*). So, *its legal regulation of prejudice against non-Muslim peoples* is absolute. That divine endorsement enforces the prejudicial injunctions of Islamic *sharia* law as infallible. The second factor is the fourteen hundred years of construction, implementation, and application of Islamic *sharia* law. The fourteen hundred years explain how the gruesome violence and blatant bigotry of Islamic holy law has become so deeply embedded in Islamic culture.

These two factors assist us in understanding why peace negotiations changed nothing in Sudan. The animists and Christians of the south, the Darfurians of the West, and all the inferior peoples—"the worst of creatures"— were predestined by *Allah* to live under *sharia*.

The Koran and *sharia* demand their submission, either submissive subjugation by war (*jihad*) or a submissive subjugation by covenant (*dhimma*). Read the text.

> Fight against them who believe not in God, nor
> the last day, and forbid not that which God and

his Apostle have forbidden, and profess not the true religion, (including) those unto whom the Scriptures have been delivered (Jews and Christians), until they pay tribute (*jizya*) by the right of subjection (willing submission), and they be reduced low (feeling subdued) (Koran IX (29)).

Clearly the West needs to examine in greater depth the specifics, applications, and the fullness of Islamic holy law. From the simple fact that the Sudan fought much of fifty years of bloody war over *sharia*, killing more than a million, possibly two million, and displacing millions more, we can only conclude that *sharia* is a very, very important issue. If we really desire to understand Islam, we need to understand Islamic holy law.

A Visit with Isaac

I stepped from the hotel lobby into a cab to once again join Benjamin. As we rode into a Khartoum ghetto, I thought of how the Islamic government claims religious and political equality for every citizen. In the meanwhile, however, the non-conforming peoples of southern and western Sudan continue to suffer and die. I looked at the bin Laden Mosque and wondered, *why does America chose to blame bin Laden for terror behavior when in fact* terror *behavior has affected relationships between Islam and it non-Muslim neighbors for centuries, long before the birth of the international terrorist?*

As we walked from the cab, a strong wind blew the dry sands, fouling the air. I choked as I reached for my handkerchief to cover my eyes. When we arrived at the address for our next visit, Ben grabbed the tether strap near the back door and shook the bell as loudly as possible.

We heard from inside, "Greetings! Greetings! Come in please! My name is Isaac. I arrived late last night."[16] Isaac described his journey in detail. I listened attentively, looking for an opportunity to pose a question as to whether there were any improvements in the conditions for displaced peoples of the south who had abandoned the territory of war and moved northward. What I remembered of the Civil War in the United States is that there was a serious effort by the victorious to restore goodwill and reunite the peoples of the north and the south.

I began, "Isaac, thank you for coming. I'm grateful your travels went so well. One of my concerns is to know the current attitude and behavior of the Islamic government of the north toward the displaced peoples from the south. Are there any improvements in the relationship? Do you sense an effort toward resolution and reconciliation? What is your experience?"

Isaac replied, "Well, I now live in Medani. We were forced from our homes and escaped to the north in 1993. They call us now 'the displaced people.' I feel more uprooted and torn apart." Isaac smiled. "The experience I wish to tell you about took place in Medani, and it says a great deal about life as a neighbor to Muslims after moving out of the territory of war (*dar al-harb*). Shortly after we arrived in Medani, I was arrested because of a *tugal* that our people built to use as a gathering place for the homeless to worship. They arrested me July 15, 2002."[17]

"Why did they arrest you? You were the victims of war. You were homeless, so you built a *tugal*. So what?"

"We built our place of worship in a vacant plot of land. Then the intelligence officials from the government said to us. 'No churches may be built in the north. It is forbidden. Destroy it.' We told the government we want to wait until the rainy season passes. After the rain we will remove it. We have no other place to gather for protection from the weather. But they refused. 'No church!'

"A police officer arrested me and put me in jail. They demanded that our *tugal* be torn down. They fined me fifteen thousand Sudanese dinars. Then they arrested our pastor, Phillip Kay Lul, and the church elders. 'We will not release them until you take down the building. No new church buildings are permitted under holy law.'

"Soldiers came to capture and beat our people. We fled them in the south, and now they attacked us in the north. Our people did not want to remove the church and were willing to fight. Then the army came with their guns and machines. 'There are no new church buildings in the north. This is the land of Islam. Even today, no church buildings are permitted, not even a *tugal*.

"For five days the elders in jail were given no food and no visits. 'If you do not remove the church building, they will die of hunger.' For all of the displaced peoples from the south, there is no new church at which they can gather in Khartoum. No place to worship. We have no place to teach our children. We only had a *tugal*, but the army took it down. We are five hundred people including our children. We can buy a plot of land for fifty thousand Sudanese dinars, but we cannot build a church. We are the enemy of Islam, now the displaced enemy. We have nothing. Islamic centers control relief to the victims of the war. We receive nothing."[18]

A Visit with Stephen

As I visited with Isaac, Stephen knocked at the door and joined us. He introduced himself as a "pastor-evangelist" who came from the south in 1998 to pastor among the displaced peoples. He explained, "I was sent to the village of Renk to see to the building of a fenced compound to protect the weary and exhausted people fleeing from southern Sudan. But I discovered that Islamic holy law forbids any new churches and schools to be built in this city. No other religion is allowed to prosper in the north.

"When the government discovered that displaced people were coming into the compound, police came and captured forty people. They refused to listen to us. We followed them. We tried to convince them to let our people go, but they tortured and killed twenty-eight of them. Seventeen survived.

"They accused us of being rebels. They knew we were Christians, so they thought that by getting rid of our fenced-off area, we would be forced to go to the Islamic center. The second day, they captured twenty members of our choir because they sang Christmas Carols for another small group of Christians nearby. The intelligence officials said they were supposed to get permission from the government to sing. They put them in jail and took their permission papers away that had allowed them to move about as displaced Sudanese people.

"The intelligence officials had a small building they used for the purpose of torture. They ran a bare electrical cord around the inside, so that if people fell, they would be killed or paralyzed. The bare electrical cord surrounded fiery hot bricks. The choir members were ordered to walk on the hot bricks. If they stepped off into the water, sand, and electricity, they were electrocuted. Our choir leader was burned, but did not die. Then they took the choir people to the mufti (mayor). He told them, 'Do not attempt to build a church or a school or you will die.'"[19]

I asked, "What about the children, Stephen?"

"The parents have nothing to say. Orphaned children are not allowed to go to the church. The church is not allowed to receive displaced people. Always they are ordered to go the Islamic center, but they never receive any support unless they convert. Some American churches send relief goods to Sudan, but the military takes them and sells them in the village. The better things are not available to us. Islam controls everything. They see to it that the only way to get any help is from the Islamic centers. Pastors are not allowed.

"On Christmas Day, the intelligence officials surrounded us to hear what we were preaching against Islam. They arrested some of our men and put them in jail. The soldiers rape our girls, but they have the guns, so there is nothing that can be done. The soldiers demand two bushels of corn for each cow that we have. If the cows are not skinny, then they threaten to kill us for stealing their fair share of the corn." [20]

As Ben and I left Isaac and Stephen, I struggled to imagine how civilized people could kill, maim, and torture helpless, displaced, suffering peoples. In this case, what is the difference between the Nazi Gestapo and the Sudanese intelligence officials? I see no effort toward resolution and reconciliation, let alone tolerance. The southern Sudanese now face a life of *dhimmitude.*

A Visit with Jacob

Benjamin said he needed some coffee, so we walked to a small Arab coffee bar nearby. The cracker tasted moldy, and for the first time since my arrival, I really missed home. While we sipped our coffee, Ben explained how Jacob, our next visit, was an uncle to my friend James Khan. Coffee finished, we took a short walk to Jacob's house. Through the formal greetings with Jacob, I could tell his eyes were failing, but his memory seemed clear.

Jacob began, "I come from southern Sudan, near the town of Nasir. We lived in a very horrible situation because all of our cities were surrounded by northern troops. There was one gate in and out. The government watched you all the time, even in church. They captured our pastors and leaders. They beat and tortured them, calling them rebels.

"One day they captured the evangelists, tied them to trees, and publicly beat them during the daytime for everyone to see. When the resistance army (SPLA) came near town, the Muslim soldiers came into town and beat everybody. We chased the rebel army (SPLA) away for our safety. We are not rebels. At that time they tied a man to a stone and hanged him in the water to drown. No one dared to take his body and bury him. We lived in fear."[21]

"Was your nephew, James, living near you at that time?" I asked.

"Yes, they put him in jail and beat him. The whole town became angry and went to the jail. They shouted, 'Bring James out. Bring James out.' The police would not let him go. The night guards arranged to set him free. I brought his sister and mother-in-law to join him so that the Muslims could not kill them when James escaped. James had no choice but to flee. He said that he had no place to go. He felt as if there was no future in Sudan, not in the Muslim north. There was war in the south and west, and the communists troubled the east, so he fled through Ethiopia to a refugee camp in Kenya. That was a very dangerous journey."[22]

"What do you mean, Jacob?"

"When James was in the United Nations refugee camp, two of his friends were abducted by two Muslim men from Somali intelligence. They cut off their ears and noses and slit their stomachs so that their intestines hung out, tied their intestines behind their backs and cut off their testicles. Then they cruci-fied them, hanging their disfigured bodies still alive. When the news came to the other Sudanese Christians, they joined with the Congolese and the Ugandan refugees and attacked the Somali Muslims. That was a mistake because the neighboring town, Walda, had a population of about ten thousand displaced Muslims—all refugees escaping the fighting between the Muslim warlords of Somalia.

"In the middle of the battle, James suddenly remembered that his wife Esther had gone to a UNICEF feeding center on the United Nations compound. Only Muslims staffed positions at UNICEF, and when they heard that the Muslims and Christians were fighting, the Muslims ran to their houses to get weapons to join the battle. They chased his wife and her friend. She tripped on a wire and fell. They beat her on her back, but before they could kill her, another Sudanese man distracted them. He was killed. At that very moment, an Ethiopian man and his wife rescued Esther, protected her in their house, and the next day brought her back to James in the refugee camp."[23]

"Wow! She was not even safe at a United Nations compound." I said.

"No, the area was first settled by Somali refugees fleeing the Somali warlords. All Somalis are Muslims. As the first refugees, they established their authority. So it's not really about the United Nations. The United Nations is no better and no worse than the people they employ. The Somali people believe that Arabic is the language of *Allah* and that if a Muslim kills a Christian, he has a house in heaven. They are very militant against all Christians."[24]

"So, where do you go from here, Jacob?"

"I am weary of this life. My life is painful and very difficult. Every day I hope for the return of the Lord Jesus. I see signs of the times. I hear the sounds of Armageddon. Soon this world will be a fire ball. Jesus is coming. He will judge the living and the dead."[25]

That seemed an appropriate moment for me to move. I said, "Until then, may God bless you and keep you Jacob! I promise to bring your love and greetings to James."

I had made my last visit to a refugee in Sudan. A short time later, I gave my thanks and farewell to Ben. He took my package of notes, a few cassettes, and disposable camera. The next day Phillip carried them to his contacts in Ethiopia.

Noon was checkout time at the Khartoum Hilton, and my flight was scheduled to depart at 1 A.M. the next morning. I chose to not spend the money for another night at the hotel, but to give the balance of my cash to my new Sudanese friends. I paid my bill at the Khartoum Hilton, and that evening I rest-ed for several hours in a hammock under the open skies. Nearby was a towering minaret, an extension of an extravagant mosque. It shined powerful green and white lights around and on me. Even in the open air, Islam invaded my space.

Around 11 P.M. Ben brought me to the airport. At Sudanese security, I met a very familiar heavy set Middle Eastern woman wearing a headscarf with a gold colored jacket to her waist. She eagerly took my bags and quickly disappeared through a near-by door and was out of sight. I smiled. I knew my new friend Phil was safely in Ethiopia.

As I flew home, my mind was stuck on the offenses of Islam. Islamic *sharia* law was an obvious tool for the control and expansion of Islam. Southern Sudanese rejection of *sharia* pro-vides Islam with a legal justification for defensive terror *jihad* from the Muslim north. Every effort of peace negotiations was completely blocked to protect Islamic holy *law, the law of Allah is non-negotiable*. Even after the destruction and devastation of the south, the displaced victims were offered no meaningful reconciliation. Always with Islam, the answer is conversion or humiliation. With millions dead, millions displaced, and thou-sands in slavery how does one describe the peace and tolerance of Islam in Sudan?

Living near Islam is dangerous for non-Muslim peoples. On a neighborhood level, Islam often addresses a non-Muslim minority person, officially an unofficially, as an inferior, as a *dhimmi*, as an animal. I witnessed the attempts of Islam to manipulate and control individual, educational, political, and religious choices by non-Muslim peoples. I saw it first in north-ern Nigeria and now again in Sudan. I believe for non-Muslim peoples living near a majority population of Muslims, there is no peace or tolerance.

CHAPTER EIGHT

Journeys into Neighborhoods of Islam
Egypt

Having witnessed the effects of terror behavior in northern Nigeria and the nation of Sudan, I was excited to visit Egypt—not only as a respite from what I had observed as brutal behaviors of religious prejudice, but also in anticipation of a fresh view of what I hoped would be a more mature, more humane Islam. After all, with the exception of French and British intermittent military occupation (1798–1956), Islam has controlled Egypt since the year 641.

At the time Islamic warriors prevailed over the Egyptian people, most of the population was Christian. By as early as the Eight Century, Islam had firmly structured its authority and had begun radical increases of its subjugation tax (jizya) on all Christian communities, instituting as well formal persecutions of individual Christians.[1] As Muslim scholars constructed a codified system of legal authority, *Islamic sharia law*, specific legal applications were put in place to maintain and enforce the inferior status of all non-Muslims peoples. Some of the practical applications of those legal discriminations against *dhimmis*, in this case the Christian Copts, are cited for the purpose of illustration.

> The construction of new churches or the restoration of old ones, as well as the use of bells, banners, sacred books, and crosses...were prohibited ...the *dhimmiis* had to hold their services (worship) in silence and abstain from lamentations at funerals. Their inferior and humble dwellings and tombs had to differ from those of the Muslims in size and decay. Marriage, sexual intercourse with a Muslim woman, and blasphemy against Islam were forebidden...*dhimmis* were not allowed to exercise any authority over a Muslim and could not testify in a legal tribunal...*Dhimmis* were inferior to the Muslim, so had to differ ...in outward appearance...in early Islam Christians had to shave their brows. They were denied the use of colours...and were forbidden to wear the type of clothes...worn by Muslims...Ill-fitting and ridiculous headdresses...were easily recognized and humiliated in the streets. A little bell around the neck...made them recognizable at the public baths...Horses and camels were reserved for Muslims, the *dhimmis* only being able to ride donkeys...in other periods Christians were humiliated by being forced to ride their donkeys facing the tail."[2]

The fact that Islam dominated the Christian Egyptians in excess of thirteen hundred years furnishes us with an opportunity for some significant insights into the real, enduring achievements of Islamic *sharia* law in its control of relations between Muslims and non-Muslim peoples. Here we have an opportunity to view long-term Muslim attitudes and behaviors toward Christians who were forced to live under the legal, cultural, and political authority of Islam. So often today the behaviors of Muslims toward non-Muslim peoples are reported as reactions to political or economic triggers—but not here, not this time. Here is a near-perfect setting in which to observe the behavior of Islamic adherents toward Christians, particularly in Upper Egypt, so many miles distant from the public showcases of European and Middle-Eastern medias.

Of course, my personal challenge was once again to access, independent of Islam, the testimonies of non- Muslim peoples. A friend from Lebanon, Bassam, was able to provide a key contact person in Egypt, Michael by name, who kindly advised me of worthwhile connections within the Cairo and Alexandria areas. As my plans developed however, I sensed a need to reach deeper into the community of the Orthodox Copts.

As I was sharing that concern with my friend, Pete, he told me that his daughter, an emergency medical doctor in Philadelphia, had a doctor friend whose father was an Orthodox Copt living in Jersey City. Soon I was on the telephone, and shortly thereafter, on a plane for a two-day visit to a very special man, Monir Dawoud. In spite of his heavy schedule as a vascular surgeon, he gladly shared his knowledge and his time. We met together with the American Association of Orthodox Copts. We visited numerous Copts at a Coptic Church facility in Jersey City, and soon I was able to make contacts with other Orthodox Copts, even in Upper Egypt. I was ready for my journey.

Pete was eager to travel along, and so was my nephew, Sherwin. With tickets, visas, and plans in place, we were soon on a direct flight to Amsterdam and then off to Cairo. Upon arrival we cautiously filed our temporary address with Egyptian officials as that of the Cairo Hilton, even though we had absolutely no intention of ever even visiting the Hilton. Instead we checked into a French hotel on the other side of Cairo. Maybe it was overtime paranoia, but if the Intelligence Department of Egypt was into surveillance anything like neighboring Sudan, why not a little misdirection?

Ibrahim in Cairo

After arrival we invested several days into getting acquainted with the streets, sights, and sounds. We saw Western wares in storefront windows, tasted scrumptious cuisines at fine family restaurants, and even purchased gold jewelry. The value of the Egyptian pound make everything inexpensive. By the third day, we began to focus on our project and hailed a taxi to visit "Old Cairo." The ancient sights were fascinating. We were, however, shocked to view a mosque that stood as a public testimony to the historical violence of Islam. The mosque was built of pillars filched from different Christian cathedrals across the Middle East. In the eleventh century, Muslim warriors had plundered those cathedrals to demonstrate the supremacy of Islam.

The next morning, we visited a gentleman named Ibrahim, a young, well-educated Orthodox Copt. His eyes were black. As a matter of fact, I found his facial features typical of the Copts. As we introduced ourselves to each other, he asked us to call him "Brahim." Almost immediately, he impressed me as a very passionate, self-confident man. His command of the English language was amazing. Even more so was his working knowledge of Egyptian and Middle Eastern history. As we shared lunch, he explained that for the safety of his family, he did not wish his full name, his voice, or his photograph to be published. Later we found a quiet place in the corner of the hotel lobby for our visit.

In my efforts to understand the state and condition of non-Muslim peoples living in the culture of Islam, I was more than curious to learn about non-Muslim children in Egypt. When Christian children live within a neighborhood of Islam, what are the effects on their psyches, their attitudes, and their perceptions of life?

I asked, "Brahim, maybe we could begin by having you share with us what it was like to be a child of Christian Copts living within the culture of Islam?" Seemingly surprised by the question, he threw back his head as if to stare at the ceiling. I waited for him, and found myself scrutinizing a chandelier that shifted ever so slightly, moved, it seemed, by a draft from the revolving door at the lobby entrance.

He began, "As a young boy, I lived in the Upper regions, near Western Thebes. I still have very strong memories of several incidents in my childhood that picture the trauma of life for many children of the Christian Copts. We were always made aware that we were inferior members of Egyptian society. We learned our second-class status from our teachers at school, from the Muslims on the streets, and from witnessing the public scorn of our parents by Muslim officials.

"On my birthday, March 12, 1992, I recall an argument between a Christian man and a Muslim man on a local street corner. The Muslim insulted the Christian. It got physical. The Christian knocked the Muslim to the ground. That seemed to inflame the Muslim men. They began to throw stones at us. They captured and killed two custodians of the church. The next day, they also killed our tailor and our barber. They burned down our doctor's office. As a matter of record, forty Christians' shops were set aflame."

Sherwin interjected, "Those memories seem very fresh for an event so many years past. That surprises me because children often forget such traumatic moments of their childhood, but you seem to recall every detail."[3]

Brahim smiled. "I not only vividly remember the particulars of that terrifying experience, I also remember that for months, for years thereafter, my mother would review the terrifying details of that incident to my father."[4]

Curious, I asked whether anyone was brought to justice for those criminal acts. This time, Brahim answered swiftly.

"Muslims never prosecute Muslims for crimes against Christians. I do not know of that happening anywhere, ever, in my whole life. Islamic *sharia* law forbids it. Muhammad mocked the 'People of the Book' as liars. Therefore, the Islamic judicial system rejects any Christian testimony contrary to the word of a Muslim. Today Christian statements are impotent in the courts of Egypt. Christians cannot testify in defense of themselves, their churches, their homes, or their families against a Muslim. The legal system is a prison for Christian Copts. The Copts have no way out. They cannot go home. Egypt is home. Even for a sympathetic Muslim, what can he do against Islamic *sharia* law? Face the facts! The anti-Christian hate language of Islamic *sharia* law is recorded as the hate of *Allah*. That means the hate for Christians is immutable!"[5]

Pete apparently moved the by the vibrant passion of Brahim, asked. "Do you recall other such violence from your youth?"

"Mostly I grew up thinking this was life for Christians. It was normal. Sure, I remember other haunting incidents, and I'll share one with you. It came some years later, when my father assisted in the renovation of our village church. Islamic *sharia* law, as you may know, forbids such repairs, especially if they are looked upon as improvements of churches. In this case, it was to build an indoor toilet to replace the old medieval 'outdoor latrine.' The Muslims created a huge riot. They seized my father to pull out his beard, and then they beat him with canes. They burned church icons, several ancient paintings of disciples of Jesus. At that time I was about fifteen years of age. My mother was sobbing. I wanted to help, but she absolutely forbade me. I heard them tell my uncle, 'You pagan infidel, next time we will burn you alive.' That is some of my memory of the young years.

"In primary school, they forced me to learn texts from the Koran. Our schools are an important part of the 'Islamization' of Christians in Egypt and around the world. Even the private, Christian schools must teach children the Koran. When I was to graduate from secondary school and needed to pass my big exam, my Muslim professor came and sat next to me. He tried to make me give up and walk out of the exam. He distracted me by accusing me of paganism, of having three gods, and of being an infidel who does not believe in one God. He did that in the middle of my exam. This is the way things are in Upper Egypt. The public schools are terrible for Christian children, all the way from El Giza to the Sudan border. Christians in the villages have no power, no education, and no money. Gradually, systematically, they are being marginalized and eliminated.

"We are victims of a foreign religion invading our own country. From the years 742 to 1852, each male Christian needed to pay two gold *dinars* as *jizya* (subjugation tax) to the local Muslim authorities. Failure to pay could mean imprisonment or the forced sale of a family member into slavery. At one time they even locked up his holiness, the Pope. The Ben Ezra Temple was sold to pay the ransom, *jizya*, to the Muslims. Always the purpose is to 'Islamize' everyone, eliminate any other faith or thought. Not only do they make life difficult for the Copts, throughout the years they keep trying to force the religion of Islam on us."[6]

"What about now, Brahim? What is it like now for Christians in Egypt?"

"Well, three days ago I am told, in a small village near Idfu in Upper Egypt, a Christian diabetic was used as a guinea pig to experiment with Muhammad's theory on the use of honey as a medicine of *Allah*. Without his insulin, the young boy went into shock. That is not all. When the experiment failed, the doctor of the clinic threatened the boy's father, 'If you do not say a Christian did this, I will rape your wife in front of you.' Imagine, first the Muslim doctor risks the life of this child and then he covers up his ignorance by threatening to rape the man's wife. The tragedy is that under Islamic *sharia* law, there is nothing this Christian father/husband can do. In his inferior position, he is powerless, exactly as the Koran teaches it should be. Islam rules. These terrible things happen. Then they vanish, with no investigation, with no justice.

"It is more difficult for women who are not Muslim. They do not cover their heads, so they are obvious targets for abuse. Here in Cairo, when my wife goes to work on public transport, Muslims call her a 'whore' and an 'infidel.' Just this month (November 2004), a week ago, they screamed at her, 'What will you do after Ramadan, walk naked?' They grabbed her glasses from her face. In Heliopolis, when she was entering a drugstore, they slapped her on the back of her head calling her a 'whore.' Christians are granted no human dignity. Muslim preachers shout threats at Christian women who travel public transport. 'Hell is waiting for you,' and 'You will be boiled in steaming hot water.'

"As a teacher, I am still able to find job opportunities in the Cairo area. For Christians in other occupations, especially the unskilled workers, many are unemployed. When anyone applies for work in Egypt, he needs to show his I.D., identification card. It is much like a driver's license in Western countries. Proportionately, Christians should hold 15–29 percent of the jobs, but when they show their I.D., it identifies them as Christians, and they are told to move on. We are identified as second-class citizens."[7]

"As you consider your life, Brahim, and the life of your family, what are you going to do? What is your greatest need?"

"For myself personally, I apply every year for a university visa, but the future is black. There are only three thousand such visas available each year. Christians are most often rejected. Even a regular visa to visit the United States is out of reach for me."[8]

"That is something that I do not understand, Brahim."

"Well, it is this simple. Go to the American Embassy. Who grants visas for America? Who selects and approves the candidates? Amazing! At present, he is not an American, but an Egyptian Muslim. His name is Khalid. Why do Americans grant thousands of permanent visas to these people who hate America instead of someone like myself? Some day, I fear, America will pay for such acts. How do you, in America, select ambassadors? What are the necessary qualifications? Who governs immigration?"[9]

Sherwin leaned forward as if to console Brahim. "Angry?" he asked.

"Yes, Sherwin, it is even more than anger. It is my sense of total helplessness. My son comes home from his school in tears because his teacher told him that as a Christian he would burn in hell. This is not Europe or America where people do not believe in hell. Here Christians still believe in hell. Every true Muslim lives in fear of hell. My son believes in hell. They are terrified and they terrify my son. My wife is slapped in the back of her head at the drugstore because she has no headscarf. On the train they insult her and steal her glasses.

"As a child, my father was tortured. My uncle's life threatened. That is life for me. Not because I am stupid. Not because I do not work hard. It is because I reject the religion of Islam. If I become a Muslim, then these issues of injustice and inhumanity go away for me. That is the effectiveness of Islamic *sharia* law in the religion of Islam. It is used for conversion growth. Then I become a hater instead of a 'hatee,' then I become another one of the falling dominos in the coercion game of Islam, as it moves to dominate the world.

"You asked me, 'what is your greatest need?' I said that I want to get out of here. Another way of saying that is, I want to be free. I want to be able to make choices without threats, without personal abuse, without abuse of my wife and children, my family. In a free country, Christians can build a church—not here, except possibly in Cairo in order to bribe the United

States Congress to approve the annual grant of 2.1 billion dollars of financial aid to Egypt. Why does America do that? Why do they support this wretched system of religious abuse? Is it oil? Those American funds only increase Islamic power against non-Muslim peoples. Why not let Saudi Arabia grant Egypt 2.1 billion dollars to support this abusive Islamic system and instead use the money for refugees coming to America to escape the bigoted violence of Islam?

"In America, Muslims have the freedom to build mosques. In Upper Egypt, Christians cannot even use a speaker system to address an audience in their local church building. But the Muslims wake us up and keep us awake with their public speakers, day after day. On Fridays and Sundays in Alexandria, they shout *Allah's* hate at us for hours. If we live near a church property, their preachers scream judgments at us from 4:30–6:30 P.M., every day now for four solid years. When Christians give up and convert to Islam, there are big celebrations. When Muslims convert to Christianity, there are tortures and threats, even at times executions. Others are arrested by the state and imprisoned. I know converts who have to sneak to Christian worship. They go incognito because intelligence officials are watching them. When Christians talk back, they are killed or put in prison. We cannot speak against a Muslim teaching. It is called blasphemy.

"Why does the world not know? Why do they not care? Why do they only come to look at pyramids? Here you are, Marvin. I love what you are doing. Where is the rest of the world? Why do they not come and look for themselves? When they prance in here, in their political positions, on the arms of our Muslim leaders, exactly how much do they think they are really learning about Islam, and its treatment of non-Muslim peoples in Egypt? They get all of their information from Islam. They do not even know the Arabic language. They do not know the Koran. Where does it say in the Koran, 'do not fight?' That is ridiculous.

"What about the Islamic *sharia* law? Why is that so difficult to understand? Just take Saudi Arabia. Why can I not take a Bible into Saudi Arabia? Why do they burn Bibles in Saudi Arabia? Why can I not preach in Saudi Arabia? Why can I not build a church in Saudi Arabia? Why can I not worship in Saudi Arabia? Islamic *sharia* law forbids it. We now have almost the same laws in Egypt as they do in Sudan, in Iran, in Afghanistan, and soon in Iraq. Why did they blow up your buildings in New York and Washington? Americans violated Islamic *sharia* law in the Gulf War. Muhammad's deathbed wish was that no infidels be allowed on Arabian soil. What did America do? America placed their infidel soldiers on Aarabian soil.

"In the Hadith, what did Muhammad do to Muslims who wanted to become Christians? He killed them. Ask the Saudi's to answer my questions. Why can I not visit Saudi Arabia and take my Bible with me? Why do they teach that they are tolerant? Let them show me their love. Why can you not immigrate to Saudi Arabia, but they can immigrate to the United States? Why do Christians in Saudi Arabia need to live underground?"[10]

As I parted with Brahim, I shared his sense of helplessness. I thought of the politicians and pastors back home who promote Islam as peaceful and tolerant. I thought of how they divide Islam between moderates and fundamentalists. Clearly, all Muslims do not feel exactly the same about persecutions, humiliations, and executions of non-Muslim peoples. But that does not take away the daily pain of oppression against non-Muslim peoples in Islamic neighborhoods across the world. *The issue is not about individual Muslims. It is about Islam. Islam is not moderate or radical. Islam is Islam. Islam is a religion, an ideology, and theology that teaches hatred against Jews and Christians and all other nom-Muslim peoples. It is what it is. How do we moderate that?*

People can review the teachings of terror behavior toward non-Muslim peoples in the biographical traditions of

Muhammad and in the Koran, and then they can come to watch it practiced in Egypt. Islam has not changed. Muhammad's beheading of 700 Jewish male captives from the tribe of Qurayza in Medina has not changed. It is still there as a model for every Muslim who wishes to emulate Muhammad's hatred for Jews. The instructions from Koran IX (29) to fight Christians and Jews into submission "until they feel themselves subdued" has not changed. It is as old as the Koran. It is still there. It is Islam. Muhammad's model as an executioner and the Koran's orders to execute stand frozen in history. How do they change or moderate?

As I thought about Brahim, I thought of how readily we bypass him and his pain. As Americans how easily and completely we miss the tragic oppression of the Orthodox Copts. For example take David Lamb, the well-known author who lived in Egypt for several years and wrote a book about the Arabs. In his descriptions of Egyptian society, he mentions his visit to some Copts living in a village on the outskirts of Cairo. He uses the Arabic word, *zabbaleen*, to describe them. In fact he contrasts the filth of Christians to the cleanliness of Muslims. He wrote that Muslims are dedicated to cleanliness, and as a matter of religious practice, cleanse themselves at every prayer time, and how they "scorn" the Copts as *zabbaleen* and consider them dirty, filthy people who pursue treasure in the waste of the wealthy.[11]

Lamb's descriptions of the Christian Copts are shamefully oblivious to the cause of their second-class citizenship in Egyptian society. He appears clueless as to why the Copts were allowed into the garbage business. At one point, Lamb explains the Copts as a people who moved from southern Egypt to Cairo in the 1930s. His work is of exceptional interest regarding the Arabs, but he failed his readers when he made no connection with the history of the Orthodox Copts as the indigenous peoples of Egypt.

I mention David Lamb because I think his understanding is typical of a Westerner living in Egypt who is very attentive to Islam. He naturally listened to the Muslims on social, economic, and political issues of the day, which becomes clear from his descriptions of politics and war in Lebanon. He stood right next to the abusive religious culture of Egypt and did not see it. If Lamb missed what was happening under his nose to the Copts, or thought it of small consequence to report, or chose to ignore the issue for his personal benefits, then we may expect the same from other Americans.

After our visit with Brahim. I was more convinced than ever of the need to travel into Upper Egypt. While departing from the hotel lobby, Peter pointed in the direction of two men whom he said kept gawking our way as we visited Brahim. That evening, at a hotel restaurant, we saw them again, this time standing behind the kitchen's swinging doors. They found us. An adrenalin rush set me up for a sleepless night. I thought about the miserable life of Brahim as I watched, hour by hour, flickering reflections of a local streetlight darting wildly from corner to corner on the ceiling above.

Bernard in Cairo

For the next day, we had arranged a visit with Bernard, a former member of the Muslim Brotherhood. In phone conversations, he instructed us to wait in the hotel lobby for the arrival of his secretary in a black Toyota. He also mentioned that our cell phone was being monitored. We were under surveillance. A little while later, a black vehicle with a woman driver pulled up and motioned to us.

Bernard explained that he and his brothers joined the Muslim Brotherhood at a very young age. As part of a good Muslim family, he diligently studied the Koran and the Hadith. At a young age, he already struggled with verses of the Koran that taught the killing of Jews and Christians and the need to humiliate them by way of the *jizya*. Most troubling to him were the Koran's claims to Islamic superiority. He said, "I was not glad with those verses. The idea was to teach me that nobody was good enough outside Islam."[12]

As we visited, I searched the office for any clues about Bernard's connections. I could see he was an organized man. I had little acquaintance with the "organization" concept. I never knew whether to honor or tease my fastidious friends. As I searched the room, I spotted nothing from which to identify Bernard's business or his purpose and was soon convinced the office served as nothing more than a shell. Obviously his Christian ministry was secretive. His thick glasses not only kept me from reading his eyes, but also protected his anonymity.

For no reason, really, other than the darting streetlight reflections the night before, my mind drifted away to think of Michael, the man who put me in contact with Bernard, a teacher from Cairo. Suddenly Bernard hit his desktop with the flat of his hand, Pete and Sherwin never seemed to flinch. I hoped that my body had not exposed how much that whack of his hand had shocked my exhausted spirit. Bernard raised his voice: "It was obvious to me as a young man that we were not the best. We were not the best in art. We were not the best in technology. We were not the best in science. The best was in the West. We all wanted educational visas to study abroad. If Islam was the super religion, then why was everything associated with Islam inferior?"[13]

Now that Bernard suddenly had my full attention, I asked him, "What was the reason for your conversion to Christianity from the Muslim Brotherhood? Was it the claim of Islamic superiority?" To me, that seemed a bit of a stretch.

Bernard paused, twitching his lips. "That was part of it, but there were more important factors. I was troubled that Muhammad brought people to love death instead of life. Islam is always about dying, dying for Islam. Islam raises young people to kill and to die because they will go to paradise. I was also troubled by the lowly position of women in Islam. According to Islam, hell is mostly filled with the women."[14]

It must have been my sleepless night. Soon I found my mind drifting again. Bernard's reference to women in Islam reminded me of the controversial issues about "women in ecclesiastical office" within so many of the Christian churches. I thought of the terrible anger by both adversaries, pro-women in office and anti-women in office. How pathetically many of us in that debate had missed the real heart of authority—that of the Spirit, illustrated so well by Jurgen Moltmann in *The Church in the Power of the Spirit*. I shook myself for the reckless comparison. The new Testament really establishes the independence and equality between a man and a woman. In the marriage context, the husband is told, "Husbands love your wives, just as Christ loved the church and gave himself up for her..." (Ephesians 5:22).

"Muhammad had nine wives," said Bernard. Then he added, "One was only six years of age. But my greatest struggle with Islam is that Muhammad killed so many people, a prophet whose hands were covered with blood. I struggled with those ideas of violence. I love all human beings, even if they have a different language, a different skin color, or a different religion. It is better with that kind of God, a God of love. I treat my wife as God created her, not as ownership. Eternal life has to be more than a nightclub where the men who died in *jihad* get to sneak off into the distant mist of paradise to have sex with virgins, located near rivers of wine.

"As I studied the Koran, I began to see Islam as a religion made for Arabia, for Arabian people, warrior tribes looting caravans, a male religion, owning lands, owning women, and owning livestock. All of these teachings that make up Islam today were in Mecca before Islam. They worshipped at the Kaba in

Mecca before, and they travel to worship at the Kaba in Mecca after. They fasted before, and they fasted after. They prayed before, and they prayed after. Islam is no more than a pagan religion of Muhammad's ancestors with some influences stolen from the Jews and Christians. The significant change is that they had three gods before and one god after. But that is even confused in the Koran as is told in *The Satanic Verses*.

"As I struggled with the teachings of Islam, I began to read the Bible. Islam calls it a corrupt book. It says, 'Love your enemies,' when Islam says, 'Kill your enemies.' It taught me that marriage is sacred and holy, not a product of consumption. I looked for weak spots in Jesus, like I saw in Muhammad. Finally, in 1984, I chose to follow the Jesus way. Then I had to make a decision: to go abroad or to risk being killed and persecuted. I decided that I had seen the light. It was not right to take the light away, and contribute to the darkness.

"I remained in my country and began to evangelize my friends. That is when persecution began. Four years later (1989) ten of my friends came to understand and follow Jesus Christ. Soon thirty-five to fifty of us, as converts, were meeting together. With the larger numbers, we began to evangelize in public places. We acted as if we were living in a land of freedom. Three of us were arrested. We spent one year in jail. We were tortured, hanged, and electrified. Normally the sentence for converting to Christianity and evangelizing in Egypt is eight years in prison. But because of political pressure by Amnesty International and the former President Bush, we were released in one year and officially black-listed with the Egyptian authorities."[15]

I said, "Bernard, you are obviously in the struggle of your life. As you promote the ideas of Christianity, you oppose the way of Islam. As you face Islam today, what would you identify as its greatest weakness?"

He replied, "There are no freedoms. It is as if you are in a coffin. Islam rejects any open criticism and any real freedoms from *sharia* law. That is the great weapons of defense in Islam. If Islam accepts criticism and freedom, it will be destroyed. Before 9/11, Islam consistently presented itself as the religion of peace and tolerance. Nobody in Egypt—Muslim, Christian, or atheist—believes that anymore. Since 9/11 Christian converts are staying in the country instead of fleeing. Now a Christian's flight from Egypt is viewed almost as traitorous, for evangelical Christians. It is like sending away our weapons. Every new Christian is light in the darkness. Christians are growing wise, working undercover, and marching for freedom.

"We now have many NGOs (Non-Governmental Organizations) present in our society. That is necessary because the Egyptian government and Islam are on the move together to repress Christians in all fields of life…politics, economics, and in any other subjects of influence. They are holding 'heavy borders' to make us desperate and needy, so as to disable us. There is an Egyptian proverb, 'If your dog is hungry, he will follow you.' Islam sees to it that as a Christian, you spend your life as a dog, less than a slave, so that you are forced to choose the way of the Crescent. But we do not fear Islam. The worst they can do to us now is to put us in prison, torture, or kill us.

"We are here because of God. We are black-listed. We are under surveillance. The power of Islam is in Egypt. Egypt produces the minds of Islam. Saudi Arabia produces the money of Islam. Nonetheless, we stand against the Arab culture and the religion of the Kaba. We are quiet Christians. We are growing in numbers. We are ready for the big battle. We are veiled and specialized. Islam is just before the knockout punch. In the Middle East there are amazing numbers of underground converts to Christianity."[16]

"Is there anything that any of us from abroad can do to assist in this battle?" asked Pete.

Bernard replied, "The first thing that American churches need to do is stand with us in our hour of need. Help the churches in Egypt with prayers and personnel. Second, demand international organizations to put pressure on Egypt for the freedom of religion. Third, the United States Congress needs to pressure our Egyptian government to grant individual rights and freedoms. Each person must have the same individual rights as another. Since Islam became the state religion oppressions of Christians has become the formal policy of the Egyptian government. Fourth, Christian children need your help so that they are not "Islamized" in our public schools. We need independent schools and tuition support for our children. Fifth, speak out in America against these oppressive evils of Islam.

"On 9/11, Islam scratched you but once. Its claws are into us every day."[17]

Suddenly I heard the ringing of a bell. Without explanation, Bernard stood, shook hands and left the room. We were asked by the secretary to please wait and remain seated. I felt encouraged by Bernard's commitment and ambition. In the middle of surveillance, threats, arrests, torture, and the general oppression of his people, Bernard appeared unswerving in his pursuit for individual freedoms in Egypt. Amazingly, I heard him say, "Islam is just before the knock out punch." As I sat waiting, I thought most about his conviction, "If Islam accepts open criticism and real freedoms, it will be destroyed."

Sherwin must have been reflecting on the same thought. Leaning over he asked, "What do you guys think? Is there any validity to that claim, 'If Islam accepts criticism and freedom, it will be destroyed?" Then he carried on, "Seems to me that is a very difficult question to answer because there are so few, if any, real public criticisms of Islam anywhere today, and there is obviously no freedom in Egypt. Back home, there is no serious analysis of Islam. Of course, there are some of the more radical radio talk shows. But our leadership is silent. We are not seriously engaging and critiquing Islam in our dialogues. So there is little data available to help make a sound judgment."

The secretary returned and invited us out a side door. As she drove us back to our hotel, I was interested to follow up on Sherwin's remarks. I said, "Outside of insignificant data available from which to make good judgment, I think that the strength of Islam all these years is probably where we will find the greatest weakness of Islam. I find the premise true in almost every other situation of life. Isolation has kept Islam strong for hundreds of years, separated from contrary influences. So it seem that diversity could weaken Islam by causing Muslims to compare their religion to other religions and ideologies. The question is how can we make freedom a reality in Islam? Islamic *sharia* law says no! It nurtures Muslim contempt for the whole non-Muslim world."

We walked from the car and carelessly proceeded to our now favorite corner of the hotel lobby. Sherwin was eager to add another thought: "I think the concept is generally true that we find the weakness of an ideology exactly opposite of its greatest strength. I think that the major strength of Islam is its *sharia* law. It prescribes behavior. It enforces behavior. It controls behavior. To the Muslim, all of the legality, all of the legalism, all of that enforcement and endorsement, is the will of *Allah*. That is powerful!"

Sherwin continued, "Now, following your theory, that means that the critical weakness of Islam is the opposite of Islamic *sharia* law. What is that? There is so little freedom in Islam! It is not the lack of democracy as we had mistakenly designed for Iraq. Through the centuries, the people of Islam have mostly lived by a democracy of consensus. What is really missing in Islam is freedom! Is it possible to attract Muslims to experience freedom so that they will throw off the shackles of Islamic *sharia* law? What do you think, Pete?"

"Well, I have my doubts," Pete answered. "Islam has trapped these poor Muslims for nearly fourteen hundred years. It's their culture. It's their community! Breaking out is something that will not happen on an individual basis in the Middle East. They hold each other hostage. But in the West, I think it may be possible. For example, if I was a Muslim woman in the West, I would be angry a the gender bias of Islamic *sharia* law! They must ask, 'Why are we classified as inferior, when women of the West are not? Why do we need to wear Arab garb and headscarves in the Western Word? Why are we forbidden to marry a non-Muslim man, when Muslim men are allowed to marry non-Muslim women? Why do the men get seventy-two places in paradise to meet virgins, when we are lucky to escape hell?"

"But Pete," answers Sherwin, "even in America the cultural controls are still there. I watch the Muslims in my area. The only time they make contacts with non-Muslim peoples is in pursuit of jobs, money, business, converts, or to fill such needs as welfare, medicine, education, and the like. When I stop to think about it, Islam is the very opposite of the American melting pot. In every place around the world where Islam holds cultural-political authority, it rejects the freedoms of the First Amendment. In America, we have guarantees: freedom of speech, freedom of the press, freedom of association, and freedom of religion. Think of the contrast!

"Islam forbids any speech critical of Islam, by press or person. Criticism is blasphemy. Islam forbids freedom of association with non-Muslim peoples. Any religions other than Islam are subjugated and penalized. It is not only in the law of Islam. It is embedded in the culture of Islam. Muslims think and behave this way. For hundreds of years now they have replicated the behavior of former generations. They have become victims of their own history and their own religion."

That night, as I crawled into bed I reflected on the theories of Bernard. When placed under serious (accurate) criticisms, will Islam collapse and self-destruct? *We do not know. But we do know* that Islam will fight back, and in their minds, justifiably so. Some Europeans and Americans seem frightened by that possibility. As Americans we are free to criticize Islam, but that does not mean we have the necessary understanding of Islam, or the courage, to do so.

For myself, for the first time, I had heard someone claim that *an Islam exposed is an Islam deposed*. Maybe Islam knows that as reality, far more clearly than non-Muslim peoples. I speculated. Maybe that is why Islam is so defensive. Maybe that is why Islamic *sharia* law forbade criticism of the Koran and Muhammad throughout the history of Islam.

Without doubt Islam is very vulnerable, as is evident when we begin to examine its history of violence and bigotry against the Copts, Berbers, Armenians, Serbians, and Assyrians, to name a few. Furthermore, if we read its teachings of intolerance and its injunctions of violence against Christians and Jews in the Koran, and if we see that intolerance and violence modeled by Muhammad in the biographical traditions, why would we sympathize or support Islam? Closing my eyes, I mulled over two questions. Do we have a moral obligation to spread the facts of Islam's core beliefs, its culture of hate, intolerance, and coercion? Or is the exposure of those realities oddly immoral in the "global village" of today?

John and Liza in El Giza

Our taxi dropped us near a designated address in El Giza. John and Liz were standing by their door, ready to greet us. They invited us to join them around the table to share crackers and tea. Liz spoke great English and was quick to assist John when necessary. As we exchanged the routine introductions and pleasantries, John eagerly told us that they had just received an official invitation to attend their son's high school graduation in Jersey City. John's euphoric spirit told me that the invitation meant more than a son's high school diploma.

As we listened, we learned that Elizabeth's family had been in the jewelry business for hundreds of years. For many of those years, under British occupation, they had been very success-ful—but times change. As was the case in other Middle Eastern countries, when the foreign occupation ended, the attitudes and behaviors of the former culture eventually resumed. Through the past twenty years, life for non-Muslim peoples had become more oppressive around Cairo.

Signs of pain an depression deeply marked John's scarred and weary face. "In 1992, my uncle was killed not far from here, on Saudi Street," he said, "In 1994, my father-in-law was attacked in his jewelry store and shot in the leg. They stole his money and jewels. To make the looting legitimate Muslim behavior, they also demanded his conversion to Islam. They seem to think that they have the moral authority to loot our properties because we are Christian infidels. When that hap-pened, it was enough for my father-in-law. He signed a proxy for my wife to run everything. He was finished. He went to Jersey City, U.S.A.

"Liz and I had worked in the family business for years, so business operations were routine to us. But one evening in 1998, we closed our store for the day. We carried a big bag of gold. Four men followed us. Obstructed us. 'Give us what you have.' So we gave them our gold. We filed a complaint with the local police. Three months later the case was closed and archived as 'criminal anonymous,' even though the police knew the thieves, no action was taken. A local Islamic group attacks Christian jewelers as their business."[19]

Sherwin could not help himself, "What are you talking about, John? Why do you call stealing 'a business'?"

Liz explained, "It is like an auxiliary to *jizya* in the minds of some Muslims. I think you understand that, the forced subju-gation payments by Christians (infidels) to Muslims. *Jizya* is paid as humiliation money. Islam believes that all money and all possessions are from *Allah*, as the Creator God, and therefore, all material things rightfully belong to his people, the Muslims.

In that sense, stealing our gold or looting our treasury is a sacred business that honors the God of Islam. Usually they target our stores at the open or the close of the business day."

John continued, "In the year 2000, our son was in the ninth grade. I gave him a ride to school as I was on my way to the store. So after school I went to pick him up, but he was not there. Some one had come and told him that I was unable to come so he was going to give him a ride home. He took him to an undisclosed area. My son was very frightened. We received a message. 'We kidnapped your son. Pay us a ransom of 25,000 pounds.' They knew we had money. They told me, 'If you report it to the police you will be killed.' After paying the ransom and receiving back our son, I reported it, but as usual it was archived 'criminal anonymous.' Fearful for our son's safety, we sent him to the United States to live with our parents."[20]

"I suppose, John and Liz, that you know the Europeans talk of these kidnappings and thefts from jewelers as the efforts of organized crime," I said. "A university student from Berlin, Debra, told me that these criminal activities are like organized crime everywhere else in the world and have nothing to do with Islam, *per se*. What do you think of that?"

Liz answered, "I think that is typical European. The French and the Germans consider themselves the think-tank of the world. What they should realize is that organized crime does not demand conversions to Islam. Organized crime does not justify behavior on the basis of the Koran. Organized crime does not have Muslim police who refuse to enforce the laws against Muslim thieves who steal from infidels. Organized crime does not singularly identify infidel business for theft and ransom. The Germans are once again parroting Muslim deception. The problem of injustice is that the Egyptian judicial system answers to Islamic *sharia* law. If they know so much, why do the French and Germans refuse to institute Islamic *sharia* law in their own countries?"[21]

I smiled at Liz. "Oops," I said. "From what I just heard, I have the feeling that question is not a fresh one for you?"

Liz laughed. "Well, it is irritating that students from European universities get 'diversity credits' for coming to Egypt to dialogue with Egyptian Muslims. They are educated as Muslim sympathizers."

For John, the discussion was irrelevant. He persisted in this explanation of life under the authority of an Islamic Egypt. "Our next experience with theses criminals of Islam came on Sunday, shortly after attending church. We drove home. I told my wife and my daughter to go upstairs while I parked the car. Ten minutes later, I knocked on the door. It opened and I was shocked to see men with machine guns surrounding my wife. They put a tape over her mouth. They were monitoring me. They knew I had the rest of the jewelry in our home. Fearing for our lives, I gave them the key to the safe. I did not resist, but they hit me on the head and I lost consciousness. They took everything and ran away. Once again our report to the police was archived and the case was filed 'criminal anonymous.' They said that there was no evidence."

Liz explained, "We are special targets because we serve in the church. The government targets all Christians to become Muslims. A recent tactic of Islam in Egypt is to seduce Christian women and entice them to convert. 'We give you many things, why should you live in humiliation?' John and I try to educate our women to resist these enticements. I will give you an example of how our Christian women are treated by Muslim men.

"A family friend of my father called us. 'Please help us, our daughter was abducted.' She was twenty-five years of age, good at her job, a quick and very efficient worker. Then she was abducted. She was blindfolded and taken to an unknown area. An *emir* (local leader) had fallen in love with her. He wanted her. She told him that a Christian is prohibited to marry a non-Christian. As a Muslim he argued that was permissible in Islam even if she did not convert. She was emphatic that she would not marry him. So they wrapped her with rope around her legs. But they did not want to permanently damage her because the *emir* wanted her beautiful for his pleasure. They tortured her three days to force her to write down a statement that she had converted to Islam. Eventually she broke down and signed so that they would release her. Then they abandoned her in a desert area. When people saw her, she asked them to take her to the nearest church.

"In church she asked for help to reach her family and told them not to ask her any questions. So her parents got her. For two weeks she was unable to talk, so her family called a doctor and a priest to check her, for she feared she had lost her virginity. She felt violated and had fits of psychological trauma. The doctor examined her, and she was still a virgin. Later the police sent her a notice that she had converted to Islam. As a Muslim she was told that she could not live with her Christian parents because they were unclean. Fortunately her father had some money and connections. He told them. 'If you do not correct this record, I will escalate this matter to the level of the President.' In her specific case, she was left at home.

"In other cases, Muslims abduct young Christian women, take photos of them naked, and then threaten to show them to the family or to post them in the woman's village. So the women, in shame, convert to Islam and wear the veil. In other situations, some stores owned by Muslims have installed video cameras. When the Christian girls are changing clothes, they take pictures, unbeknown to the girls. Then they alter the pictures. They put men with them and blackmail the girls.

"The latest method of trapping and coercing Christian women began four months ago. Muslims started raffles and calling Christian women, 'You have won the raffle, come and claim your gift.' The woman comes and signs for her gift, but in reality she is signing a statement that she converted to Islam.

Now she is viewed as a Muslim by the state, and Islamic *sharia* law says that she may no longer live with unclean Christians. Sometimes these women do not know what to do. In addition to the false documents, they and their families are threatened. They are afraid. So out of desperations, they convert. Once a person converts to Islam, Islamic *sharia* law forbids that person to leave Islam and convert back to Christianity.

"Whether you are at work, at school or walking down the street, they see you have a crucifix or you are not covering your head, so they call you an infidel. When Muslim men walk down the street, they curse and spit at you, even throw acid at you. That is increasingly a problem. Through these terror tactics, they try to force Christian women to forsake their real identity and to act like Muslim women. On special Christian days of celebration, such as Easter and Christmas, when women are walking home from church, some Muslims carry acid in small spray bottles, and casually spray the skin of a Christian woman. In a crowd, the woman does not realize what has happened until her skin begins to turn raw."[22]

I asked, "Liz, is there any protection for these women?"

"Well, on our church program, we are trying to teach them caution and that they can confide in us. Other than that there is nothing. Unless, of course, they dress like Muslims but that also has risks because it can be used as evidence against them along with forged documents to prove that they have indeed converted to Islam. The truth of the matter is that the Egyptian police and especially agents in the department of intelligence are all Muslim. The state religion is Islam. In that sense, the state endorses this treatment of Christians as instructed by Islamic *sharia* law. For fourteen hundred years, Islam has threatened and coerced Christian women. When fathers and husbands object, they are dealt with.

"The government tries to put a good face on things for the West, especially the United States. For example, at Ramadan, the Pope of the Copts and other leaders of the Christian community are invited to the annual feast. They attend out of fear for their people, and in turn they invite Muslims to Christmas celebrations. Of course we as Christian Copts see it as superficial and grist for the propaganda mill, but the Western Press is very naïve and reports these celebrations as efforts toward peace and unity."

Curious about their future, I asked, "What are you doing, John? They stole your gold. They stole your son. They stole your jewelry. What could you do? What did you do?"

John replied, "After they took everything from me, I decided to use my teaching degree to get a job. I left Giza for southern Egypt to teach in a high school. It was hell. There is no life there for a Christian. No job, no money, no value, and no honor. Right now our hope is that when we attend our son's graduation in Jersey City, we will be granted asylum. I cannot live here any more. It is all about converting to Islam, the 'verse of the sword,' IX (29). Christians must convert or face daily threats, violence, and humiliation. We are viewed as animals. That is our experience. By Islamic *sharia* law, we are meal tickets for the Muslim population."[23]

Just then our taxi driver knocked at the door. It was time to move along. As we said our goodbyes, Liz asked for a prayer that God bless their future request for asylum. In the quiet of the apartment we held hands, sharing tears of solidarity and praying for God's blessing of safety, travel, and permission to live in a land of freedom. Parting, we made promises for the future. In a painful silence we rode back to our hotel.

Round Table Dialogue in Alexandria

Finally our hopes for a visit into Upper Egypt were taking shape, Bishop Wissa of the Orthodox Coptic church had offered to hold an audience with us the following week at the

Monastery of the Child. My interest was in the deaths of twenty-one Christian Copts who had been murdered in the village of Qus, part of Wissa's bishopric. I was curious as to details on the cause of the murders, and I wanted to do a follow-up on the prosecution of the criminal. While we were absent because of our trip to Alexandria, our hotel concierge agreed to purchase our train tickets for Upper Egypt. We telephoned the bishop to seal arrangements as to time and place.

In the meanwhile, Samir, a young teacher at a government school for women, kindly made arrangements for a private car and driver for our journey into Alexandria. In Alexandria, we had scheduled visits with several Christian Copts who were authorities on Islam to learn of their experiences and understanding of Islamic sharia law.

In appreciation we invited Samir to lunch. He told us that the enrollment in his school was about two hundred fifty students. He was clearly an evangelical Christian. In America he would probably be called fundamentalist because of his basic beliefs. He volunteered that he was committed to the way of Christian love in his relationship with the Muslim faculty. He said, "That is why the Muslim headmaster frequently invites me to his office to ask advice and discuss issues. When I share my faith, I always begin with the love of God. That is the Gospel.

"One of the teachers became angry at me for sharing the love of God with him. But the next day he came to school saying, 'I am not sure. I need to think.' Thinking is the beginning. Another of our teachers was very depressed. He was fearful of everything. As a teacher forty years of age. He left school and stayed in his house. People were afraid of him, even his family. He was alone. He said, 'I have no friends.'"[24]

Samir told him, "I am your friend." Eventually, in the love of Samir, he saw the love of Jesus. Samir explained, "He began to greet people again. He called his cousins for the first time in ten years. He thanked me for his 'new life.' Today he worships at different churches so that Islamic zealots cannot track him."

That evening we were invited to dinner at the home of Pastor Zeke from a nearby evangelical church. When we arrived, we were surprised to see police guarding the sanctuary. Zeke smiled and assured us that the Egyptian government assigned the police for protection against terror attacks. The food was fresh and tasty. The pastor's wife, Emily, faithful to Middle Eastern custom, repeatedly insisted that we eat to the full.

In the course of the evening, I asked Pastor Zeke about Bibles in Egypt.

"Bibles are banned in Saudi Arabia, but not here," he said. "But you cannot give a Bible or Christian literature to anyone in Egypt. That is against the laws. At the present time, you can sell Bibles in Cairo, but I think that Cairo is probably the safest place for Christians in Egypt. I hear Upper Egypt is far worse. We have some advantages here because of economic and political influence from the United States."[25]

The evening of a causal visit and good food soon passed, and we were saying farewell. Pastor Zeke hailed us a taxi and sent us off with his blessings. When we arrived at our hotel, we were exhausted and crashed on arrival.

Morning came quickly, and we were on the road to Alexandria. As we viewed the sights along a very impressive highway system, I realized that back home my family and friends were celebrating Thanksgiving Day. But for us, it would prove to be no sweet potato and turkey day. As we traveled, our driver, David, told us that he was born a Muslim, his wife and children were still Muslims, but he converted to Christianity two years ago. He did not risk attending any church and was educating himself by way of videos and cassettes. His wife was tolerant of his conversion: "She says that since my conversion, I am a better man. As for my kids, I am trying to win them through Jesus films."[26]

In Alexandria we rented rooms at a Christian hostel. Everywhere we went on campus, the air was filled with loud, very loud Arabic speech coming from a nearby minaret. Throughout the late afternoon hours, the sound was constant and very annoying, Brahim was right in what he said. I found it difficult to understand that Christians were hounded by such boisterous, incessant noise whenever they resided near a Christian facility. I suppose that policy increasingly will be put in place wherever Islam holds authority.

That evening we ate at the mess hall and visited with some Christian youth on retreat from a Presbyterian church in Cairo. I was surprised by their friendliness and willingness to sit and chat. They held strongly unfavorable opinions about the United States Army in Iraq. They viewed American action as aggressive and imperialistic. They were convinced that the United States was in Iraq for the sole purpose of stealing Middle Eastern oil. Sherwin later commented that the arguments they presented were similar to those in the film by Michael Moore, which was very popular throughout Egypt. So if Moore had any concern about whether or not his film was a success, he can rest assured that he convinced these young Egyptian Christians of American imperialism.

As we departed the mess hall, I remembered Michael Moore as he sat alone in a balcony a the Republican National Convention in 2004. Surely, I thought he exercised his freedom and injected his opinions into the American political process. But I doubted very much that he ever thought his so-called "documentary" would capture anti-American support from the Europeans and the non-Muslim Middle Easterners.

It was already early evening and we needed to confirm tomorrow's roundtable discussion on Islamic *sharia* law. As we hurried through the hallways, I noticed two men in their early thirties that we had previously seen in the lobby of our Cairo hotel. As we passed, they gazed out the windows as if watching the children at play. What was their agenda anyway?

Early the next morning, we boarded a bus into Alexandria. As we sat down, I saw a taxi pull from the curb and follow us. For our safety, we made an early exit from the bus, walked two blocks, and hailed a cab. As we drove away, Pete could see "our shadows" several car lengths behind. "Please, go around the block," I said to the taxi driver, rotating my finger in the motion of a circle. He understood and we lost them. A few blocks later, we jumped from the cab and walked to our destination. We found three men waiting for us.

James was tall and slender. His smile reflected a gentle spirit. Alexander was a little shorter and heavier. His eyes flickered curiosity and his face passion. Titus was by far the shortest, heaviest, and oldest of the three. He spoke softly and with authority. All three were Orthodox Copts, schooled abroad, held doctorate degrees, and spoke English.

"So where do we wish to begin in this discussion of Islamic holy law (*sharia*) in Egypt?" I asked.

Titus was eager to speak and offered the opinion that it was important for us to first address a few significant political changes in Egypt throughout the past fifty years.

Titus said, "When I was a young boy we lived under the authority of the British. With the rise of communism came the leadership of Nasser. Egypt aligned itself with the Soviet Union, in the fifties, when the British forces departed. At that time, French law still governed Egypt. When the British withdrew, the theme of the people on the streets was, 'Long live the sign of the Crescent and the Cross,' a battle cry of united Muslims and Christians against the occupying forces of Britain. When the Brits withdrew, however, the Muslim Brotherhood demanded that Egypt return to its past as a truly Islamic nation, even though the Constitution of 1932 stated that 'everyone is equal.' Nasser's commitment to communism had no room for an Islamic state, and he imprisoned the Muslim Brotherhood.

"Eventually, Sadat became President. As a strong adherent of Islam, he freed the Muslim Brotherhood. Later, of course, they assassinated him when he agreed to officially recognize the legitimacy of the state of Israel. During his reign, however, he allowed *sharia* to become the foundation of Egyptian legislation and Islam was officially adopted as the state religion.

"In the constitution, 'everyone is equal,' but the adoption of Islam as the state religion totally contradicted that article by teaching that Christians are inferior human beings. At that point, equality and religious freedom were totally crushed in Egypt. In recent years, Egypt has returned to its abusive behavior of the past. Christians were once again persecuted as infidels and enemies of *Allah*."[27]

Alexander passionately broke into Titus' historical reflections with a biblical reference: "They will put you out of the synagogue; in fact a time is coming when anyone who kills you will think he is offering a service to God" (John 16:2). That is the poison of Islam. They kill us and think they do God a service. With the adoption of Islam as the state religion, the Egyptian authorities turned Islam's hate loose on all Christians."[28]

"But," Titus clarified, "the Islamic Code (*sharia*) was not applied uniformly in all areas of Egypt. Nonetheless, a transition took place in which Egypt progressively ignored French law, which protected the rights of Christians, and implemented Islamic holy law, that was increasingly used to punish Christians as inferior human beings."[29]

"Excuse me. Alexander, but this discussion relates to my experience in Nigeria," I interjected. "When I was in Kaduna, some of the Muslim leaders justified *jihads* against Christians because Christians had objected to the implementation of (Criminal Code) Islamic *sharia* law. As I understood Islamic *sharia* law, it was constructed by Muslim scholars based on teachings from the biographical traditions of Muhammad and the Koran. These are the two main sources for the content of

Islamic *sharia* law. According to the Christians of Nigeria, the implementation and application of Criminal Code *sharia* law would be oppressive and restrictive to the Christian community. Were they correct? The Muslim leaders in Kaduna said the Islamic *sharia* law only affects Muslims. *How does Islamic sharia law affect non-Muslim peoples?"*

"It's punitive," said Alexander. "It endorses and legalizes a culture of oppression and persecution. It punishes Christians for their rejection of Muhammad as a legitimate prophet in the Christian tradition. Hundreds, thousands of Christians have been killed since Islam was adopted as the state religion and followed Islamic *sharia* law." [30]

"Can you illustrate some of the practical specifics from Islamic *sharia* law that might affect Christians?" Pete asked.

"Marriage in Egypt serves as an example," said Titus. "Under Islamic *sharia* law, a Muslim man can marry a woman of any faith. The woman is not forced to change her religion. But, as an example of *sharia's* punitive character, if she remains a Christian, she cannot receive any inheritance from her husband. In addition, her children must legally be raised as Muslims. In fact, these days Muslim men are advised at their mosque to marry infidel women, especially if they have a child. That way the woman, the child, and future births are all Islamic numerical growth instead of Christian." [31]

James commented on the subject of women in general, making the point that a woman who is a Christian Copt does not cover her head. For her to do so these days is for her to dishonor her identity. *Sharia* states that a woman must cover her head at all times n public places. Therefore, Coptic women are obvious targets in a Muslim society and are cursed and spit on when they travel. They are called whores. Even in this simple way, *sharia* makes life more difficult for a non- Muslim person.

"Islamic *sharia* law controls social relationships," said James. "Just compare Muslim society to American society. In

America everyone is equal by law. In Egypt, there is a culture of hate for infidels, which is learned at home, in the mosques, and public schools. Our schools teach the superiority of the Muslim over the Christian, even in grammar school. Islamic holy law demands that non-Muslim people must submit to Islam. That is true on a personal level. You must submit and honor their authority. The law is based on Koran IX (29). They are superior. In a famous Hadith, it teaches Muslims, 'Do not pass greetings to Jews and Christians. Whenever you meet them force them to the other side of the street. Put obstacles in front of them.' *Sharia* enforces this culture of intolerance.

"A friend of mine, Lati, applied and was accepted at the police academy. He is strong and smart. At the end of training, he received a documented letter. He was officially rejected because of a tattoo on his wrist; it was a tattoo of the Coptic cross. Many of us have that tattoo of the cross.

"When the Muslims came into Egypt under the second Caliph in 641, Muslims humiliated Christians by forcing them to wear heavy crosses around their necks so that Muslims could spit on the cross when they passed by. The crosses weighed five to ten pounds and, because of the weight, routinely cut off the blood supply and left a blue mark on the clavicle. So the Christian Copts became known as Blue Bones. In resistance and out of pride, many of us put the blue bone cross tattoo on our wrists to remind us of our ancestors. But *sharia* forbids the showing of the cross, so if you wear a cross in a Muslim society, you may legally be unemployed. The cross offends Islam."[32]

Titus spontaneously professed, "The cross of Christ stands at the center of our religion. I believe he was crucified for me. We confess the cross. We are proud of the cross. We wear it on our right arm, the arm of power, to show that we receive our power from God."[33]

"*Sharia* controls education," said Alexander. "I grew up in a nice neighborhood. We were very poor. We really learned to love our enemy. We loved life as a gift from the Lord, not because we were worthy, but because God gave life. We tried to harmonize with the community. I played with Muslim friends on the streets. I was very happy. Then one day the kids tied my hands together. They said, 'You are a *kafir*.' That is an Arabic word meaning death and torture, loosely translated 'infidel.' I was only seven years old. They tied my hands. They beat me. I was mocked as a Christian who worships the cross. They treated me as a cockroach. I was not human to them. These are seven and eight-year-old Muslim children. Islamic holy law instructs them that as Christians we are inferior.

"Already as a seven-year-old, I learned that was normal life for a Christian. We had about 50–60 students in our class. One day they kicked out the Christians during the religious period. Christians were told to clean up the streets and the school grounds. But I did not go out. I learned the Koran. I memorized many chapters (*suras*). One day the teacher came to class and said, 'We are going to talk about *Sura* (Chapter) Nine of the Koran today. We will talk about the People of the Book. Christians and Jews are the People of the Book. Christians believe in three gods, god the Father, god the Mother, and god the Son.' I raised my hand and said. 'That is not true. We believe in one God in three persons, God the Father, God the Son, and God the Holy Spirit.' My teacher came and physically beat me. I cursed him and spit at him. The police were called to school.

"The officer in charge came and scowled at me, 'So you think you are a big shot? I can crush you like I crush an ant. From now on, during religion, get the hell out of school.' That is when I really started to study Islam. I decided to be an authority while I was at it.

"Let me give you another example. I had one buddy, a loving friend. He was very nice. He respected me. For several days, he was absent from school. I missed him. So, I went to his house to see if anything was wrong.

"His father greeted me at the door and asked, 'What is your name?'

'My name is Alexander.' I answered.

'My son is sleeping. Please do not ever come to see him again!'

"That was my best friend. His father only needed to hear my Christian name, and he saw me as a *kafir*. That is life under Islam. That is life under *sharia*. That is normal. Its like a dog beaten since he was a puppy. After a while, the dog starts to act like a rabbit. When Muslims see your cross, hear your name, they spit in your face. To them that is human. That is normal. That is what Muslims do to a *kafir*. That is what their parents did and that is what their grandparents did. All of that behavior is endorsed by *sharia*."[33]

James added, "Those kinds of attitudes and behaviors are embedded in the Muslim culture. But they are more than a custom. They are found in the Hadith and the Koran, the religious authorities of Islam. Many of them have been translated into the Islamic holy law. Let me give you an example of how *sharia* is used in the Islamic culture to oppress Christians.

"The biographical tradition of Muhammad shows that the women of non-Muslim men and the possessions of non-Muslim peoples are there to be looted and possessed by the followers of Islam. I recently applied for asylum on behalf of a woman now in the United States. She is a beautiful woman. Her Muslim neighbor saw she was so beautiful and said that she should not be married to a *kafir*. He was infatuated with her. He would wait for her to leave her residence, and then he would follow her and try to seduce her. He offered her money and a beautiful home. He told her she did not belong with an infidel guy. He even tried to rape her.

"She did not tell her husband because she thought they would kill him when he defended her honor. A year later, the Muslim neighbor obtained a certificate from the government office claiming that she converted to Islam, so the police went to her house to take her away. Her husband asked why she had to leave. 'A Muslim woman by *sharia* law cannot be married to a Christian. She is a Muslim.' He was powerless to do anything. They took his wife in front of his own eyes.

"He went to complain to the government officials, 'She is a Christian.'

'What proof do you have? They asked. He showed them her certificate of marriage. Even then because almost all the police are Muslim, no one was there to help. So the neighbor was allowed to keep the Christian's wife. Six months later, through the church and church records, we were able to get a visa and got her out of the country to the United States. The laws of Egypt are discriminating laws. All legislation is now based on *sharia*. For example, all young men are drafted as soldier into the army for three years, but if you memorize parts of the Koran, you serve one-half the time as do other soldiers."[34]

"Identification cards of Egypt," explained Alexander, "are used to enforce *sharia*. In the center of the card, the government prints your religion. Sometimes they identify a rich Christian and they intentionally print Islam on his I.D. His children are of course Christian. As a registered Muslim, *sharia* forbids his Christian children to inherit his money and properties. All of his wealth then goes to the local mosque and Islam. In Egypt that is called 'double death.' If after he is registered as a Muslim, he attempts to convert back to Christianity, he is officially an apostate. Apostasy according to *sharia* is punishable by death. A Muslim who converts to any other religion is at risk of being killed. On the other hand, if a man such as this remains a Muslim, then he and his family die the deaths of poverty, so its is called 'double death.'"

"Islamic holy law also prohibits church repair and church construction."

Alexander described how under *sharia*, churches need a presidential decree for repairs. "That is harder than reaching the moon. Even if the president does make such a decree to build or repair a church, *sharia* says that it must be ten kilos, six miles, from a mosque. So the Muslim *mufti* issues a decree that they plan to build a mosque in that vicinity, canceling the president's order. Or if Muslims simply make it a prayer site, then according to *sharia*, no church construction is allowed.

"At one point when the international press challenged the president of Egypt, Hosni Mubarak, on the issue, he said that he was going to build the Christians fifty churches at his own expense. We are still waiting for the first block to be laid for the first church to be built. Hate and intolerance are a legal activity in Islam. They plant mosques in the middle of a Christian community. They turn the speakers so high so that you cannot sleep, and you cannot study. They harass you every day in the name of *Allah*."[35]

"*Sharia* uses taxes in Egypt to punish Christians," said James. "According to *sharia*, if you build a mosque in your building, say your house, then you do not have to pay taxes. That of course is not true of churches, so the money of the Christians' taxes go for the expenses of the imams, mosques, and *jihad*, but no taxes go for Christian churches and priests. Under Nasser the government claimed all private property. When Sadat became president, he returned the properties of all the Muslims, but *sharia* allowed the Islamic government to withhold certain Christian properties. In addition the government under Nasser sold treasures from Christian museums to international museums. The funds all went to Islam."[36]

As the time for our visit was coming to a close, Alexander made the point that the specifics of the Islamic holy law are established from the will of *Allah* as recorded in the Koran. So for a simple understanding of *sharia* law, you really only need to read the Koran.

However, James warned that to understand the Koran, one needed to understand the concept of abrogation. He said, "An eleventh century Hadith teaches it is absolutely necessary to understand the concept of abrogation in order to accurately understand the teachings of the Koran. Abrogation means the cancellation of an earlier text when it is contradicted by a latter test. In other words, in the case of a contradiction, the message last recorded is the message that remains binding and authoritative. That means that the reader really needs to pay critically close attention to the dates/events of when Muhammad received the message to be certain of its actual authority."[37]

Titus added, "Readers dependent on translations of the Koran need to be cautious because some publications now intentionally exclude the dating of events. The Koran, as you know, is not printed in chronological order, so when you pick up certain paperback copies of the Koran in English, you have no idea of which text speaks authoritatively. The reader becomes vulnerable to an interpretation and advice from a Muslim."[38]

We gathered addresses, made promises of future correspondence, and embraced one another. We then joined David, our driver and we were off to Cairo. The traffic was light and our discussion centered mostly on *sharia*.

CHAPTER NINE

Journeys into Neighborhoods of Islam
Qus, Egypt

Early Thursday morning, we boarded the train out of Cairo. I enjoyed watching passengers as they settled into their seats. Some dressed Middle Eastern, but many were wearing Western-style jackets and pants. I saw only a few women on the whole train, and there were no Anglo-Americans aboard except for us, the three men seated near the rear of the last car. Behind us were two men whose faces were safely tucked behind newspapers. So as to not attract greater attention, we sat silently as we raced along the Nile River, appreciating a panorama of small farm villages and magnificently cultivated landscapes. We were traveling in luxury, with an occasional pause for passengers to get on and off. This was no Amtrak.

After some five hours, we reached our destination and stepped from the train. Suddenly six Egyptian police confronted us. Our translator guide was visibly shaken. Behind us we saw the familiar faces of two intelligence agents. Both of them began shouting and pushing at us, making a commotion. A crowd of villagers began to gather, signaling danger. As my mind raced for any possible exits, a young, tall, and very handsome clergyman dressed in a black robe moved between the police and us. He was unmistakably our contact person, Father Paul, chauffer of Bishop Wissa. In a clear but normal voice, he gave the order, "Go to the blue Mercedes now."[1]

Within seconds we were inside the bishop's Mercedes. Pete kept saying, "Lock the door, Marvin." I set my bag on the floor. "I don't think you locked the door, Marvin." He reached over to push down the lock. We were already moving away from the crowd. But red lights were flashing and an eerie European siren was sounding. We were in a police chase. The road was one and one-half lanes wide, cluttered with pedestrians, donkey carts, and people-packed lorries (trucks). When I looked over Father Paul's shoulder, the speedometer read one hundred twenty kilometers per hour.

After fifteen very long minutes, we pulled into a walled monastery, and a very large black medieval gate dropped behind us. Father Paul, seemingly unfettered by our concerns, invited us to come inside. After the chase of our lives, we found ourselves sipping tea and sitting together on luxurious furniture in a magnificent great room with twenty to thirty-foot high ceilings. Father Francis soon joined us, a soft-spoken amicable priest who had schooled in western Canada. His family had fled Egypt after the Suez massacres (January 4, 1952), when Muslims, following Friday prayers, dragged nine Christians through the streets with butcher hooks and then burned them alive in the Saint Antonious Coptic Church.

In Canada Francis had earned his Ph.D. in psychology and later returned to Egypt to aid and serve his people. As we visited, we realized that our recent, traumatic incident was a way of life for these people. Father Paul told us that he had been run off the road on three occasions. He believed that all three were efforts to kill Bishop Wissa. He reassured us, "Don't worry about the police." While father Paul was still speaking, a priest of the monastery entered the grand lobby and signaled him.

When Father Paul returned, he was less enthusiastic. "We have two intelligence agents at the gate demanding to see your passports."

"That is not good." I said. "My passport has visas from Nigeria and Sudan as well as Egypt."

Father Paul momentarily twisted his lips and shrugged his shoulders. "Just give me your passports and I will copy the passport information and your visas to Egypt. That will serve the purpose. They do not need your actual passports." Soon he returned with our passports, saying, "Finish."[2]

In the meanwhile, Father Gabriel from Qus joined our little band. His special interest was current world events. I found it difficult to imagine living in Upper Egypt and studying day-by-day global affairs. At the moment my interest, however, was a massacre that took place in Qus. I asked, "Tell me Father Gabriel, what is life like for children in your region?"

He replied, "Islam poisons little children's minds in their early years of school. 'I will not play with you because I am a Muslim. Muslims do no play with Christians.' Today the Germans are having the same problem with Muslim students in their school systems. Islam is just the opposite from America, where you try to teach acceptance of diversity. Here at early ages they teach religious isolation and supremacy. That attitude and behavior permeates the mind of Islamic society. The worst areas for Christians are Giza to Luxor to Aswan. The Christians in these areas are truly marginalized and helpless. No authority listens. The families are kept illiterate. There is no external support. Thy are trapped. The police, the judges, and other officials are all Muslims. The children are victims. Schools are in ill repair. The teachers are Muslims. The curriculum is Muslim. To bring children to these schools is to offer them up to Muhammad. The real choice for parents is illiteracy or Islam.

Christian students are forced into Muslim cleansings, Muslim prayers, and the memorization of the Koran. That process is correctly described as Islamization."

"What about adults, Father Gabriel?" I asked.

He explained, "In Qus, a Muslim neighbor killed his Christian neighbor. What happened to the Muslim? Nothing! He was acquitted! He was set free! He said, 'I did this for *jihad*.' That meant it was a holy killing. In Qus Christian children are told by adult Muslims, 'I hate you.' That is reality. Living in the villages you see this bold prejudice all the time. There are many examples.

"One Muslim woman was bleeding and a Christian took her to the hospital. They were of the same blood type, but the Muslim could not accept the blood because it was *kafir* blood. In a village near Qus, there was a fire that destroyed many farms, fields of grain, and produce, so the government gave assistance. But the assistance all went to the Muslims—a big truck of flour, pasta, sugar, and tea. Not a small part was given to the Christians, nothing!"[3]

Father Paul hurried into the lobby, "They want to know why Marvin was in Sudan." Everyone turned to look at me.

I said, "They knew that I was in Sudan when I received my visa to Egypt, why didn't they ask then? Why are they so afraid now? Tell them to stop the harassment." Father Paul smiled and went for the door.

That evening we were invited to the residency of the bishop. Father Francis served as our translator. Sherwin ran a video camera, and Pete managed a small cassette recorder. We stood in respect as Bishop Wissa entered the room, and then we exchanged formal greetings. Father Gabriel accompanied him. The two of them were the spiritual leaders and protectors of the Copts in Qus at the time of the massacre and therefore preferred to make a joint testimony.

According to Father Gabriel, on August 14, 1998, two young Christian men of Qus, Samir Oweida Hakim and Karem

Tamer Arsal, were murdered. The Christian community suspected five young Muslim men as possible culprits and did not view the murders as a religious crime. However, the police immediately said to Father Gabriel that a Christian was responsible for the murder. "They soon began to round up Christians," he said.

Bishop Wissa continued, "They started taking our people to the police station, twenty to forty of them, torturing them with unbelievable tortures. They did not distinguish whether it was a man or a woman, children or elderly. It made no difference. The reason for the torturing was to get them to testify against a certain Christian to prove he was the killer. That person's name was Buktor, a Copt name for 'Victor" in English."[4]

Troubled by the behavior of the local police and local intelligence, the bishop appealed to a top intelligence officer. He told him, "If you are looking for a killer, that is your business, but you are torturing my people. What have the children and the elderly to do with this? If the killer is a priest, by all means take him, but do not torture my people."[5]

In response the director of intelligence in Qus became angry with the bishop for consulting a higher authority. He told Bishop Wissa, "As for the torture of Christians in Qus, you have seen nothing yet. There is plenty more to come." His threat was clear and public. He went on to mock the idea of justice. He said, "I know for a fact that Buktor and his family committed the crime." But then, out of the other side of his mouth, he offered to look the other way if Christians were ready to offer up a scapegoat in place of Buktor.[6]

Imprisonment and torture continued!

Two weeks later, one of the priests serving in Qus died, and the bishop went to pay his final respects. While there, he asked to see the daughter of Buktor, the accused man. A rumor had been manufactured that the murder victims, Samir and Karem, had raped her. As an act of revenge, her father, Buktor, killed them. The police defended their whole case on the basis of that rumor. When the daughter agreed to accompany the bishop in order to visit a medical doctor, he took her to the village of El Balyana outside of Qus, across the Nile River. The doctor certified that the daughter was still a virgin, proving the rumor untrue. *Nothing changed.*

On Thursday, September 17, 1998, the bishop again visited the intelligence authority of higher rank. When he was asked, "Why me?" the bishop answered, "I will not discuss the issue with a person who threatens me and my people with more torture and greater violence."[7] He requested the officer to please visit Qus in person because words could never explain what was happening there. So he came and visited the victims one by one. He saw how the son and daughter of Buktor had been tortured. How they had tortured the girl with electrical wires. During the officer's interrogation, the daughter began weeping and found herself unable to finish her story. The intelligence officer asked that the case against Buktor be closed. Since Buktor's arrest, thirty-three days had passed.

Amazingly this was not the end of the case.

On the same day, a Christian man by the name of Shibub, formerly tortured to testify against Buktor, was now charged with the crime of murder. According to the bishop, "Soon they started torturing Buktor to testify against Shibub."[8] At that time, they took two Christian military interns and tortured them, along with a third person who refused to testify against Shibub. One of the interns succumbed to fear and turned his testimony against Shibub. Then the police announced that Shibub was the killer.

Later the father of the intern that testified against Shibub came to Bishop Wissa and told him that his son was emotionally unstable and that he felt guilty because he falsely testified in the case of Shibub, so Bishop Wissa sent one of the priests to El Minya, which is the area where the two men were being trained, to ask for a leave so that he could come to restate his testimony. They arrived back in Qus on October 6, 1998. The next day they testified at the intelligence department, where the whole incident started. On October 7, the case against Shibub was closed.

Then the unbelievable was committed.

On October 8, actually 7 according to the bishop, the intelligence department began investigating why the interns left their unit. Even though the two testified that they had never seen or met Bishop Wissa, the intelligence department decided to put the two in jail. On October 19, the bishop was asked to appear at the intelligence department. They told the bishop that the interns had admitted that Wissa instructed them to change their testimony.

The investigation was closed as follows.

Five charges of terrorism were filed against his Grace, Bishop Wissa. The punishment for those charges ranges between ten to fifteen years of imprisonment. Wissa told me, "These charges are still filed against me until this minute." His lawyer described it as "putting a sword to his neck as a option for the future," an effort to intimidate Bishop Wissa to stop trying to protect his people. They sentenced Shibub to fifteen years imprisonment. Shibub remains in prison today.[9]

The fulfillment of the threat.

The director of intelligence in Qus had threatened Wissa, "As for the torture of Christians in Qus, you have seen nothing yet. There is plenty more to come."[10] That threat became reality beginning on December 31, 1999 with a fight between a Christian merchant and a Muslim customer. The merchant went to the police station to report the incident. By the time he returned, a Muslim crowd had rioted and destroyed his whole store.

The situation was volatile. The police asked the priests to instruct their people to stay at home. They did, but Christians' stores were pillaged and burned, on Sunday Christians went to worship. That is when the full attack exploded. By twelve o'clock, Father Gabriel was in El Balyana, the seat of the bishopric, for an emergency visit with Bishop Wissa. Telephone calls were also coming in from Qus. The sounds of gunfire and bullets could be heard from the telephone all the way across the room. Father Paul drove Wissa and Gabriel back to Qus...a one-hour drive. Qus was in flames.

The department of intelligence requested Pope Shenouda III to send a bishop to Qus to calm down the Christians. "Imagine," said Wissa, "We are being assaulted and they request a bishop so that we be calmed."[11] When the designated bishops arrived, the governor told them it was a normal situation where only five people were killed. The bishops asked to see for themselves. They found twenty victims. Eight were killed out on the farms and twelve were killed in the residential area. A young Christian boy was also shot to death on the spot while riding his bicycle. The killers threatened the family, so the father agreed to testify that a car struck his son, and the boy was not recorded among the other dead. Of the eight found in the field, one was alive long enough to identify the killers. This was on Sunday, January 2, 2000.

Religious executions!

On Tuesday, January 4, seventeen corpses were brought into the church. Two corpses had already been buried, another person was so totally burned away that only one small bone remained, and the boy on the bicycle was excluded. All were buried as martyrs. When I inquired why they were buried as martyrs, I was told that in each case prior to the killing "the Christian victim was told to convert to Islam. When the offer was rejected, the victim was executed."[12]

The burial of the executed victims as Christian martyrs is supported by the findings of a human rights organization, Center of Religious Freedom. For example, in its published report, *Massacre at the Millennium,* four armed Muslim men tackled a young deacon departing from the Copt church after holy mass. He was taken into a nearby field, forced to kneel as a Muslim at prayer, and then instructed to convert to Islam. When he refused, he was shot in the head. They also forced his younger sister, whom they may have confused as his wife, to lie next to her brother's body and executed her.[13]

The government tried to explain the executions as a conflict in which twenty Christians were killed and one Muslim. Wissa added, "That was not true of course. There were twenty-one Christians. A Muslim was killed, but that was twelve kilometers away, in another incident, an accidental shooting."[14]

"So how did this really begin? I know there was a threat, but was there a prior meeting? Was there a prior discussion of such violent behavior?" I asked.

Bishop Wissa then explained that prior to the killings, deliberations by the Muslims began on a Saturday evening during Ramadan Feast. After they broke their fast at sunset, the deputy director of intelligence asked the Muslim elders, "Why are you fearful of Christians?" The deputy said, "I have sent one person to kill eleven Christians, he was only in prison one hour. What is stopping you from taking action against Christians in Qus?"

Eighteen Muslims stood up in opposition. They argued, "The end is not pleasant. We want to be excluded." They were called "hypocrites of Islam." The result was the assault. The bishop said, "I had access to this information for some time, but did not release it for the sake of those who withdrew. But now an independent magazine has documented all of the details."[15]

The director of intelligence was ready to indict Father Gabriel for the massacres and interrogated him for ten hours, 9:00 P.M. until the next day. Thirteen charges were filed against him. Six Muslims charged that Father Gabriel shot at them when they were crossing a bridge to the Islamic Institute in Qus. When they were asked to explain why they were all crossing the bridge at that time that day, each one said that he had come to pick up family members from the institute. However, they lied. They forgot that the day they claimed Father Gabriel shot at them was a holiday weekend, Sela, and there was no school that day. Father Gabriel made the point. "There is a old Arabic saying, 'Lying has legs.'"[16] We laughed together.

Finally, after all the false charges, with increasing international disgrace, with growing interest by human rights organizations, the intelligence department issued a decree charging ninety-six persons, out of which thirty-eight were Christians and fifty-eight were Muslims.

Taken by the absurdity of the charges, I asked, "How many Muslim properties were destroyed.?"

Father Gabriel and Bishop Wissa answered emphatically, "None, not one."

And I asked again, "How many Muslims were killed?"

Again they responded, "None, not one,"[17] So Christians were charged for burning and looting their own properties and killing their own people.

The prosecution continued into December 2000.

Then the judge ordered all the defendants into the court and addressed them: "We are close to the Christmas and Ramadan feast.[19] I propose a peace agreement." He picked out a Christian and a Muslim in court and had them shake hands, and all ninety-six defendants were released. The only person held and charged was the Muslim who had accidentally shot and killed another Muslim twelve kilometers outside of Qus. All the others were let go. Even the criminals who had burned, assaulted, and murdered were set free. No convictions! No imprisonments! No sentences were ever issued. Just like the director of intelligence had predicted.

The testimonies of the witnesses who had seen the actual murders and the actual shootings were denied. The forensic evidence was altered to state that all of the killings were committed with sharp weapons, knives, machetes, and swords. No guns were used in the killings.

Two Christians testified in court against the person they saw commit the killings. "They said the name exactly," according to Bishop Wissa. "They knew. The name is in the file."[20] But the intelligence officers placed information in the file that the accused person was a patient in the hospital at that time and therefore could not have been responsible for the killings.

Twenty-one Christians were killed and no one was held accountable. The Egyptian government and the Egyptian President had detailed knowledge of the crimes of murder, pillage, torture, and false indictments against the Christians of Qus. From the record, it is clear that Christians of Egypt are as oppressed by Islam as they are in northern Nigeria, and Sudan.

Why the public humiliations, the fraudulent indictments, the extreme tortures? They were all used to protect what? The answer can be nothing other than Islam. The Center for Religious Freedom performed numerous interviews among residents of Qus. Both Muslims and Christians testified that the call to terror *jihad* came from the minaret of the mosque next door to the church. Over the loud speakers Muslims were instructed to take up their weapons and "kill the Christians." The Muslims soon responded shouting, *"Allahu-Akbar."* They entered the church with violence, destroying the floor coverings, breaking windows, shooting and destroying the sacred images and paintings, and stealing the donations.[21]

Those of us from the West are encouraged to believe that this is simply sporadic, impulsive behavior—that it has no religious source, and no culture modeled by the ancient authorities. Of course this behavior is not the nature and inclination of every Muslim believer. But where was the opposition, even by the police? Why was the church prohibited from repairing the damages? The state and living conditions for Christians under Islam are so unbelievable, it is difficult for an American to even image.

But Qus is a window for the Western world to see true Islam at work. There was no justice for the Copts of Qus. No justice from the Qus officials! No justice from the Cairo officials. No Egyptian authority was courageous enough to offer justice to the Copts of Qus! Egyptian officials sanctioned, by silence, by inaction, by the nodding of the head, a culture of discrimination, persecution, and execution of Christians. The failure of justice in Qus is not about fundamentalists. The failure of justice in Qus is not about radicals. The failure of justice in Qus is not about fanatics. The failure of justice in Qus is the failure of Egypt. It is the failure of the Egyptian government. It is the product of the Egyptian religion. It signifies the impotency of an Islamic nation to rise up for real righteousness. It is a window for Americans to see the influence of the Koran and the models of Muhammad and an opportunity to take their hands from their eyes.

We need to ask ourselves: What are the sources that feed this culture of discrimination and persecution?

Let me make several suggestions for consideration. *First*, we must acknowledge that this oppressive culture has for centuries suckled from both breasts of Islam, the models of Muhammad and the teachings of the Koran. We need to remind ourselves of Muhammad's deportations, beheadings, and terror attacks against animals, Jews, and Christians. We need to look again at the teaching of terror behavior in the Koran. "Fight against them who believe not in God, nor the last day, and forbid not that which God and his Apostle have forbidden, and profess not the true religion (including) those unto whom the Scriptures have been delivered (Jews and Christians), until they pay tribute (*jizya*) by the right of subjection (willing submission) and they be reduced low (feeling subdued)" (Koran IX (29)).

Second, we must acknowledge that the oppressive culture feeds at the trough of a "supremacist religion." Egypt adopted Islam as its state religion in 1984. Consequently the teachings of Islam, that all non-Muslim peoples are inferior and must be treated as such, are now supported and practiced by the state. *Third*, we must acknowledge that the sociopath culture of Islam is able to feed on Christians by the use of the Egyptian identification card. The card identifies each Christian and thereby facilitates the isolation and marginalization of Christians by Muslim officials of the Egyptian state and Egyptian religion. *Fourth*, we must acknowledge that this oppressive culture is enabled by support from the local police and government intelligence agencies. Only followers of Islam are appointed to positions within the intelligence agencies. That type of employment discrimination solidifies the faith and behavior of the oppressors against the oppressed.

A *fifth* contributing factor—although it may not be considered a cause for the failure of justice for Christians in Qus—is that the Copts history tells us they have been oppressed and persecuted since the Islamic invasion of 641.[22] Roman Catholics are oppressed, but they have the Vatican. Anglicans are oppressed, but they have the Queen of England. Presbyterians are oppressed, but they have Westminster. The Egyptian Copts have no foreign recourse. They are truly the indigenous Egyptians. As Father Gabriel said, "There is no way to fight back. There is no way to justice." Here we have fifteen million Christians trapped in the Guantanamo Bay of Egypt without a whimper from the world.

What can we do about this state-endorsed culture of religious oppression?

First, let Egypt excise from its state religion the teachings to fight Christians and Jews (non-Muslim peoples) into submission and humiliation, Koran IX (29), as well as all the other messages of the Koran that feed a culture of dehumanization and bigoted violence. *Second*, let Egypt desist from printing people's religion on their identification card. Let them begin to honor human equality and the freedom of religion. *Third*, let

Egypt desist from forcing its state religion on non-Muslim students in its educational system. *Fourth*, let Egypt impose and enforce a quota that requires the 20 percent of the Egyptian population that is Christian to also hold 20 percent of all government employment nationwide. Strangely enough, these are items one might think belong on the agenda of the United Nations.

The Return Home

The testimonies were lengthy and detailed and of course everything doubled in time because of translation. Nonetheless, at the close of the interview, Father Gabriel and Bishop Wissa seemed enthusiastic for their people and their faith. We said our good-byes and retired for the night. At 2 A.M. Father Paul drove Bishop Wissa from the monastery to a new location. That night our guide asked our prayers for his safety and that of his family.

The next morning, the local police taxied us to the train depot, an arrangement made between them and the monastery. We saw no intelligence agents. The police even offered to shake hands, and it made me wonder if several of the police were possibly Christian, a rare exception, but possible according to several sources.

We were still suspicious of the intelligence agency and decided to step off the train early at a depot several stops before the one designated by our tickets. Who would be waiting for us? Who was following us now? When the train stopped, we hurried to the ticket counter to purchase new tickets. Sure enough, we no more than had the tickets in hand and two intelligence agents were demanding tickets for the same destination. Then they followed us aboard the next train. We tried the same routine again with the same response. On our third effort, we hurried from the train depot to catch a taxi. So did they.

We stopped shortly down the road, and they shot by us. We lost them temporarily. As we returned to our hotel, we figured our real problem was to preserve our records. We were warned that the Egyptian government had legal authority to confiscate all cameras, pictures, recordings, and any other personal items. The next day we gave our cameras, video recorder, videotapes, tape recorder, cassette tapes, and handwritten notes to a reliable contact who will forever remain anonymous. When she returned to her country, she was to mail them to a North American address, which would, in turn, mail them to my address. Six weeks later, I received all of my materials and information.

The next evening, in order to identify exactly who were the newly assigned intelligence agents, we decided to risk crossing six lanes of freeway traffic. Sure enough, two men and one woman followed us. Once we crossed the freeway, we entered a pizza restaurant and sat on the second level near the window so we could watch the Egyptian agents. One of the agents, looking up at the window, slipped and fell off the curb. Later, when we returned to the hotel, we thought to trick our new agents into thinking we were staying several days longer. We extended our reservations and went to our room. However, at 12:30 A.M., we appeared in the lobby for a quick ride to the airport. We completely surprised them. By the time they arrived, we had cleared security and customs and were sitting in the safety of the international transit section of the airport, waiting to board our flight to Amsterdam.

Visiting Qus Again

In March 2006 I accepted an invitation to present my interviews with Bishop Wissa to a joint conference of the United Copts and the International Christian Union at the Dag Hammarskjöld Conference Room at the United Nations (Appendix F). In the days that followed, Islamic nations were able to force the conference off-site to Newark. With an apology from our United Nations Ambassador, John Bolton, the conference nonetheless met on the scheduled days. During my speech, Egyptian President Mubarak's representative walked out. When an intermission was called, I had opportunity to meet and interact with other speakers and guests. The Christian Copts present were grateful to tears and insisted on kissing my ring. Professor Saad Eddin Ibrahim from the Ibn Khaldun Center in Cairo was not so gracious. In our brief encounter, he poked his finger into my ribs and called me a "dangerous man." He vehemently objected to my accusations against Islam. He assured me that he could find identical teachings in the Bible to the one I identified in the Koran. He viewed the criticism of Islam as highly improper.

Since that time, I have occasionally reflected on the professor's remarks. I had never before been called a dangerous man. I will not be silent when I see that the teachings of the Koran and the models of Muhammad enjoin terror behaviors against the innocents of Nigeria, Sudan, and Egypt. In my opinion, any non-Muslim person in the West who fails to make the obvious connection, cause and effect—that is, the teachings of Islam to execute terror behavior against non-Muslim peoples and then its practice—is shamefully unschooled in Islam or is possibly an adherent of intolerance toward Jews and Christians.

I found the professor's attack on the Bible interesting. He did not attack the truth of what I said about the Koran and Muhammad. Instead he shifted the attention to the Bible and Christianity. I noticed that technique in other discussions with Muslim leaders. For the most part, I think that is rhetorical small talk. I have yet to visit a Muslim who admits that he reads the Bible. They believe they have the superior revelation. In effect, they say, "Why should we waste time reading the Bible when it is a corrupted revelation. We have the real thing." Islam forbids the reading of the Bible. Bibles are trashed and burned in Saudi Arabia and Iran. Regarding Saad Ibrahim's point, the Old Testament certainly has instructions of violence, but the

New Testament abrogates, fulfills, and transforms those teachings through the person of Jesus of Nazareth, the Christ, as shown in this verse: "You have heard that it was said...but I tell you..."(Luke 5). The Bible does not instruct discrimination and persecution. In fact the parable of the Good Samaritan (Luke 10:25–37) teaches the exact opposite. When individuals try to use the Bible for such perverse behavior, churches of all stripes immediately condemn them. When does Islam apologize, reject, condemn, and make restitution for terror violence by Muslims against non-Muslim peoples? The Bible and the Koran are two different books. I think journalists and politicians who report on the clash between the civilizations of Islam and the post-Christian West are miserably ill equipped when they have failed to read these two books.

The professor blames the politicians for the discrimination and persecution of Egyptian Christians. Americans seem vulnerable to owning that error for we see politicians as the framers and enforcers of legislation and laws to protect individual freedoms. We are also inclined to view the eradication of individual freedoms in other nations as political. However, in nations heavily populated by Muslims, the religion of Islam establishes Islamic law to rule and restrict the freedoms of people. In Saudi Arabia, Iran, Egypt, Sudan, Syria, Pakistan, Iraq, and Afghanistan that is done by official state policy, whereas in other nations, Turkey and Indonesia, it is done culturally.

Even in Iraq, where thousands of Americans have been killed and wounded to establish a democracy, the new government approved Islamic *sharia* law as the basis of its legislation. The approval guarantees the continuation of terror behavior against the indigenous Chaldean, Assyrian Christians. As can be seen from Nigeria, Sudan, and Egypt, Islamic *sharia* law codifies and enforces attitudes and behaviors against Jews and Christians as inferior creatures: no new churches, no repair of churches, no new cemeteries, no promotions, no jobs, no education, no authority, no assistance, children forced into Islamic curriculums in public schools, special taxes, no inheritance, torture, murder, rape, and intimidations, to name some.

The professor dismisses the prejudice and terror behavior against Christians as the fault of political leaders. That flies in the face of the facts. Such acts of legal intolerance and legal terror violence have occurred in Egypt for fourteen hundred years under a variety of political leaderships: the Caliphs, the Mamluks, and the Sultans are some. The source of terror behavior is clearly not political, but religious. Politicians may at times have the power to limit and control these laws of prejudice, as was true under the Abbasid Caliphate. Eventually, however, such political systems collapse under the cultural and spiritual pressure of Islam when it wishes to enforce the inferior status of Jews and Christians.

Currently—in the case of terror behavior in the states of Nigeria, Sudan, and Egypt—all three of these nations have different political leaders and different political systems. So the political system is not the primary cause of persecution and oppression. What these three nations have in common is the religion of Islam and Islamic *sharia* law. The religion of Islam is the common source of bigoted oppression.

CHAPTER TEN

*Journeys into the Heart of Islam
Journeys End*

I began my journeys dedicated to explore whether two specific forms of terror behavior are, in fact, legitimate practices within the religion of Islam: terror war (*jihad*) and terror subjugation (*dhimmitude*). For that purpose, I chose a search method by which I could independently investigate, as much as possible, from outside the bias circulated by Western advocates and Western sympathizers for Islam. Initially I reviewed the two great ancient authorities that stand at the heart of Islam to search for models of terror behavior in the life of Muhammad and for teachings of terror behavior in the text of the Koran. Then I began personal journeys into the heartland of Islam to explore the current attitudes and behaviors of Islam toward non-Muslim peoples to determine whether they are consistent with the instructions of the ancient authorities.

On my first journey to review the life of Muhammad, I was shocked to observe specific models of terror behavior. That is not to say that this violent behavior toward the unbelievers (*kafirun*), especially the Jews, is a novel subject to the faithful followers of

Islam. Terror behavior and miraculous performances by Muhammad are general knowledge within the Muslim world. My focus, of course, is singular in nature. I am interested in the subject of terror behavior, not the miracles and miraculous journeys ascribed to Muhammad by the traditions and the Koran.

As a non-Muslim, I am deeply troubled by my findings. Muhammad's terror executions and deliberate *jihads* against Jewish and Christian villages were not simple violent acts of personal rage, but pious acts of profound devotion to his God. *Allah* consistently challenged Muhammad to commit extreme acts of terrorism against the enemy. For example. By way of angel Gabriel, *Allah* ordered Muhammad and his followers to behead six to nine hundred adult male prisoners of the Jewish tribe of Qurayza. He said that he would make them tremble.[1]

I understand Muhammad's hatred for the polytheists of Mecca, since they were the great oppressors and persecutors of Islam. But how did Jews and Christians make the prophet's hate list? *Clearly the answer is the Jewish and Christian rejection of Muhammad's claim that he was the fulfillment of prophecies from the Torah and the Gospels.* He preached to the Jews that he was the long sought-after prophet proclaimed by Moses, "The Lord your God will raise up for you a prophet like me from among your own brothers. You must listen to him" (Deuteronomy 18:15).

Muhammad stated that he was from the lineage of Abraham and therefore a brother to the Jews. But the Jews made it very clear to Muhammad that the fulfillment of the prophecy was to come from the line of Isaac, the true line of brotherhood in Judaism, not from Ishmael, the son of Abraham's slave woman, Hagar. When the Jews rejected Muhammad as a genuine prophet within the religion of Judaism, it was perceived as an intolerable offense to the honor of the prophet, *Allah*, and Islam. As the Jews proved themselves intractable in the rejection of Muhammad as their prophet, acts of terror behavior against the Jews began, first against the tribe of Nadir in 625, next against the tribe of Qurayza in 627, and then against the tribe of Khaybar in 628, and so forth.

In the case of the Jewish tribe of Khaybar, Muhammad, not long after his flight to Medina, had challenged them by letter to receive him as the fulfillment of the divine prophecy (Deuteronomy 18:15) and to convert to Islam. Eventually, in the year 628, Muhammad led his military to surround Khaybar. In the early morning hours, when he heard no evidence of conversion to Islam, no Muslim call to prayer, he offered his prayer of *jihad* and attacked Khaybar, crying, "Allahu Akbar." Islam decisively conquered and then subjugated Khaybar, as well as the neighboring Jewish tribe of Fadak. In his military (militia) exploits, Muhammad attacked many independent Jewish villages scattered throughout the fertile regions of the Hejaz in western Arabia. In his conquests, he gathered great amounts of booty from the Jewish tribes, which enabled Islam to finance a mighty cavalry of warriors.

Similar to his behavior with the Jews, Muhammad also claimed himself as the prophetic fulfillment of Jesus' prophecy, "When the Counselor comes, whom I well send to you from the Father, the Spirit of truth, who goes out from the Father, he will testify about me" (John 15:26). Muhammad viewed himself as the Counselor. He did not understand that in the Christian creeds, "the Counselor" was the Holy Spirit. Muhammad actually thought that the Trinity consisted of God the Father, God the Son, and God the Mother (Mary). Christians, along with the Jews, were targeted with violent reprisals for their rejection of Muhammad as their prophet and Islam as the religion of truth.

Muhammad finally conquered Mecca in January of 630. He then bribed his former enemies (Sufyan, Khalid, and others) to convert to Islam and join him in his military conquest of the world. With his new allies, he began his broadest efforts yet to expand Islam. Christian communities mostly stood defenseless before Muhammad, with the gradual, but constant, erosion of Byzantine (Eastern Roman Empire) power. When he and his warriors arrived at the city gates of Christian Tabuk with the threat of *jihad* (October 630), the only realistic alternative for the leaders of Tabuk was to surrender and to subjugate themselves to the supremacy of Islam and pay the subjugation tax, the *jizya*. That march against Christianity (Christendom) took no serious interlude until the defeat of Islam by the Austrians (Hapsburgs) in Vienna in 1683. Today, of course, we are witnessing its revival.

Many people of America ask, "Why do they, Islam, hate us so much?" The answer is very simple. The Judeo-Christian civilization refused to believe that Muhammad was the fulfillment of prophecies by Moses and Jesus. That is the meaning of unbelievers, the *kafirun*, in Islam. The culture of Islam has fed it hatred on that rejection for fourteen hundred years. This my not be simple to understand, but one must remember that the rejection of Muhammad as the prophet of *Allah* by Jews and Christians was viewed as one of the most, if not the most, heinous crime ever perpetrated by humanity and was thereafter trumped within Islamic culture against the unbelievers. In a way, it has similarities to the repetition of the Pharisees' (Jews') call to crucify Jesus of Nazareth, the Christ, within the culture of Christianity. Sadly that repetition of Jewish rejection has also been used throughout history to motivate acts of bigotry and violence by Christians against Jews.

My second journey was to review the ultimate authority of Islam, the Koran, as to its teachings of terror behavior and terror subjugation. The Koran teaches violence against the unbelievers (*kafirun*), especially forms of coercive violence to frighten and to intimidate Jews and Christians (terrorism) so that they will convert or submit to Islam. For example, observe several texts that were initially injunctions of *Allah* to terror *jihad* against the oppressors of Islam, the polytheists of Mecca.

"Fight in the religion of God against those who fight you…kill them…this is the reward of infidels (who suppress faith)" Koran II (191, 192).

"Prepare against them what force you are able…strike a terror into a enemy of God…" Koran VIII (60).

"Say to the unbelievers…that if they persist, the exemplary punishment of former opposers of the prophets is already past, and the like shall be inflicted on them." Koran (VIII (38).

"I (*Allah*) will cast dread (terror) into the hearts of the unbelievers: Therefore strike off their heads. And strike off all the ends of their fingers" Koran (VIII (12).

In these texts of the Koran, one can read divine instructions to Muslims to terror war (*jihad*) against the polytheists. In fact within the context translators effectively use the English word "terror" to define the meaning of *jihad*. When the Jews rejected Muhammad as an authentic prophet in the line of Judaism, *Allah* declared that the Jews and polytheists were evil equals: "Thou shalt surely find the most violent of all men in enmity against the true believes (Muslims), to be the Jews and the idolaters…" (Koran V (82)), and, "When that came to them which they knew to be from God, they would not believe therein: Therefore the curse of God shall be on the infidels" (Koran V (89)). Once the Jews and polytheists were joined together as equal evils, *Allah's* instructions of terror war (*jihad*) against the unbelieving polytheists could reasonably be applied to the unbelieving Jews.

Soon Christians were charged for the crime of hiding the revelations of the Gospel about the coming of Muhammad

(John 15:26): "O ye who receive the scriptures, why do ye clothes truth with vanity, and knowingly hide the truth?" (Koran III (71)). Eventually, when Islam had accumulated sufficient wealth and arms, a plan was set in place and then executed to terror *jihad* against the Christians of Tabuk and Duma, three hundred miles from Medina.

Several moths after the *jihad* (631), *Allah* stated his support of Muhammad's subjugation of Tabuk and Duma. In the Koran, he sets forth a very clear policy of terror war (*jihad*) and terror subjugation (*dhimmitude*) against all peoples who reject Muhammad as the prophet of God and Islam as the religion of the truth. This text of the Koran comes near the end of Muhammad's life (June 632). Here *Allah* abrogates the few early words of the Koran that had offered friendship toward the people of the book. In order to understand the current injunctions of terror behavior against Jews and Christians (non-Muslim peoples), which were never abrogated, every non-Muslim needs to remember and evaluate the following text: "Fight against them who believe not in God nor the last day, and forbid not that which God and his Apostle have forbidden, and profess not the true religion, (including) those unto whom the Scriptures have been delivered [Jews and Christians], until they pay tribute (*jizya)* by the right of subjugation (willing submission) and they be reduced low (feeling subdued)" (Koran IX (29)).

In this text, the injunction to "fight" is the primary command of *Allah*. It is a ceaseless fight. It says, "until" non-Muslim peoples are subjugated, i.e., "pay the *jizya*." Terror war (*jihad*) then is viewed by Islam as a perpetual declaration of war led by *Allah* and his prophet. When non-Muslim peoples live as neighbors to the faithful of Islam, they eventually face coercive violence and/or threats of violence. Currently that is the experience of many neighbors in the vicinities of Chechnya, Sudan, Ethiopia, Kashmir, Bosnia, Zamboanga, Thailand, northern

Nigeria, and Israel, to name some. It seems reasonable that the world will eventually view terror behavior advances from within other heavily populated citadels of Islam presently located in Belgium, Denmark, England, France, Germany, the Netherlands, and Sweden.

In text IX (29), the text of the sword, there is more than an injunction to prosecute terror *jihad*, (terrorism). It is also an injunction to practice terror *dhimmitude* (terrorism). It says "until" they pay the tribute (*jizya*) and rightly subjugate themselves as inferior and show that they are low of spirit, totally defeated. Muhammad had initially implemented a form of terror subjugation in response to the terror stricken requests of the defeated Jews from Khaybar and Fadak (628). Two year later, the prophet adopted and modeled terror subjugation as an alternative for enemies of Islam who were facing the threat to terror *jihad*. In the case of Tabuk and Duma, the defenseless Christian leadership, "feeling themselves subdued" elected to "willingly submit" to the covenant (*dhimma*) of subjugation ("pay the *jizya*"). As the year passed, specifics of subjugation for Jews and Christians were further defined into a codified legal system (*sharia*). Muslim scholars constructed detailed legal applications from the words of *Allah* in order to maintain and enforce the inferior status of unbelievers (*kafirun*).

When Jews and Christians rejected Muhammad as a legitimate prophet within their respective religions, *Allah* declared terror war (*jihad*) against them as enemies of Islam, i.e., until they willingly subjugated themselves to his supremacy (*in lives of dhimmitude*). The subjugation affirmed in the eyes of Islam that *Allah* punished the people of the book to demonstrate to the world that Muhammad was the legitimate fulfillment of the Jewish and Christian prophecies.

Allah and his prophet condemned the basic principles of the Christian Creed (Apostles' Creed). They rejected Jesus as the Christ: "God hath not begotten issue; neither is there any other god with him" (Koran XXIII (91)). They rejected the heart of the Gospel, i.e., atonement through the cross and the resurrection: "Yet they slew him not neither crucified him..." (Koran IV (157)). They rejected the Trinity: "They are certainly infidels, who say, God is the third of three. For there is no God, besides one God" (Koran V (76)).

Allah also attacked the character of the unbelievers. He condemned to hell the Jews and Christians as liars who had refused to acknowledge Muhammad as the prophet of God. He commenced to dehumanize them so as to make them more vulnerable subjects to the hate and violence of his devout followers: "Verily, those who believe not, among those who have received Scriptures [Jews and Christians], and among the idolaters, shall be cast into the fire of hell, to remain therein forever. These are the worst of creatures" (Koran XCVIII (6)). In that same method of dehumanization, *Allah* is said to have transformed some of the cursed unbelievers into "apes and swine" (Koran V (60)).

In establishing the Islamic battle lines against the unbelievers, *Allah* proscribed any relationship with Jews and/or Christians. They remain frozen within the original perception of *Allah*, isolated as non-humans, non-believers, and non-Muslims. Many within the Muslim world today continue to view Jews and Christians through the eyes of *Allah*, through the ancient spectacles of the Koran. Current events are still viewed by many Muslims through this fourteen-hundred-year-old prism. "Muslims are not to take Jews and the Christians as their friends and protectors. If they join them, they become one with them" (Koran V (53)).

From my first and second journeys into the heart of Islam, I have no doubt that Muhammad, modeled and the Koran instructed terror war (*jihad*) and terror subjugation (*dhimmitude*). From the ancient authorities, it is clear that Islam views Jews and Christians as the enemy, the *kafirun*. So why do many of our American pastors, politicians, and educators teach us that Islam is a religion of peace and tolerance? From where did they access their information? Furthermore, why do they, through the past six years, fail to substantiate those claims of peace and tolerance with real evidence from the life of Muhammad and the Koran? An obvious answer is that they have listened to the Western advocates of Islam and failed to review the ancient authorities.

As I journeyed along the way, I was at times fascinated by propaganda from the Western advocates of Islam. Numerous essays have been published to persuade the American people that Islam is not a religion of terror behavior, but one of peace and tolerance. Many books and articles by Muslim scholars distort the past by use of half-truths, clearly efforts to deny, recast, and rewrite the early years of terror *jihad*, in order to halt inquiry and make *jihad* more suitable to the Western culture. In some cases, materials of the biographical traditions of Islam were manufactured so as to take the sting out of terror behavior. For example one Muslim scholar wrote that Muslims and Jews, and Muslims and Christians, united together in terror *jihad* and fought side by side against common enemies. That may have been some Muslim dream, but that is not a reality of history. Many of these publications by Western advocates of Islam imply that the relationship between Islam and the people of the book was cordial and had a common purpose.

Did Jewish and Muslim armies really fight side by side against a common enemy? There is no such evidence in the Ishaq account, even though the Muslim scholar identifies Ishaq as his primary source. The fact is Ishaq did record the drafting of an agreement by Muhammad, which he in turn offered to the Jews of Medina, that they fight jointly against the warriors of Mecca. But did that ever happen? There is no such evidence. Did the Jews accept the agreement? There is no such evidence. According to Ishaq, any relationship with the Jews was already in jeopardy within the first twelve months of Muhammad's arrival in Medina. In the seventeenth month, Muhammad suspended Jerusalem as the *qibla* of Muslim prayers and substituted in its place Mecca. He also changed the day of worship from the Jewish Sabbath to Muslim Friday Prayers. Within three years of his arrival, Muhammad laid siege against the Jewish tribe of Nadir and then had them exiled from the region. At that point, terror *jihad* against the Jews was well underway. Why do Western advocates of Islam labor so diligently at propagating such an inaccurate view that blurs the actual models of terror behavior in the biographical traditions of Islam?

Did Christian and Muslim armies fight side by side in *jihad* against a common enemy? To make the case, one Muslim scholar offers as evidence a note from the historical writings of al-Tabari in which a commander of the Muslim forces offered to temporarily release subjugated Armenia from its payment of *jizya* if they would provide Armenian mercenaries to join with Muslim solders in the prosecution of terror *jihad*. He makes no mention as to whether such an agreement was ever consolidated, and it appears unlikely. In the essay, he intentionally omits that ten years after the death of Muhammad (632), the Islamic military had marched eleven hundred miles north of Medina to *jihad* and subjugate Christian Armenia on the Caspian Sea (642).In light of Islam's military aggression against Armenia, how does any scholar reasonably argue that its relationship with Armenia demonstrates the peace and tolerance of Islam? His material is so absolutely bogus. Some data is factual, but is then used to distort reality. Why do Muslim scholars wish to mislead the West? Why do they seem so fearful to expose the real Islam?

To further confuse the historical accuracy or terror behavior, the same author fails to mention that sixty-two years after the initial terror subjugation of Armenia, a caliph's son gathered the Armenian leaders into the Saint Gregory church in Naxcawan and the Church of Xran on the Arexes. His soldiers locked the church doors, set the churches on fire, and burned them to death. How can anyone in the name of scholarship promote the prosecutors of such behavior as the leaders of a world religion that espouses peace and tolerance? In my opinion, such essays are not a cute and humorous tweaking of realities for subtle implications: They are deliberate deception. Why are Americans and other Westerners so vulnerable to such misinformation by Western proponents of Islam? I believe there is at least a partial explanation for such vulnerability, and I call it "the missing link."

The Missing Link

As I complete my journeys into the heartland of Islam, I am more than ever aware of our great need in America (the West) to understand the religion of Islam. For more than five decades, Islam was a non-subject in the Western world and simply off the screen at our colleges and universities. In my college and post-graduate experience, studies of Islam were superficial to non-existent, even though my major interest was ancient-medieval history. At that time, the sixties and seventies, Islam was for America the other world, the third world, and an irrelevant world. Our major interests were the World Wars, the Bolshevik Revolution, the growing power of the Soviet Union, and the powerful struggle between Marxism and Capitalism.

I believe my formal educational experience duplicates that of many other Americans. Since I began my journeys, I have encountered numerous, in my opinion, well-rounded, well-read, well-educated people, very often elderly people, who are asking, "What is Islam? Who are these Muslim peoples?" or, "Where did they come from all of a sudden"? Those are fair questions for Americans to ask these days.

The fact is that Islam was a non-subject for many decades because Islam was for decades a minor actor in world affairs. After the Ottoman Muslims' effort to exterminate the Armenian

Christians (1885–1915), the military power of Islam totally disintegrated. In fact militant Islam began its steep decline centuries earlier when the Austrians defeated the Ottomans' siege of Vienna (September 12, 1683). For centuries soldiers of Islam had battled for control over Hungary and Central Europe. Finally "Christian Europe" halted the onslaught. The signing of the peace treaty of Carlowitz (January 26, 1699) brought a "profound" change between Christianity and Islam.[2]

For hundreds of years, the Ottomans had been victorious in their military aggression against Eastern and Central Europe. With the Austrian victory at Vienna, the tables were turned. It was the beginning of a long stretch of retreat by Islam and military advances by Christian Europe.[3]

Without an understanding of radical imperialism by Islam for more than a millennium (628–1683), how can we as Americans gather an accurate understanding of military violence within the religion of Islam? When knowledge of Islamic history is limited to little more than momentary flashes, then we become extremely vulnerable to distortions and falsehoods by Western advocates of Islam. *From the subjugation of Khaybar to the defeat at Vienna, followers of Islam fought victoriously to rule the whole world as the dar al-Islam. Those one thousand years of war against the world by Islam seem to always be the missing link in American textbooks.* The careless omission of one thousand years of Islamic imperialism not only enables Muslim scholars to distort Islamic history to the West, but is also enables them to distort the realities of Western imperialism.

The missing link permits Western proponents of Islam to manipulate history by denying a thousand years of imperialism, and then on the contrary, to complain of the Crusades as the efforts of Western imperialism. Likewise they protest the Europeans' military occupation of subjected regions of the collapsed Ottoman (Islamic) Empire as Western imperialism.

Those of us from the West need *first of all* to understand that the Crusades were no more than a limited retaliation against Islam after four-hundred-sixty-six years of its military aggression into North Africa and Europe. Is there any reasonable person who wishes to explain why the retaliation of the European military (the Crusades) was such a terribly offensive act when they had suffered under Islamic *jihad* and *dhimmitude* for four-hundred-sixty-six years (630–1096)? *Secondly*, we need to better understand the European's colonization of Islamic regions hundreds of years later, but let me first ask, what is an Islamic region? When does a region become Islamic? How many years previous did Islam need to conquer the territory? Twenty years? One hundred years? Five hundred years? One thousand years?

So what about European colonization? When the Hapsburgs (Austria) crushed the Islamic armies, at Vienna, what was the expectation of the next scene? Does anyone really anticipate that the Hapsburgs would then lay down their weapons and say, "Islam can keep the rest of the territory that they conquered the last several hundred years?" What kind of fairytale do the Western Muslim scholars want to write here? After Carlowitz the two great "Christian" powers, Austria and Russia, began campaigns to regain territories previously lost to the imperialistic stretch of the Islamic military. Between the nineteenth century and World War II, many other regions of Islam fell to the Western European military. That colonization, whether one likes it or not, was something of a normal military process. As Islam lost its power to control certain subjugated segments of its Empire, the Dutch, English, French, and Spanish filled the power vacuum.

Many years later, following World War II, these Islamic regions occupied by the Europeans were slowly but surely granted independence (1946–1970). A generation or two later, Islam slowly began to reassert its imperialist policy, probably from the established models of Muhammad and teachings of the Koran. The divine duty to rule the world seems to have re-ignited first among Muslim scholars. Then it spread to small terrorist militias, which began to take up the cause. By the year 1979, the spirit of war (*jihad*) spilled over into the realm of government. An Islamic revolution, led by the cleric Ayatollah Khomeini, took down the Shah of Iran, and now, after twenty-five years, Islam is developing nuclear weapons. Currently Iran is committed to rule the world (not a new idea) and threatens to annihilate the "Jews" (Israel) and the "Christians" (American) (not a new idea). We can expect more governments to fall. It appears that military force alone is presently main-taining the status quo of the governments of Egypt, Saudi Arabia, Kuwait, and Pakistan—politicians quasi-friendly to America. Meanwhile the Muslim nations with so-called secular governments, such as Turkey, Iraq, and Indonesia, are increas-ingly committed to Islamic domination of the non-Muslim world by *sharia* law through the ballot box, which of course means no Bill of Rights.

So in answer to the questions so many Americans are ask-ing, "What is Islam?" "Who are these Muslims?" and "Where did they come from all of a sudden?" Many of these Muslims are serious adherents to the teachings of the Koran and are emulators of the models of Muhammad. We must remember that Islam has been knocking militarily at the door of the "Christian" West, now America, for nearly fourteen-hundred years. Many of us missed the terror *jihads* in the textbooks of our classrooms, and we missed them again in the early years of our lives because militant Islam, thanks to the European colo-nization, was still out on a very long hiatus, the length of sev-eral generations. For many of us, it was only 9/11 that served as a warning that they are back.

In response to 9/11, American attention had focused on terror groups and terror cells. Americans soon learned to call them "radicals" and "fundamentalists." America declared war against terrorism. Our politicians, pastors, and journalists made certain to include among the terrorists those who were non-Muslim people so as to not offend Isalm. In my daily newspaper, *The Desert Sun,* the bold headline of one Sunday edition was "Christian Terrorist Captured." I am still waiting for the *Sun* to mention a "Muslim Terrorist." Why is America responding this way in spite of the instructions of the ancient authorities to terror *jihad* against Jews and Christians, which were then followed by a millennium of imperialistic *jihad* against Western and Eastern Europe?

Is the American leaderships' failure to address terror behavior in the religion of Islam simply a good military tactic? After all, who wants to fight 20–25 percent of the world's population? So did Western leaders possibly manufacture divisions among the enemy, the radical ones and the moderate ones? It seems no one really knows whether there are one billion radicals and two-hundred million moderates or one billion moderates and two-hundred million radicals. But in the mind of America, they are at least divided between the true and the untrue. So America can be friends with the true and enemies with the untrue, i.e., if they can determine who is who.

Militarily and politically, the manufactured division may be a working strategy in a very difficult situation, but disastrously, somewhere along the way, the facts and the flaws of the position will need to be exposed. Then what? Again why do our politicians focus attention almost solely on terror groups and political groups within Islam? Is it fear? Why not search for the reality of terror behavior within the religion of Islam by studying the ancient authorities of Islam? Why not do so in a public forum? Let the people of the West learn together. Let Americans discuss, debate, and argue with each other. We have done that before, free speech is a part of American democracy! How does our nation go wrong by publicly struggling to determine among each other what are the realities with regard to an alleged enemy? Or are Americans simply too inept to process such issues these days? We admit that our educational system has failed us, but to that degree? Is Islam a subject solely and wisely submitted to political elitists? I think not!

Furthermore, in our interest to uncover the realities of terror behavior in Islam, it does make sense to journey into the heartland of Islam to view the actual attitudes and behaviors of Muslims toward non-Muslim peoples. Clearly such journeys can assist Americans in their understanding of Islam and can also clarify whether the models of terror war (*jihad*) and terror subjugation (*dhimmitude*) in the ancient authorities are being replicated within the neighborhoods of the Islamic heartland today.

Journeys into the Heartland

In my search method, I visited three specific locations in Nigeria: Kaduna State, Kano State, and Plateau State. In all three regions, I collected evidence, heard testimonies, and witnessed devastation of terror behavior perpetrated by followers of Islam. In Kano, Islam holds a Muslim majority of 95 percent, so I found it no surprise that the small Christian minority, 3 percent, suffered from an open practice of Islamic supremacy that marginalized them and forced them into an inferior status socially, educationally, economically, and politically. Even though Nigeria is a democracy, Christians testify that the culture of Islam supports the implementation of an "unwritten code" of terror subjugation (*dhimmitude*).

As an example, Christian children are not admitted into the public schools unless they change their names from Christian to Muslim. According to several professional educators, " That is true throughout the whole educational system, primary to university." In the public school curriculum, Christian children are bullied to memorize the Koran, perform Islamic cleansings, and repeat Muslim prayers. Young female students must wear the Islamic headscarf. In the words of a local resident named Simon, "Children are forced into Islam."

Other, more obvious, examples of a public policy established to rank Christians as creatures of inferior status, a policy easily confirmed, is the official practice of denying requests and appropriate honors for Christians and the Christian community. Permits to construct churches are repeatedly denied, permits to repair churches are denied. Permits to re-build churches, even after they have been burned down by followers of Islam, are denied. A permit to purchase land for a Christian cemetery is repeatedly denied. Corpses are presently buried with other corpses or shipped out of state. Normal promotions for Christian workers, including professionals, are denied. Christian programming that is broadcast each Sunday by national television networks is denied, sabotaged on a weekly basis by Muslim officials. Scholarship to Christian students for advanced studies in Europe and America are denied.

In addition there is active terror *jihad*, as evidenced by the sacking and burning of the churches and houses of Christians (1980–2006). Terror *jihad* in Kano State is issued and executed by Islam for so-called justifiable reasons. For example, in Kano, Nelson told us that in Kazura, two months before, they burned down thirteen churches because a Muslim accused a Christian girl of insulting the prophet. And Simon remembered the Bunke evangelistic meetings of 1991, which were viewed as a threat to evangelize Muslims, and thus the killing of Christians began.

He saw thirty dead bodies. One pregnant woman had her baby cut from her body while she was still alive. They killed the whole family. That form of terror *jihad* replicates terror behavior implemented and applied against *dhimmis* in regions of terror subjugation; but this is within Nigeria, a democratic nation with guaranteed freedoms. According to descriptions by Bat Ye'or, the conditions of Christians subjugated by Islam in North Africa in the eighteen hundreds were very similar to the conditions of Christians presently living in Kano, Nigeria. She describes how *dhimmi* churches were razed and set afire because Christians had allegedly violated the conditions of subjugated inferiors.[4]

Currently in Kaduna, the population is evenly divided between Muslim and Christian, but has been ripped by Islamic violence since 1980. In the most recent violence, almost every church in the northern section of Kaduna, with a 90 percent Muslim majority, was destroyed. The suffering of the Christians has been immense, particularly the widows, orphans, and the elderly. Public demonstrations by Christians against the implementation of *sharia* law have been used by Islam to justify terror *jihad* against the churches and the Christians of Kaduna North.

The position paper for peace (Appendix D) by the Kaduna Muslims states that the application of *sharia* law is absolutely necessary for a Muslim to be a Muslim. But the problem with Islamic holy law, at least Criminal Code *sharia* law, is that it elevates Muslims and denigrates non-Muslim peoples. That supremacist attitude can easily be understood without embracing the whole of Islamic *sharia* law. One only needs to understand that *sharia* law is constructed on the bases of the ancient authorities and thus reflects the terror behavior models of Muhammad and terror behavior teachings of the Koran.

Muslims have conducted terror *jihad* against Christian citizens of Kaduna by burning them, their homes, and their churches. Islam justifies terror *jihad* because it views the Christians as guilty of suppressing Muslim faith. Clearly the Christians object and protest against the implementation of Criminal Code *sharia* law. In the fact that Islam sees Criminal Code *sharia* law as absolutely necessary for a Muslim to be a Muslim, Christians are accused of flagrantly taking away from a

Muslim the right to be Muslim. The Christian protest is easily viewed as similar to the initial oppressor of Islam, the polytheists of Mecca, in the days of Muhammad. In answer to such obstruction and oppression, the God of Islam orders his followers to "fight for the religion of God against those who fight you …kill them wherever you find them…this shall be the reward of the infidels (suppressors of faith)" (Koran II (191, 192)).

Can Christians or Jews live securely and in freedom when they are near a large population or a majority population of Muslims, or will they eventually face terror behavior? According to Kano and Kaduna, they will face terror behavior. The strategic purpose of terror *jihad* against Christians in Kaduna is to coerce and to weaken Christian resistance to Criminal Code *sharia* law. That assessment comports with the purpose of terror behavior as defined in Koran IX (29), to fight them until there is real subjugation and a genuine sense of inferiority. The purpose of terror behavior in Islam is to "fight" the enemy—to weaken his will, to cripple his fiancés, to damage his life view, to damage his faith, to demonstrate the supremacy of *Allah*, and to force those who resist the will of Islam to flee—so that the territory may be reconstituted as the redeemed land of Islam, *dar al-Islam*.

In Plateau State (2004), I collected evidence from various sources to support the many testimonies I heard of terror *jihads* against Christians living in small cities and villages on the plateau. In the case of Yelwa, all of the seventeen churches were burned to the ground. In addition, many Christians were killed, some brutally so. In one church as many as fifty Christians were captured and slaughtered, then the corpses were doused with kerosene and set afire. The *jihad* terror strike against Yelwa was no spontaneous attack, but well planned. The Muslim residents of Yelwa housed and fed Muslim mercenaries for several days without reporting them to the government authorities. After the *jihad*, the Muslim villagers refused to provide any vital intelligence to the police. In that way, they participated in the murder of their Christian neighbors. All landowners and residents of Yelwa are now Muslin. It is legitimately *dar al-Islam.*

In the village of Bolgani (2004), houses were torched. Lories, autos, and motorcycles were sprayed with kerosene and set ablaze. The chief of Bolgani said, "Over two thousand Muslim men attacked my village. They threw Molotov cocktails into our houses and on our roofs." Karkashi village was the same scene. The chairman of the Roman Catholic Church said they were attacked by hundreds of Muslim invaders, as many as two thousand. People were attacked in churches while attackers shouted, "Glory to God!" Hundreds and hundreds of Christians fled their homes by foot, in mass, down the roads and through the fields. Still others fled on motorcycles, bicycles, and on the tops of jam-packed lories. How does anyone understand this deliberate form of terror *jihad* in any way other than in light of the Koran?

Nigeria was a terrible shock of reality. I heard testimony and saw devastation of terror behavior frighteningly similar to that instructed by the Koran. I felt like the world stood still. What I had read from the ancient authorities of fourteen hundred years past came to life before my very eyes. Most troubling for me to see was that the religious policies of terror behavior were taken from the pages of a holy book, from the mysterious will of a divinity. Then they were carried out against a real world of flesh and blood human beings. I saw the fear. I saw damaged people— small, large, young, old, widows, orphans—all struggling for survival. As the Koran says, they are "the worst of creatures."

More than that, I saw the damaged followers of Islam. I saw the authority of a "divinity" that ordered Muslim believes to terrorize and to execute non-conformers and non-believers until they are no more. That bloody assignment is the divine burden laid upon the backs and hearts of Muslim men and women. My journey to Nigeria brought the ancient abstract teachings of the Koran into the bright daylight of a very real, flesh-and-blood present. When I think of Nigeria, I feel compassion for the victims of Islam, but also, strangely, for the faithful adherents of *Allah*.

Journeys into Sudan

Increasingly the world sympathizes with the Darfurians as they suffer and die under the Islamic authorities of Sudan. Interestingly television portrayals of the dead and wounded at Darfur seem staged to stimulate American compassion. I suppose that the final objective of these portrayals is to move Americans to rally for a military intervention by the Untied Nations or possibly some Western military coalition. *But who is investigating the cause of this attempted genocide?* It is assumed by many from the West that the cause is Arab-Islamic racism against the Muslim black Africans of Darfur. Is that actually the case?

Or could James Khan be correct? Is the effort to exterminate the Darfurians more than racism? Is the West once again refusing to look Islam in the eye? Is the real cause of the Darfuran tragedy a major effort by the Islamic leadership of Sudan to purify Islam from the assimilations of African tribal religions? Efforts to purify Islam have occurred in years past. For example, Jews and Christians, who initially converted to Islam under terror *jihad* were later interrogated, and in some cases exterminated, for retaining practices of their former faiths. When one understands that the Sudanese Government's institution of Islamic *sharia* law was done to control and humiliate ten million non-Muslim peoples, killing and displacing millions, then seeing the atrocities of Darfur as terror behavior carried out to purify Islam is not such a great leap of logic.

Probably the strongest argument for believing that the purpose of Darfuran genocide is to purify the religion of Islam is the overall grand design of Islam to rule Africa. The declaration of Islamic *sharia* law in September 1983 was the first act of Sudanese Islam to preparer to take the continent. With Christian control gone in the south, Islam firmly controls the largest African nation, i.e., largest in landmass. More importantly, with its central location on the continent, southern Sudan can be used as a conduit for the movement of automatic weapons, militias, and slave-suicide bombers into citadels of Islam within neighboring non-Muslim states. The Muslim Egyptians, Saudis, and Libyans now have land access to the whole of Africa. As Islam proceeds toward their divine objective to dominate the world, it is reasonable to conclude that they desire to purge African Islam from its assimilations of tribal religions, leading to genocide in Darfur.

Darfur is the most recent terror tragedy of Sudan. Since 2006 it seems to obscure the twenty-plus years of official terror *jihad*, declared in 1983, by its Muslim rulers against the non-Muslim peoples of the south, but Darfur pales in comparison. On my journey into Sudan, I was focused on the twenty years of official state policy that resembled in many ways the terror behaviors taught by the ancient authorities of Islam. Although I was severely restricted in my travels by threat of imprisonment, I was able to listen to testimonies of victims who had been motored into Khartoum undercover. They shared experiences of living near and under the authority of cultural, religious, and political Islam in Sudan. They witnessed terror war (*jihad*), and upon defeat and flight, many of them experienced life eerily similar to that of terror subjugation (*dhimmitude*).

Obvious to everyone, the terror war (*jihad*) against the southern animists and Christians was the work of the Islamic government in Khartoum—but support was not limited to Khartoum. Assistance of automatic weapons and military aircraft to aid the terror *jihad* was provided by Saudi Arabia, Iran, Iraq, and Libya. When one begins to understand that Islam is the perpetrator of the terror *jihad* against the non-Muslim south—not politicians *per se,* but the religion of Islam by its demand to impose and apply Islamic *sharia* law on non-Muslim peoples—then it seems impossible that American leaders are actually promoting Islam as a religion of peace and tolerance.

The twenty years of *jihad* against a resilient south were waged for only one purpose: to govern the state of Sudan by Islamic *sharia* law. That is no statement of tolerance; that is about the need of Islam to control the thoughts and behaviors (for *Allah*) of all peoples. The Islamic *jihad* against the south began in 1983 and spanned over twenty years because the Islamic government of the north refused to cancel (freeze) Islamic *sharia* law. As a matter of record, when the president of the north seemed prepared to freeze Islamic *sharia* law in order to bring an end to the *jihad,* the religious leaders executed a coup d'etat (June 30, 1989) and Colonel Bashir took the political leadership.

According to the policy of using *jihad* "only on defense," the *jihad* against the south was viewed by Islam as legitimate *jihad* because the Christians and the animists (polytheists) of the south had refused to submit to Islamic *sharia* law, which Islam claimed is absolutely necessary in order for a Muslim to be a Muslim (Appendix D). The so-called tolerance of Islam seems to work as follows. If Islam has a majority or near majority population, then Islam has the right democratically (according to Islam, *the obligation!)* to implement and apply *sharia* law. If a non-Muslim submits to this codified system of legal prejudice against him, then he can remain as a legally coded inferior creature/person within his home (Islamic tolerance). However, if a non-Muslim opposes the application of *sharia* law, then he has suppressed the faith of Islam, and he becomes subject to defensive terror *jihad.* It is a no-win situation for the Christians, Jews, and other non-Muslim peoples. It is terrorism at work.

Some peace activists see all war as terror war, so they fail to see the terrifying ugliness of terror *jihad.* But in Sudan, Islam brought new meaning to the word "terror." While peace lovers all over the world support Islam in it tears over the crime of Muslim men naked in an Abu Ghraib prison, they must not ignore the horrifying, terrifying treatments against men like Raphael. *Imagine the barbaric cruelty: crucified, burned off fingertips, hot peppers stuffed up his rectum, and thrown into the forest to be eaten by wild animals. Or envision the helpless friends of James Khan in the United Nations refugee camp in Kenya. There the Somali Muslims took refugees, cut off their ears, cut off their noses, slashed their bellies, tied their intestines behind their backs cut off their testicles, and then crucified them.*

Every bit as troubling as the experiences of terror *jihad* are the crippling experiences of Christian refugees under the early forms of terror subjugation (*dhimmitude*) in Sudan. Imagine Tsol who was imprisoned because he accepted the position offered by the elders of the Dinka tribe to be teacher of their exiled, orphaned children. He was imprisoned because he opposed the forced education of the Koran upon non-Muslim children in the Sudanese schools. Or imagine Isaac, who was tortured because he built a tugal (a house of sticks and mud) for fleeing Christian refugees from the south so that they could gather for worship out of the heat of the sun. The police and soldiers warned the fleeing refugees that there are no new churches in the north. It is the land of Islam. In the village of Renk, police tortured and killed twenty-eight for singing Christmas carols without permission. Troubling also are reports that no assistance was permitted through any world relief agencies; even the Sudan Lifeline was shut down. Aid was distributed only through Islamic centers. In my visits, "displaced persons" repeatedly told me that at the Islamic centers, Islam prostituted itself by trading relief assistance for conversions.

From my experience in Sudan, I must conclude that terror *jihad* remains an active part of religious Islam. Once a non-Muslim, a Christian, subjugates to the authority of Islam, he is an inferior, a second-class citizen, submitting to a life of *dhimmitude*. He has only two opportunities to restore his rights and or his freedoms: to flee or to convert. From what I have seen in Nigeria and Sudan, it is clear that an important tool for the expansion of Islam is the use of Islamic *sharia* law. Islam argues *sharia* law is necessary for a Muslim to be a Muslim, and they also deny that *sharia* law has any negative effect on Jews, Christians, and non-Muslims. But the teachings of the Koran disagree, and the laws of *Allah* disagree. The *kafirun* are viewed as a despicable people. The evidence shows that *sharia* law is a nasty tool that cuts short the freedoms and ambitions of a non-Muslim.

I depart from Sudan with a reminder to my readers that the activities of Islam in Sudan are not rare and unusual behaviors. They are consistent with the terror *jihads* of Islam through history. For example, in her studies of the decline of Eastern Christianity under Islam, Bat Ye'or reports that in the ninth century, Muslim armies subjugated the Christian cities of Bari, Messina, and Modia between 842 and 844 and later besieged Rome in 846. Al-Abbas of Tunisia looted and destroyed Castrogiovanni, Castania, Syracuse, Noto, and Ragusa of Sicily between 853 and 854. He destroyed the harvests and took thousands of captives to be sold on the slave markets of the Middle East. In Syracuse thousands of Christians were killed in the year 878. In Taormina the residents were executed in 902. Massacres, human trafficking, looting, and the destruction of churches, cathedrals, homes, and farmlands by the armies of Islam are well documented and were common in Europe, Africa, and Asia for centuries.[5]

Journeys into Egypt

Northern Nigeria is presently experiencing efforts by Islam to increase and expand its territory, the *dar al-Islam*, through implementation and application of Islamic *sharia* law in Kaduna. Farther south, terror war (*jihad*) is the means used to frighten and expel Christians from regions of Plateau State. In the far north, aspects of terror subjugation (*dhimmitude*) are unofficially in practice. In Sudan the major terror war (*jihad*) against the indigenous peoples of the south is nearly complete, and the application of terror subjugation (*dhimmitude*) is being put in place to verify inferior status. The annihilation of Darfur seems the last chip to fall before Sudan and its Islamic neighbors can really focus an expansion of Islam into its citadels within Ethiopia, Kenya and the Congo.

In contrast terror war (*jihad*) came to Egypt as early as 641 and the practice of terror subjugation (*dhimmitude*) shortly thereafter. Egypt today gives an opportunity for those of us from the West to view and measure the attitudes and behaviors of Islam toward its indigenous peoples, the Christian Copts. After nearly fourteen hundred years, Christians are still subjected to the terrors of murder, torture, imprisonment, and other forms of mental and physical abuse done to them in order to maintain and enforce their inferior status as *dhimmis*.

There is no freedom of religion in Egypt. There is no freedom from Islam in Egypt. Little Christian children are forced to memorize the Koran in the public schools and private schools, even segments of the Koran that deprecate and humiliate their parents, their families, ands their churches. Muslim teachers frighten little Christian children with threats from the Koran that they will burn in hell. Others are forced into ceremonial washings, recitations of Islamic prayers, and the wearing of typical Muslim headscarves.

On the streets, Muslim adults call out to Christian children, "I hate you." This is reality. This is Islam's attitude toward Christian children. They are the *kafirun*. They are the children's children of a long line of unbelievers who allegedly lied and covered over revelations of Muhammad within the Gospels of Jesus. To Islam they were and are the worst of creatures. In the Muslim culture they are animals, "apes and swine."

Christian women cannot ride public transport without risking insults from adult Muslim males, who call them "whores" and whack them on the back of their heads. Christian churches are closed without explanation. New churches are forbidden. Church improvements, including toilets with running water instead of outdoor latrines, are not allowed. Advertisements for job opportunities in public newspapers clarify, "Christians need not apply." These behaviors are not exceptions, but are increasingly the rule of Egypt. Islamic *sharia* law is deeply embedded in the Islamic culture. Muslims do not need to research the law books to determine appropriate behaviors toward Christians. Parents and grandparents have modeled terror subjugation of the *dhimmis* for generations, for fourteen hundred years. Terrorism is embedded in the religion. It lives and breathes in the religious culture. Terror behaviors are nurtured in the mosque, emboldened by the culture, justified by Islamic *sharia* law, and authorized by the Koran.

Although many in the Western world consider the state of Egypt as secular, in the mid-1980s Egypt adopted Islam as it state religion. Under British rule, the practice of persecution was fed mostly by the culture of Islam, but with the official adoption of Islam as the religion of state, all the forces of the state are legitimately used to endorse religious oppression. Identification Cards identify the religion of every Egyptian resident and thereby enable Islam to facilitate oppression and marginalize Christians in education and employment. In addition only followers of Islam are appointed to positions within the intelligence agencies, so only Muslims investigate and enforce punishments against Christians.

The evidence I gathered in Egypt, Sudan, and Nigeria testifies to the practice of terror war (*jihad*) and terror subjugation (*dhimmitude*) by faithful followers of Islam today. Following my journeys, I am more than ever troubled by many of our leaders' declaration that Islam is a religion of tolerance and peace. What is the basis for that declaration? The life of Muhammad models terror behavior. The Koran teaches terror behavior. A millennium of history portrays terror *jihad* by warriors of Islam against the European continent, in the West, in the South, and in the East. Today, in the neighborhoods of Islam, the heartland, terror behavior is on public display. It stretches from the small village of Qus to the large state of Iran. How can our political and religious leaders responsibly dismiss the evidence that indicts Islam?

Summary Thoughts

I began my journeys into the heart and heartland of Islam with prayers and hopes that in some small way my efforts might contribute to (1) a greater openness toward public discussions on the actual teachings and behaviors of Islam, (2) an increased awareness of our nations' need to secure the protection for individual freedoms, (3) an increased assistance to non-Muslim victims of Islamic violence, and (4) an awakening and emancipation of Muslim peoples who have been enslaved by the legalistic tyranny of Islam (*sharia*), a bondage that seems to have haunted them since the death of Muhammad.

At journey's end, I am convinced that America needs a greater openness toward public discussions on the real teachings and behaviors of Islam. Through the early years of American isolationism, there was little interest or knowledge in foreign politics and foreign religions. When America became a significant player on the world stage (World War I), Islamic power (Ottoman Empire) had collapsed, and Europeans occupied Muslim lands. As a consequence, America never really knew Islam.

In this vacuum of knowledge, political and religious leaders now seem eager to teach America that Islam is a religion of peace and tolerance. But they try to teach America by slogan without serious documentation. Why? Clearly they are wrong. Have they been misinformed? Is there some sinister purpose? Political correctness, oil dependency, and political favor aside, why do they endorse a policy of disinformation? Why do they reject the teachings of the Koran? Why do they reject the non-Muslim victims suffering under Islam?

The American people deserve more. Open the Crescent curtain for American viewing. Listen to the victims! Americans need to witness the brutal, bigoted treatments of non-Muslim peoples, observe the chilling evidence of terror behavior, *jihad* and *dhimmitude*, listen to the testimonies of refugees fleeing Islam, and understand the coercive features of Islamic religion, law, politics, and culture. Does America endorse this brutal behavior? Is this what we want in America? In light of feeble politicians, Americans (we the people) need to push this issue into the public forefront at every available opportunity. "Explain, Mr. President, the meaning of Koran IX (29)!"

At journey's end, I am convinced that American freedoms are on a collision course with Islamic holy law (*sharia*). Americans need to know that *sharia* rejects freedoms of religion, freedom of the press, and freedom of speech. That is the evidence gathered in northern Nigeria, southern Sudan, and throughout Egypt. That is the open public policy in Saudi Arabia and Iran. *Sharia* does not alter from territory to territory, from Muslim to Muslim. Sharia is not governed by the will of the people. It is governed by the immutable will and word of *Allah*. It is non-negotiable. *Sharia* is the basis of legislation among all Islamic nations, including Iraq and Afghanistan. *Sharia* is more than an instrument for legal religious control of Muslim peoples; it is also a legal instrument formulated to regulate the inferior status of non-Muslim peoples within Islamic regions.

Islam *jihads* against non-Muslim peoples to implement Criminal Code *sharia* law in Kadunda. Islam *jihads* against non-Muslim people to strengthen the practice of *dhimmitude* in Kano. Islam *jihads* against non-Muslim peoples to redeem non-Muslim land in Plateau State to the *dar al-Islam*. Islam *jihads* to implement and apply *sharia* on the non-Muslim peoples of southern Sudan. Islam *jihads* to enforce the life of *dhimmitude* on "displaced" Christians of southern Sudan. Islam *jihads* to enforce a life of *dhimmitude* on the indigenous Christian Copts (of Egypt).

In light of this behavior, why do politicians immigrate into America adherents of *sharia* by the hundreds of thousands? For a Muslim to be a good Muslim, *sharia* must replace American laws. By what method(s) have our politicians evaluated the various codes of Islamic *holy* law and their effects on individual freedoms? Where is that official evaluation? How valuable are American freedoms?

At journey's end, I have seen the wounded, broken victims easily camouflaged by Islam behind the Crescent curtain. Many suffer in tears of silent dignity. Why do some religious leaders praise a religion of such oppression? Why do they argue that only some of the more radical Muslims perpetrate such violence? That is exactly not the point. It is not about what every Muslim does or does not do. It is about what Islam (*sharia*) instructs them to do. In my visits and studies, I did not once, not once, uncover leaders of Islam (political or religious) who seriously condemned terror *jihad* and compensated those looted or offered healing to those wounded. The point is Islam teaches terror behavior. When the really committed (radical) believers execute its instructions, they remain free to strike again an again. Islam is the enemy.

Churches in America need to understand the bigotry, and more importantly the oppression, that Islam perpetrates against Jews, Christians, and other non-Muslim peoples. Churches need an awareness of those suffering victims behind the Crescent curtain so that they can champion the compassion of the Gospel. Churches need to publicly identify and hold accountable perpetrators of such violence against the innocents. At the same time, church leadership needs to stop closing their eyes to refugees fleeing *jihad* and *dhimmitude*. For churches to ignore the wounded at the side of the road is for them to abandon their basic values of goodness, truth, justice and decency.

At journey's end, the religion of Islam entraps Muslim peoples. Many Muslim people are not enthusiasts for *sharia* violence, but they are trapped within Islamic regions and acquiesce in silence. Many faithful Muslim women from the West and within the Middle East struggle to flee the legal gender bigotry of *sharia*. Muslim men in non-Muslim nations fear the loss of their freedoms through the implementation and application of *sharia*. Others within the Islamic world do not even understand the concept of freedom. They are taught that freedom is an occasion for disobedience instead of an opportunity for a genuine obedience exercised from the human heart. The Islamic world needs freedom. But how can they obtain, even imagine, freedom when Americans reject their entrapment and endorse their oppressive religion as one of tolerance? How can Muslim people be really free?

In a similar discussion concerning the law and the children of Abraham, Jesus of Nazareth, the Christ, said, "The truth will set you free" (John 8:31–47). Freedom is in the truth. Tell the truth. How ironic that politicians who wish American freedoms on Muslim peoples praise and endorse the religion of Islam (*sharia*), which rejects those freedoms. How ironic that religious leaders who wish to convert Muslim peoples to the ways of Jesus Christ praise and endorse Islam (*sharia*), which stipulates socio-economic punishments (possible execution) for such conversions. The **truth** will set them free. Lies will hold them hostages.

END NOTES

Chapter 1

1. Bernard Lewis, *Islam and the West* (New York: Oxford University Press, 1993), 121.
2. Ibid., 123.
3. Ibid., 13.
4. Manal Abdul Aziz, "Islam under Attack in Europe." *The Egyptian Gazette,* Nov 29, 2004, 51–54.

Chapter 2

1. Ibn Ishad, *The Life of Muhammad: Apostle of Allah*, trans. Edward Rehatsek and ed. Michael Edwards (Chatham, Great Britain: The Folio Society, W&J Mackay and Co. Ltd, 1964), 66.
2. Ibid., 113.
3. Ibn Warraq, *Leaving Islam: Apostates Speak Out*. (Amherst, New York: Prometheus Books, 2002), 89–99.
4. John Glubb, *The Life and Times of Muhammad* (New York: Cooper Square Press, 2001), 225.

5. Ibn Ishaq, *The Life of Muhammad: Apostle of Allah*, trans. Rehatsek, 129.

6. Alfred Guillaume, trans., *The Life of Muhammad: Apostle of Allah: A Translation of Ibn Ishaq's Sirat Rasul Allah* (Oxford: Oxford University Press, 1955), 464.

7. Ibn Ishaq, *The Life of Muhammad: Apostle of Allah*, trans. Rehatsek, 256.

8. Bat Ye'or, *The Dhimmi: Jews and Christian under Islam* (Cranbury, New Jersey: Associated University Presses, 1985), 51–77.

9. Bat Ye'or, *The Decline of Eastern Christianity under Islam: From Jihad to Dhimmitude* (Cranbury, New Jersey: Associated University Presses, 2002), 69–88

Chapter 3.

1. Abdullah Yusus Ali, *The Holy Quran Text, Translation and Commentary*, Vol. 1 (Cambridge, Massachusetts: For Hafner Publishing Company, New York, U.S.A. 1946), 246.

2. Bernard Lewis, *The Middle East: A Brief History of the Past 2,000 Years* (New York, NY: Touchstone, Simon and Schuster, 1997) 233.

3. Morteza Mutahhari, *"Jihad": The Holy War of Islam and Its legitimacy in The Quran*, (trans. Mohammed Salman Tawhidi (Tehran, Iran: Islamic Propagation. Organization, 1989) 8.

4. Ali, *The Holy Quran Text, Translation and Commentary*, (footnote 206), 76.

5. Lewis, *The Middle East: A brief History of the Last 2,000 Years*, 211.

6. Bat Ye'or, *Islam and Dhimmitude: Where Civilizations Collide* (Lancaster, U.K.: Madison, Teaneck, Farleigh, Dickinson University Press. 2002), 89–90.

7. George Braswell W., Jr., *Islam: Its Prophet, Peoples, Politics and Power* (Nashville, Tennessee: Broadman and Holman, 1996), 45.

Chapter 4

1. Sherwin Heyboer, interviews 27 by author; KLM (Dutch Airlines Airborne; 17 March 2004.

2. Muhammad Ati and Ali Maui, interview 7 by author and Paul Kortenhoven; Starbucks in Dearborn, Michigan; 31 August 2003.

3. Luke Jonji and Mark Ahula, interviews 9 by (recorded); HEKAN guesthouse on Kaduna, Nigeria; 21 March 2004.

4. Ibid.

5. Reverend Marki, interview 11 by author (recorded) HEKAN headquarters in Kaduna, Nigeria; 21 March 2004.

6. Pastor James, interview 12 by author; Church of Christ in Kaduna, Nigeria; 21 March 2004.

7. Mary Jeames, interview 13 by author (recorded); Kaduna, Nigeria; 22 March 2004.

8. Joseph Gyang, interview 14 by author (recorded); Kaduna, Nigeria; 22 March 2004.

9. Joen Alamba, interview 14 by author (recorded); Kaduna, Nigeria; 22 March 2004.

10. Mshenil Ssjmbia Wimi, interview 15 by author (recorded); Kaduna, Nigeria; 22 March 2004.

11. Laitu Jonatham, interview 16 by author (recorded); Kaduna, Nigeria: 22 March 2004.

12. Bishop Vacuba, Interviews 17 by author and Sherwin Heyboer (recorded); Kaduna, Nigeria; 23 March 2004.

13. Ibid.

14, Martha Toon, interview 18 by author (recorded); Kaduna, Nigeria; 23 March 2004.

15. Habib Umar Mahmud and Kabiru Buhari Saleh, interview 19 by author (recorded); Kaduna, Nigeria; 23 March 2004.

16. Ibid.

17. "The Kaduna Peace Declaration of Religious Leaders," August 22, 2002.

18. "Position Paper Submitted by the Kaduna State Muslim Community on the Application of Shari'a Legal System on Muslims to the Inter-religious Leaders Committee on the Application of Shari'a Law in Kaduna State," 18 January 2000 (unpublished document with signature under Appendix D).

19. The Position Paper of the Christian Members of the Committee of inter-religious Leaders on the Application of Sharia-Law in Kaduna State (unpublished document with signatures under Appendix C).

29. Reverend Joseph Hayab (State Secretary of the Christina Association of Nigeria), interview 22 by author and Sherwin Heyboer (recorded); Kaduna, Nigeria; 24 March 2004.

Chapter 5

1. Ms. Rebecca Koba, interview 23 by author and Sherwin Heyboer; Jos, Nigeria; 24 March 2004.

2. Ibid.

3. Reverend Adaki, interview 31 by author and Sherwin Heyboer; Jos, Nigeria;. March 2004.

4. Ibid.

5. Bulus Gambo and Jerry Datim, "Crazy Fanatics Invade Southern Plateau," *The Light Bearer* (March 2004), 18–19.

6-8. Reverend Adaki, interview 412 by author and Sherwin Heyboer, Jos, Nigeria, 30. March 2004.

10. Chief of Bolgani Village, recorded videotape of *Jihad* destruction of Bolgani and other villages of Plateau State. 23-25 March 2004.

10-17. Ishaku Kera (graduate student at Bayero University) interview 25 by author (recorded); Kano, Nigeria; 26 March 2004.

18-19. Donven Maden, interview 25 by author (recorded); Kano, Nigeria; 26 March 2004.

20-23. Pastor Nelson, interview 26 by author (tour of city and Christian cemetery); Kano, Nigeria; 27 March 2004.

24-26. Simon Kohn, interview 27 by author; Kano, Nigeria; 28 March 2004.

27. Yakubu Pouwi, interview 27 by author; Kano, Nigeria; 28 March 2004.

28. Farouk Isah Yahaya, interview 28 by author (recorded); Nigeria; 28 March 2004.

29. Saxone Akaine, "Sharia Panel Faults Report on Polio Vaccine; AllegesDivision in Government Team," *The Guardian* (22 March 2004:1, 4

30. Farouk Isah Yahaya, interview 28 b author (recorded); Nigeria; 28 March 2004.

31. Bat Ye'or, *The dhimmi: Jews and Christians under Islam* (Cranbury, New Jersey; Associated University Presses, 1985) 58.

32. Bat Ye'or, *Islam and Dhimmitude: Where civilizations Collide* (Lancaster, U.K.: Madison, Teaneck Farleigh, Dickinson University Press, 2002), 87–88.

Chapter 6

1-6. James Khan, interview 36 by author; Pasadena, California; 15 April 2004.

7. Pastor Tom, interview 37 by author; airborne between Nairobi and Khartoum; 1 July 2004.

8,. Sudanese officer, remarks at registration desk, Hiltons; Khartoum Sudan; 3 July 2004.

9-18. Benjamin Dee, interview 38 by author; tour Khartoum, Sudan; 2 July 2004.

19-21. Chaplin Thomas, interview 35 by author; women's prison, Khartoum, Sudan; 3 July 2004.

22-36. John Tang (trans. Uncle Nathan, interview 39 by author (recorded); Khartoum, Sudan; 4 July 2004.

37. Bernard Lewis, *The Middle East: A Brief History of the Last 2,000 Years,* 109,..

115, 124–1228, 302; also Kenneth Scott Latourette, *A History of Christianity* (New York, Evanston, and London: Harper row Publishers, 1953), 614.

Chapter 7

1-6. Isol Mafti, interview by author; Khartoum, Sudan; 5 July 2004.

7-10. Gabriel Jodi, interview 41 by author; Khartoum, Sudan; 5 July 2004.

11. J. Millard Burr and Roberty O. Collins, *Revolutionary Sudan, Hasan al-Taburi and the Islamist State, 1989-2000.* (Boston: Brill, 2003), 10.

12. Ibid., 246–7.

13. Mohammad El-Amin Kalifa, *Ten Years of Peace Making in Sudan* (Khartoum, Sudan: Khartoum University, 2000), 19.

14. Ibid., 30.

15. Ibid., 44.

16-18. Isaac Doolia, interview 34 by author (recorded); Khartoum, Sudan; 6 July 2004.

19-20. Stephen Iokik, interview 46 by author; Khartoum, Sudan; 6 July 2004.

21-25. Jacob Khan, interviewed by author; Khartoum, Sudan; 6 July 2004.

Chapter 8

1. Kenneth Scott Latourette, A History of Christianity, 320.

2. Shawky F. Karas, *The Copts Since the Arab Invasion: Strangers in Their Land* (Jersey City, NJ: American, Canadian, and Australian C. Coptic Association, 1985) 9–10.

3-10. Ibrahim Akul, interview 49 by author, Sherwin Heyboer Jr., and Peter Bulthuis; Cairo, Egypt; 14 November 2004.

11. Ibn Ishaq, *The Life of Muhammad: Apostle of Allah,* trans. Edward Rehatsek, 129.

12. David Lamb, *The Arabs: Journeys beyond the Mirage* (New York: Vintage Books, A Division of Random House, Inc. 2002,

45.

12-17. Bernard Jona, interview 50 by author, Sherwin Heyboer Jr., and Peter. Bulthuis; Cairo, Egypt; 15 November 2004.

18-23. John and Elizabeth Phata, interview 53 by the author; El Giza, Egypt; 16. November 2004.

24. Samir Pus, interview 54 by author; Cairo, Egypt; 17 November 2004.

25. Pastor Zeke, interview 55 by author; Cairo, Egypt; 17 November 2004.

26. David Barrus. Interview 56 by author; Cairo to Alexandria, Egypt; 18 November 2004.

27-38. Titus Duna, Alexander Shaart, and James Shiaky; interview 60 by author,. Sherwin Heyboer Jr. and Peter Bulthius; Alexander, Egypt; 20 November 2004.

Chapter 9

1-2 Father Paul (chauffer of Bishop Wissa) interview 57 by author; Monastery of the Child, Upper Egypt; 23 November 2004.

3. Father Gabriel, interview 58 by author (recorded); Monastery of the Child, Upper Egypt; 23 November 2004.

4-12. Bishop Wissa and father Gabriel (trans. Father Francis), interview 59 by author (recorded); Monastery of the Child, Upper Egypt; 23 November 2004.

13. *Massacre at the Millennium: A Report on the Murder of Twenty-one Christians in AI-Kosheh, Egypt and the Failure of Justice* (Washington, D.C.: Centre for Religious Freedom, 2001), 6

13-20. Bishop Wissa and Father Gabriel (trans. Father Francis), interview by author (recorded); Monastery of the Child, Upper Egypt; 23 November 2004.

21. *Massacre at the Millennium*, 43–4.

22. Karas, *The Copts Since the Arab Invasion: Strangers in Their Land.*

Chapter 10.

1. Ishaq, *The Life of Muhammad: Apostle of Allah*, 129.

2. Lewis, *The Middle East: A Brief History of the Last 2,000 Years*, 276.

3. Ibid., 277.

4. Bat Ye'or, *The Dhimmi Jews and Christians under Islam*, 58.

5. Bat Ye'or, *The Decline of Eastern Christianity under Islam From Jihad to Dhimmitude*, 50–52.

SELECTED BIBLIOGRAPHY

Akaine, Saxone, "Sharia ;panel faults report on polio vaccine. Alleges division in. government team." *The Guardian* (Lagos, Nigeria), (22 March 2004): 1, 4.

Armstrong, Karen, *The Battle for God: A History of Fundamentalism*. New York: The Random House Publishing Group, 2000

Abashiya, Chris Shu'aibu, and Ayuba Jalaba Ulea, *Christian and Islam: A Plea for Understanding and tolerance*. Jos, Nigeria: Holma (Nig) Ltd., 1991.

Azia, Manal Abdul. "Islam under attack in Europe." *The Egyptian Gazette* (Cairo, Egypt), (29 November 2004): 51–54.

Bistawros, Bakeg T. *The Coptic Christians of Egypt Today: Under Threat of Annihilation*. Virginia: Regent University, 1996.

Braswell, George W., Jr. *Islam: Its Prophet, Peoples, Politics and Power*. Nashville, Tennessee: Broadman and Holman, 1996.

Burr, J. Millard and Robert O. Collins, *Revolutionary Sudan, Hasan al-Taburi and the Islamic State, 1989-2000*. Boston:

Brill, 2003.

Caldwell, Christopher. "Daughter of the Enlightenment." *The New York Times,* 3 April 2005.

Center for Religious Freedom. *Massacre at the Millennium: A Report on the Murder of Twenty-one Christians in Al-Koshenm, Egypt and the Failure of Justice.* Washington, D.C.: Center for Religious Freedom, 2001.

Dau, Isahia Majok. *Suffering and God: A Theological Reflection on the War in Sudan.* Limuru, Kenya: Kolbe Press, 2002.

Demessie, Loeke M. "Sudanese Rebels Issue Demands for Resuming Talks with Government." *The Desert Sun.* (Palm Springs), (17 July 2004 A 21).

French, Howard W. *A Continent for the Taking:' The Tragedy and Hope of Africa.* New York: Alfred A. Knopf, 2004.

Gambo, Bulus and Jerry Datim. "Crazy Fanatics Invade Southern Plateau." *The Light Bearer.* (Jos, Nigeria), (March 2004): 18–19.

Glubb, John. *The Life and Times of Muhammad.* New York: Cooper Square Press, 2001.

Guillaume, Alfred. *The Traditions: An Introductory Study of the Hadith Literature.* Beirut, Lebanon: KHaya Book and Publishing Company S.A.L. (Reprinted by permission of Oxford University Press from the original edition of 1924), 1966.

Guillaume, Alfred, trans. *The Life of Muhammad: Apostle of Allah: A Translation of Ibn Ishaq's Sirat Rasul Allah.* Oxford: Oxford University Press, 1955.

Jeffrey, Arthur. *Materials for the History of the Text of the Quran.* Cairo: Oriental Institute Baroda, 1938.

Karas, Shawky F. *The Copts Since the Arab Invasion: Strangers in Their Land.* Jersey City, N.J.: American, Canadian, and Australian C. Coptic Associations, 1985.

Kalifa, Mohammad El-Amin. *Ten Years Of Peace Making In Sudan.* Khartoum, Sudan: Khartoum University, 2000.

Laffin, John. *The Dagger of Islam.* New York: Bantam Books, 1980.

Lamb, David. *The Africans.* New York: Vintage Books (A Division of Random House), 1987.

——— *The Arabs: Journeys Beyond the Mirage.* New York: Vintage Books (A Division of Random House), 2002.

Latourette, Kenneth Scott. *A History of Christianity.* New York, Evanston, and London: Harper & Row, 1953.

Lewis, Bernard. *Islam and the West.* New York: Oxford University Press, 1993.

——— *The Middle East: A Brief History of the Past 2,000 Years.* New York, N.Y.: Touchstone, Simon and Schuster, 1997.

Lumbard, Joseph E,B, *Islam: Fundamentalism and the Betrayal of Tradition (Essays by Western Muslim Scholars).* Canada: World Wisdom, 2004.

Molaty, Tadros Yacoub. *Introduction to the Coptic Orthodox Church.* Alexandria, Egypt: St. George's Coptic Orthodox Church, 1993.

Moltmann, Jurgen. *The Church in the Power of the Spirit.* Translated by Margaret Khol. New York, Hagerstown, San Francisco, London: Harper and Row, 1977.

Mutahhari, Morteza. *"Jihad": The Holy War of Islam and Its Legitimacy in the Quran.* Translated by Mohammed Salman Tawhidi. Tehran, Iran: Islamic Propagation Organization, 1989.

Parker, Michael. *Children of the Sun: Stories of the Christian Journey in Sudan.* Limuru, Kenya, Kolbe Press. 2000.

Rajab, Ahmed: "Winning the Peace." *The BBC: Focus on Africa,* April-June 2004: 14-15.

Rehatsek, Edward, trans. *The Life of Muhammad: Apostle of Allah.* Abridged and edited by Michael Edwardes. Chatham, Great Britain: The Folio Society, W & J Mackay and Co. Ltd. 1964.

Talban, Alfred. "Winning the Peace." *The BBC Focus on Africa,*

April-June 2004: 10-13.

Van Gunsteren, Herman. *"Angst is de olie van tirannie."* *Vrij Nederland,* 20 November 2004, 51-54.

Warraq, Ibn Q. "Islam and Freedom." *Commentary,* December 2004: 23-28.

Ye'or, Bat. *Islam and Dhimmitude: Where Civilizations Collide.* Lancaster, U.K.:

Madison, Teaneck, Farleigh, Dickinson University Press, 2002.

—— *The Decline of Eastern Christianity Under Islam: From Jihad to Dhimmitude.* Cranbury, New Jersey: Associated University Presses, 2002.

—— *The Dhimmi: Jews and Christians Under Islam.* Cranbury, New Jersey: Associated University Presses, 1985.

UNPUBLISHED SOURCES
INTERVIEWS

Jos, Nigeria

Adaki, Reverend. Interview 31 by author and Sherwin Heyboer. *Church of Christ, Yelwa, Plateau State.* 30 March 2004.

Bolgani Chief (videotape of *jihad* destruction of villages in Plateau State), 23-24 March 2004.

Jonji, Luke and Ahula, Mark (Ministry supervisors *Hadaddiyar Ekklisiyar Kristi A Nigeria, HEKAN*). Interview 8 by author. 20 March 2004.

Koba, Rebecca (Secretary World Relief). Interview 23 by author and Sherwin Heyboer. 25 March 2004.

Zarko, Benjamin, Benjamin Tadi, and Paul Doku (reports and pictures of *jihad* destruction in villages in Plateau State). Interview 30 by author. 25 March 2004.

Kaduna, Nigeria:

Alamba, Joen. Interview 14 by author (recorded). Kaduna,

Nigeria, 22 March 2004.

Gyang, Joseph. Interview 14 by author (recorded). Kaduna, Nigeria, 22 March 2004.

Hayab, Reverend Joseph (State Secretary of the Christian Association of Nigeria). Interview 22 by author and Sherwin Heyboer (recorded). Kaduna, Nigeria, 24 March 2004.

James, Pastor. Interview 12 by author. Gilliam Church of Christ, Kaduna, Nigeria, 21 March 2004.

Jeames, Mary. Interview 113 by author (recorded). Kaduna, Nigeria, 22 March 2004.

Laitu, Jonathan. Interview 16 by author (recorded). Kaduna, Nigeria, 22 March 2004.

Mahmud, Habib Umar and Kabiru Buhari Saleh (Muslim educators). Interview 19 by author (recorded). Kaduna, Nigeria, 23 March 2004.

Marki, Reverend. Interview 11 by author (recorded). Hekan Headquarters, Kaduna, Nigeria; 21 March 2004.

Toon, Martha (board member, YMCA). Interview 18 by author (recorded). Kaduna, Nigeria, 23 March 2004.

Yacuba, Bishop. Interview 17 by author and Sherwin Heyboer (recorded). Kaduna, Nigeria, 22 March 2004.

Wimi, Mshenil Ssjmbia. Interview 15 by author (recorded). Kaduna, Nigeria, 22 March 2004.

Kano, Nigeria

Kera, Ishaku (graduate student, Bayero University). Interview 25 by author and Sherwin Heyboer (recorded). Kano, Nigeria, 28 March 2004.

Kohn, Simon. Interview 27 by author. Kano, Nigeria, 28 March 2004.

Nelson, Pastor (Tour of Kano and Christian Cemetery). Interview 26 by author. Kano, Nigeria, 27 March 2004.

Pouwi, Yakubu. Interview 27 by author. Kano, Nigeria, 28 March 2004.

Yahaya, Farouk Isah. Interview 28 by author (recorded). Nigeria, 28 March 2004.

Khartoum, Sudan

Dee, Benjamin (Guide for tour of Khartoum). Interview 38 by author. Khartoum, Sudan, 2 July 2004.

Doolia, Isaac. Interview 45 by author (recorded). Khartoum, Sudan, 6 July 2004.

Ioki, Stephen. Interview 46 by author. Khartoum, Sudan, 6 July 2004.

Khan, Jacob. Interview 47 by author. Khartoum, Sudan, 6 July 2004.

Jodi, Gabriel. Interview 41 by author (partial recording). Khartoum, Sudan, 5 July 2004.

Mafti, Tsol. Interview 47 by author. Khartoum, Sudan, 5 July 2004.

Tang, John. (Translator Uncle Nathan). Interview by author (recorded). Khartoum, Sudan, 4 July 2004.

Thomas, Chaplin. (Chaplin Women's Prison of Khartoum). Interview 35 by author. Khartoum, Sudan, 3 July 2004.

Toni, Pastor. Interview 37 by author. Airborne between Khartoum and Nairobi, 1 July 2004.

Sudanese Government Official. Registration Desk, Khartoum Hilton; Khartoum, Sudan, 1 July 2004.

Cairo, Egypt

Akul, Ibrahim. Interview 49 by author, Sherwin.Heyboer Jr., and Peter Bulthuis. Cairo, Egypt, 14 November 2004.

Barrus, David. Interview 56 by author. Cairo to Alexandria, Egypt, 20 November 2004.

Duna, Titus, Alexander Sha`art and James Shiaky. Interview 60 by author, Sherwin Heyboer Jr., and Peter Bulthuis. Alexandria, Egypt. 20 November 2004.

Jona, Bernard. Interview 50 by author, Sherwin Heyboer Jr.,

and Peter Bulthius. Cairo, Egypt, 15 November 2004.

Phata, John and Elizabeth. Interview 53 by author. El Giza, Egypt, 16 November 2004.

Pus, Samir. Interview 54 by author. Cairo, Egypt, 17 November 2004.

Zeke, Pastor. Interview 55 by author. Cairo, Egypt, 17 November 2004.

Upper Egypt

Gabriel, Father (Priest from Qus). Interview 58 by author (recorded). Monastery of the

Child, Upper Egypt, 22 November 2004.

Paul, Father (Chauffer of Bishop Wissa). Interview 57 by author. Monastery of the Child, Upper Egypt, November 2004.

Wissa, Bishop and Father Gabriel (translator Father Francis). Interview 59 by author (recorded). Monastery of the Child, Upper Egypt, 23 November 2004.

Other

Heyboer, Sherwin. Interview 27 by author. KLM (Dutch Airlines) Airborne. 17 March 2004.

Khan, James. Interview 36 by author. Pasadena, California, 15 April 2004.

Ati, Muhammad and Ali Maui. Interview 7 by author and Paul Kortenhoven. Detroit, Michigan, 31 August 2003.

<small>UNPUBLISHED SOURCES</small>

DOCUMENTS

Gyang Document: Description of items and values lost to *jihad* by Mr. Joseph Gyang. *Wadennan an sune da an kone ran* 22nd February, 2000. Classified: Appendix A.

Peace Document, "Kaduna Peace Declaration of Religious Leaders" signed by eleven Muslims and eleven Christians and the Governor Alm. Ahmed Mohammad Makarfi. Classified: Appendix B.

Christian Document on *Sharia-Law*: "THE POSITION PAPER OF THE CHRISTIAN MEMBERS OF THE COMMITTEE OF INTER-RELIGIOUS LEADERS ON THE APPLICATION OF SHARIA-LAW IN KADUNA STATE." Classified: Appendix C.

Muslim Document of Shari'a Legal System: "POSITION PAPER SUBMITTED BY THE KADUNA STATE MUSLIM COMMUNITY ON THE APPLICATION OF SHARI'A LEGAL SYSTEM ON MUSLIMS TO THE INTER-RELIGIOUS LEADERS COMMITTEE ON THE APPLICATION OF SHARI'A LAW IN KADUNA STATE." Classified: Appendix D.

Prison Program Document: "PRESBYTERIAN CHURCH OF THE SUDAN, WOMEN DEPARTMENT, PRISON PROGRAM ON 2ND JULY 2004 TIME FROM 10:00-12:00 A.M." Classified: Appendix E.

International Christian Union Document: "International Conference on 'Democracy in the Middle East and Preserving Christians and Other Minorities' Future Existence" At the Holiday Inn, Newark Airport Hotel on June 19 and 20, 2006. Classified" Appendix F.

Mr Joseph Gyang
House Address
CK No 3 Shehu Shagari Road
U/Rimi Kaduna,

APPENDIX A Mr. Joseph Gyang

OR

Church Address
HEKAN Church
U/Rimi
P.O. Box 5028
Kaduna.

22nd February, 2000.

WADANNAN SUNA KAYAN DA AN KONE RAN 22ND FEBRUARY, 2000.

1.	Three bags of maize	₦ 4,500.00
2.	Three beds	7,500.00
3.	Three matress	7,500.00
4.	Four cushion chairs	10,000.00
5.	Two boxes	10,000.00
6.	One radio cassette	4,000.00
7.	Standing fan	1,500.00
8.	One wall clock	600.00
9.	Four children	
10.	Four curtains	1,500.00
11.	Ten plates	2,000.00
12.	Eight pots	4,000.00
13.	Two tables one	1,000.00
14.	Rug carpet	5,000.00
15.	Stand one	1,000.00

Total   =   ₦68,500.00

22-2

THE KADUNA PEACE DECLARATION OF RELIGIOUS LEADERS

In the name of God, who is Almighty, merciful and compassionate, we who have gathered as Muslim and Christian religious leaders from Kaduna State pray for peace in our State and declare our commitment to ending the violence and bloodshed, which has marred our recent history.

According to our faiths killing innocent lives in the name of God is desecration of His Holy Name, and defames religions in the world. The violence that has occured in Kaduna State is an evil that must be opposed by all people of good faith. We seek to live together as neighbours, respecting the integrity of each other's historical and religious heritage. ;We call upon all to oppose incitement, hatred, and the misrepresentation of one another.

1. MUSLIMS AND CHRISTIANS of all tribes must respect the divinely ordained purpose of the creator by whose grace we live together in Kaduna State, such ordained purposes include freedom of worship, access to and sanctity of places of worship and justice among others.

2. AS RELIGIOUS LEADERS, we seek to work with all sections of the community for a lasting and just peace according to the teaching of our religions.

3. WE CONDEMN all forms of violence and seek to create an atmosphere where present and future generation

will co-exist with mutual respect and trust in one another. We call upon all to refrain from incitement and demonization, and pledge to educate our young people accordingly.

4. THROUGH THE CREATION of a peaceful state, we seek to explore how together we can aid spiritual regeneration, economic development and inward investment.

5. WE ACKNOWLEDGE the efforts that have been made within this State for a judicial reform and pledge to do all in our power to promote greater understanding of the reform, so that it can provide a true and respected justice in each of our communities.

6. WE PLEDGE to work with the security forces in peace keeping and implementation of the Declaration in the State.

7. WE ANNOUNCE the establishment of a permanent joint committee to implement the recommendations of this declaration and encourage dialogue between the two faiths, for we believe that dialogue will result in the restoration of the image of each in the eyes of the other.

These declarations are binding on all people in the state, from this day of 22nd August, 2002 and agree that any individual or group found breaching the peace must be punished in accordance to the due process of the law.

1. ARCH. BISHOP B. A. ACHIGILI

2. ELDER SAIDU DOGO

3. BISHOP JOSEPH BOGOBIRI

4. BISHOP A. B. LAMIDO

5. REV. Y. B. SIDI

6. REV. HABU MARI

7. PASTOR J. AJAYI

8. REV. PETER AHMED

9. REV. JESSY ADAM

10. EVANGELIST JAMES M. WUYE

11. MR. E. B. YERO

1. ALH. JA'A FARU MAKARFI

2. SHEIKH ZUBAIRU SIRAJO

3. SHEIKH YUSUF S. RIGACHIKUN

4. SHEIKH UMARU SULEIMAN

5. MAL. MUHAMMAD A. SA'ID

6. MALLAM IBRAHIM NAKAKA

7. IMAM MUHAMMAD S. ISAH

8. MALLAM HAMZA A. IBRAHIM

9. IMAM MUH'D N. ASHAFA

10. ALHAJI IBRAHIM KUFENA

11. ALH. BALARABE JIGO

SIGNED
His Excellency
ALH. AHMED MOHAMMED MAKARFI

APPENDIX C

<u>THE POSITION PAPER OF THE CHRISTIAN MEMBERS OF THE COMMITTEE OF INTER-RELIGIOUS LEADERS ON THE APPLICATION OF SHARIA-LAW IN KADUNA STATE.</u>

INTRODUCTION

The debate on the application of full Sharia Law and an accompanying separate legal system to administer it has been a recurring issue in the constitutional and legal history of this great country Nigeria, first in Northern Nigeria and gradually assuming national importance.

Let us go down memory lane to briefly trace the development and the positions so far taken.

1.0   The application of Islamic Personal Law and not Sharia Law in the Northern part of Nigeria is as old as the defunct "Alkali" Courts that were in existence in the Northern Region of Nigeria (now the Northern States). Those courts were applying the Islamic Personal Law in civil litigation e.g marriage and inheritance that affected Muslims. Of course the same courts were handling cases inrespect   customary matters affecting non-Muslims.

2.0   Criminal maters were governed by the Penal Code. When the late Sir Ahmadu Bello, the Sardauna Sokoto was the Premier of the defunct Northern Region of Nigeria he was wise to realise that it was not possible to apply the Sharia Law fully in the then Northern Region in view of the diversity of ethnicity and religion in the Region. Consequently, he commissioned some ronown jurists headed by Professor J.N.D Anderson, a British and formerly Professor of Oriental Laws at the University of London to produce a legal code that would govern criminal matters. This code, though contained provisions of the Sharia Law, was modified in the manner that would suit the peculiar nature of the northern region of Nigeria in terms of diversity of ethnicity and religion. The legal code thus produced by the team of eminent jurists was called the Penal Code which has been in the northern part of Nigeria. It is indeed very pertinent to quote the words of S.S. Richardson Esq in respect of the report of Professor J.N.D. Anderson's Panel as recorded in page one of part one of the introduction to notes on the Panel Code Law. The words are as follows:.

.   "The most important of the Panel's recommendation was that it was
necessary for a self-governing Northern Region to establish a criminal
law which would gain international acceptance, which would apply
uniformly to all persons living within the Region, which will not
discriminate against any section of the community and which would
be generally acceptable throughout the Region"

Furthermore in enacting the new code into law the intention of the
Government in introducing the reforms were clearly stated in the words
of the Late Sir Ahmadu Bello Saurdaunan Sokoto and Premier of the
Northern Nigeria as follows:

   "it is necessary if the self governing region was to fulfil
   its role in the Federation of Nigeria and command respect
   amongst the nations of the world".

3.0   A glance at the Republican Constitution of 1963 will reveal that the
application of the Sharia Law was restricted to the Islamic Law.

1.0 Then came the drafting of a new constitution of Nigeria in 1976/1977. Some Muslims insisted that the application of the Sharia must be total and that it must be included in the Draft Constitution.

There were heated debates on the matter which nearly rocked the deliberation of the constitution Drafting Committee. After critical and mature consideration by the committee it was agreed that the provisions of the 1963 constitution should be adopted, namely, the application of the Sharia Law should be restricted to Islamic Personal Law. The Draft Constitution was debated by a Constituent Assembly. The issue of Sharia almost rocked the corporate existence of Nigeria as one entity. However, sanity prevailed and it was agreed that the application of the Sharia should be confined to Islamic Personal Law.

5.0 In 1989 another constitution was promulgated for Nigeria by the then Federal Military Government. But before the promulgation the issue of Sharia almost rocked the deliberations of the then Constituent Assembly that was established to consider the Draft Constitution that had been produced by the Political Bureau. The hotly contested Sharia debate was finally halted by the Military Government of General Ibrahim Babangida which took the Sharia matter out of the hands of the Constituent Assembly and declared it a "no go area".

5.0 In 1994/1995 another attempt in producing a new constitution for Nigeria was made. During that exercise, undertaken by the National Constitutional Conference, the issue of Sharia Law also came up. After heated debates it was decided that the application of the Sharia Law should be restricted to Islamic Personal Law. Unfortunately, the 1995 Draft Constitution was never promulgated into Law.

7.0 During the tenure of the immediate past Military Regime of Gen. Abdulsalam Abubakar the 1999 Constitution of the Federal Republic of Nigeria was promulgated. In the new constitution the application of the Shaira Law has been restricted to Islamic Personal Law as can be seen in Section 262.

8.0 The Christian Community has decided to give the above summary in order not only to trace the development of the Sharia controversy but also to show that because of the impracticability of the full application of the Sharia Law, it is the Islamic Personal Law that has been in existence.

9.0 Now that some of our Muslim neigbours have renewed the demand for the full application of Sharia'Law, the Kaduna State Government has decided to constitute a committee, consisting of Christians and Muslims, to consider the practicability or otherwise of the full application of the Sharia Law in Kaduna State.

9.1 The Christian Community, before making its viewsknown, would like to seize this opportunity to commend the Executive Governor of Kaduna State, Alhaji Mohammed Ahmed Makarfi for the mature and wise way he has decided to handle the issue of the Sharia Law. We, the Christian Community in Kaduna State have always believed that dialogue is the best and most appropriate method of tackling any problem.

9.2 However we want to clarify some grounds arising from the address and terms of reference given to the committee by the Governor. This has to do with the terms used namely "application" as against our preferred use of "implication". Thus taking the whole address our understanding of the term of reference would clearly mean the implication of the application of Sharia Law and legal system on Muslims in Kaduna State.

10.0   Also before making our views and stand known, we would like to address the following issues.

10.1   RELIGION AS A WAY OF LIFE

Some of our Muslim Neighbours have always maintained that Islam is a way of life. We respect their stand. However, we Christians want to make it abundantly clear, in case some people do not know, that Christianity is not only a way of life but life itself. For Christianity is Jesus Christ who in the Gospel by the Apostle John Chapter 14 vs. 6 says "I Am the Way, the Truth and the Life. No. one comes to (GOD) the Father except through me". Consequently Christianity governs every aspect of the life of its adherents, thus the Apostle Paul in 1st Corinthians 10 vs 31 says that Christians are commanded that even their eating or drinking be done the Christian way with the aim to glorify God, not to talk of activities like going to court.

10.2   A LEGAL CODE FOR RELIGION

a)   Some of our Muslim neighbours maintain that the Sharia is the legal code given to Muslims by Allah. The Christian Community respects their assertion.   However, we would like to point out that we Christians have in the Holy Bible a legal code given by God. In fact we are even enjoined not to take to our disputes to any court that are manned by non-Christians as is recorded in 1st Corinthians Chapter 6. Therefore, ideally Christians are not supposed to go to the Law Courts that are being operated in Nigeria. These courts are not Christians courts. But Christians attend such courts simply because these courts have been established since the British Colonial times as a compromise and panacea for peaceful co-existence, over the years, thus we Christians have not insisted in having our own courts run by the Government. Rather we have our ecclesiastical adjudicating panels administered by us.

c)   We are also not unaware that even among Muslims there are many schools of Sharia namely Hanbah, Hanafi, Maliki etc with only the Maliki applicable in Nigeria. What will the Muslims themselves do now with so many sects like Shi'ites becoming more powerful in Nigeria? Or will we have Algeria, Egypt, Iran, Iraq, Pakistan and other violent prone Islamic feuds e.g Abacha vs El-Zakakky and the Maitatsine era repeated in Nigeria in a larger scale with more devastating impact?

0.4 THE "FOREIGNNESS" OR OTHERWISE OF CHRISTIANITY AND ISLAM

some of our Muslim Neighbours have held that Islam is an indigenous religion but Christianity is not. The Christian Community would like to point out that both Christianity and Islam are "foreign" to Nigeria. While Christianity was brought by the Western World, Islam was brought by the Arab World. Hence, both must be seen either as "Foreign" or "Indigenous".

5 THE POPULATION OF CHRISTIANS AND MUSLIMS IN KADUNA STATE.

Some of our Muslim neigbours have maintained that there are more Muslims than Christians in Kaduna State. We wonder where they have obtained their figures from. The truth of the matter is that there are no accurate and reliable figures for the population of Christians and Muslims in Kaduna State not to talk of Nigeria as a whole. Hence, it is advisable not to begin talking of "Majority" and Minority" group. However, even if for the sake of argument it is accepted that there are more Muslims than Christians in Kaduna State, does such a situation warrant the introduction of measures that would not augur well for peaceful co-existence in Kaduna State? Will the insistence of any dominant group on having its way ensure peace in the State? We believe that the example of the situation in Northern Ireland should be a lesson for us in Kaduna State, Muslims and Christians alike.

1.0 Having commented on the above issue we would like to state some of the implications of the application of Sharia in Kaduna State.

1.1 IT WILL DESTROY THE UNITY OF THE STATE IN PARTICULAR AND NIGERIA IN GENERAL

Hitherto the people of Kaduna State have been living under one Constitution, i.e. the Constitution of the Federal Republic of Nigeria. If the Sharia Law is adopted the Constitution of our Muslim neighbours must certainly be the Quran and other religious books of Islam. This would mean that it is only the non-Muslims that would be governed by the Constitution of the Federal Republic of Nigeria. How can two groups of people living within the same territory be governed by two separate constitutions? Will such a situation unify or divide the people?

1.2 IT IS A WAY OF MAKING NIGERIA AN ISLAMIC REPUBLIC THROUGH THE BACK DOOR.

Some of our Muslim neigbours hold that they are only asking for the full application of Sharia and not that they are asking for an Islamic State. To the best of our knowledge there is not a single territory or country having a full application of Sharia and yet not being an Islamic territory or country, The game here is simply this: Let us start with the full application of Sharia. Once that is established then the declaration of an Islamic State is a foregone conclusion

11.3 ITS APPLICATION WILL CERTAINLY AFFECT THE NON-MUSLIM AND EVENTUALLY RESULT IN ANARCHY IN KADUNA STATE AND NIGERIA AS A WHOLE

a) It is a pity that some of our Muslim neigbours have deceived some Nigerians by claiming that the application of Sharia will affect only Muslims. Nothing could be far from the truth: Even the application of the Islamic Personal Law which is in practice now has been affecting many non-Muslims, especially in the Northern States. We know of many Christians with Muslim parents who could not inherit the properties of their parent simply because they were Christians and the Islamic Personal Law, contrary to Section 42 of the 1999 constitution of the Federal Republic of Nigeria, forbids such Christians and in fact all non-Muslims from inheriting properties of their Muslim parents.

b) But a great problem would certainly arise if the application of Sharia Law is extended to criminal matters. Suppose there is a criminal case between a Muslim and a non-Muslim which court do they go to? The non-Muslim cannot go to Sharia Court since he is not a Muslim. On the other hand the Muslim may refuse to attend a Common Law Court by insisting that being a Muslim he is governed totally by the Sharia. Where do we go from there? Anarchy of course. Hence, it is an absolute deception to hold that the application of the Sharia will affect only Muslim, for they do not live in isolation. Laws have territorial jurisdiction governing all those resident therein and not binding only individuals in isolation who as it were hang them on their necks for identification and punishment.

1.4 IT WILL CURTAIL, IF NOT COMPLETELY ELIMINATE, FREEDOM OF RELIGION AND CONSCIENCE AS ENSHRINED IN SECTION 38 OF THE 1999 CONSTITUTION of the Federal Republic of Nigeria. Anyone that is at home with the Sharia Law knows that the punishment for any person who changes from Islam to any other religion is instant death.

1.5 IT WILL CURTAIL, IF NOT ELIMINATE COMPLETELY, THE RIGHT OF THE INDIVIDUAL TO PROPAGATE HIS RELIGION AND IDEAS AS PROVIDED FOR IN SECTION 38 OF THE 1999 CONSTITUTION: of the Federal Republic of Nigeria. It is an indisputable fact that where the Sharia is in practice there cannot be the propagation of any religion other than Islam.

1.6 IT WILL CLEARLY VIOLATE THE CONSTITUTIONAL PROVISION OF THE RIGHT TO FREEDOM FROM DISCRIMINATION BY VIRTUE OF ETHNIC GROUP, SEX, PLACE OF ORIGIN, BIRTH, RELIGION OR POLITICAL OPINION.

It is well known that when the Sharia is fully applicable, non-Muslims are confirmed to second class status with no right to hold certain public offices. The non-Muslims will only be protected citizens subject to paying jizhya tax. Furthermore, the evidence of non-Muslims and women under the Sharia Law will not carry equal weight as of Muslim males.

12.0 Having enumerated some of the implications of applying Sharia in its fullness let us now consider the options that are available:

12.1 Demand for the removal from the present constitution the provisions having to do with Islamic Personal Law. To us Christians such a demand will be just since apart from Islam there is no other religion that is given such a favoured place in the Constitution of a country with a plurality of religions.

12.2 Demand that Christians as well as other non-Muslims in the country be allowed to be governed by their own religious laws and that government must take responsibility for the administration of such laws.

12.3 Demand that each religious group in the country be given its separate territory so that it can practice its religion without any inhibition whatsoever.

12.4 Hence Sharia is an Islamic Legal System, it will only be wise for the Muslims to advocate first for the establishment of a pure Islamic political system (State) which will implement the Islamic Legal System in an Islamic State instead of demanding for only the aspect of the Islamic System in a religiously pluralistic system. To do otherwise is calling for oppression, confusion and anarchy.

12.5 Accept the continuation of the status quo i.e only the Islamic Personal Law can continue to exist as provided for in the 1999 constitution of the Federal Republic of Nigeria.

13.0 THE STAND OF THE CHRISTIAN COMMUNITY IN KADUNA STATE

Having critically and objectively considered all the options and their implications, for the sake of peaceful co-existence, the stand of the Christian Community is as follows:

13.1 It is now pertinently clear that the Sharia controversy has always been and remains a national issue. It is constitutional and only within the ambit of the National Assembly and not a state legislative or executive function. Therefore, we urge the Kaduna State Government to hands off this matter completely and refer the agitators to the National Assembly or the Constitutional Courts. Same advise goes to the Kaduna State House of Assembly which has been led by the nose to ignite this fire that is threatening the corporate existence, peacefulness, tolerance, and the liberality with which Kaduna State is known but also which has had its fair share of ill reputation as religious violence prone state - a legacy every right thinking person or government will want healed and not handed over to our youth and children.

13.2 We demand that Government, as a matter of urgency, establish the Customary Court Appeal for Non-Muslims in the State as provided for in the 1979 and 1999 Constitutions of Nigeria.

13.3 We demand that Government completely overhaul and reform the judicial institutions administering Islamic Personal Law and Customary Law in the State i.e the Area Courts to remove the obnoxious apartheid practice that has existed in all form ranging from appointments of judges, compositions and jurisdiction of the said courts.

13.4 AS TO THE APPLICATION OF SHARIA IN KADUNA STATE. THE BOTTOM LINE, WHICH IS ABSOLUTELY NON-NEGOTIABLE, IS THAT THE STATUS QUO SHOULD REMAIN, I. E. THE APPLICATION OF SHARIA SHOULD BE THE CONTINUED APPLICATION OF ISLAMIC PERSONAL LAW ADMINISTERED BY AREA COURT AND SHARIA COURT OF APPEAL OF THE STATE AS PROVIDED FOR BY THE 1979 – 1999 CONSTITUTIONS OF THE FEDERAL REPUBLIC OF NIGERIA.

1. HIS GRACE B. A. ACHIGILI ....

2. HIS GRACE ARCH BISHOP P. Y. JATAU ....

3. MOST REVEREND BISHOP J. D. BAGOBIRI ....

4. HIS GRACE J. I. FEARON ....

5. REVEREND B. Y. SIDI ....

6. SP. APOSTLE S. B. FASANYA ....

7. REV. YAKUBU H. PAM ....

8. REV. DANJUMA MAKOSHI ....

9. REV. ABBAS DALLAH ....

10. REV. KANTIYOK A. TUKURA ....

11. ELDER SAIDU DOGO ....

12. MR. TONNY UDAH ....

13. REV. EYO E. EDET ....

14. REV. DANIEL SHAFURA ....

15. DR. C. S. ABASHIYA ....

16. BARRISTER J. ACHIMUGU ....

17. EVAN. M. OWOJAIYE ....

18. REV. BARRISTER WAKILI KADIMA ....

The following should be noted:-

a) All non-Muslim judges of Area Courts in Kaduna State have no jurisdiction over Muslims in civil matters but the Muslims judges have jurisdiction over non-Muslims.

b) Of the eleven Upper Area Courts Judges in Kaduna State only one so far is non-Muslim. Even in the predominately non-Muslim SOUTHERN PART OF THE STATE, ALL THE JUDGES OF THE UPPER AREA COURTS ARE MUSLIMS.

c) Of the over ninety Area Courts in Kaduna State only about fifteen (more or less) are Christians and non-Muslim judges

d) Non-Muslim and Christian judges in Area Courts in the State are never posted to Adjudicate in the Muslim dominated geographical half of Northern Kaduna State, but their Muslims counterparts can be found all over the predominately Christian geographical half of Southern Kaduna.

e) Abolish the criminal jurisdiction of the Area and Upper Area Courts and transfer such jurisdiction vis-a-vis the Penal Code to Magistrate Courts only. In fact this has been done in some sister states of the North e.g. Sokoto, Plateau, Benue etc.

f) Abolish with immediate effect the Appellate jurisdiction of the Upper Area Courts in regards to any matter and make appeals from all Area and Upper Area Courts to go to either the Sharia Court of Appeal or Customary Court of Appeal.

POSITION PAPER

SUBMITTED BY

THE

KADUNA STATE MUSLIM COMMUNITY

ON

THE APPLICATION OF SHARI'A LEGAL SYSTEM ON MUSLIMS

TO

THE INTER-RELIGIOUS LEADERS COMMITTEE ON THE APPLICATION OF SHARI'A LAW

IN

KADUNA STATE.

18TH JANUARY, 2000

To: · The Secretary,
Committee of Inter-Religious Leaders on
The application of Shari'a Legal system in Kaduna State
General Hassan Usman Katsina House
Kawo-Kaduna.

From: The Kaduna State Muslim Community,
C/o Jama'atul Nasril Islam Headquarters
Ali Akilu Road, Kaduna.

Subject: <u>POSITION PAPER ON APPLICATION OF SHARI'A LEGAL
SYSTEM ON MUSLIMS IN KADUNA STATE.</u>

Introduction: Shari'a across the world is more synonymous with the Muslim Community. It is our religious legal System, a divine Code of Conduct to guide our spiritual and temporal undertaking in all aspect of our life. As there used to be manual escorting any machinery or appliance from a man made factory, giving the idea of handling well and making a meaningful usage of the devices: so Almighty Allah as the Creator gives His creatures through His chosen Messenger Shari'a as a manual to guide all mankind to live a meaningful life on this earth. The application of Shari';a is a religious obligation, compulsory on muslims.

Identified Problem: As a result of the Muslim request for Shari'a in Kaduna State and the multi-ethnic nature of Nigeria, and specifically Kaduna state; There exist a deep rooted wrong perception, assumption, stereo-type, fear, misconception and mis-interpretation of the Shari'a by he Christian community and even by some un-informed Muslims, as egard its implication on the non-Muslims.

Clarification: The Executive Governor of Kaduna State Alh. Ahmad Muhammad Makarfi, while inaugurating the Committee on Inter-religious eaders on the application of Shari'a law in Kaduna State; on Thursday, 30/12/1999, requested for the need to create enlightenment and dialogue on the fear of its implication as regard the life of non-Muslims in the State, thus:

> "It has become necessary that our people sit together and examine the whole principle of law vis-a-vis the various opinion and indeed lack of enlightenment on how the legal system can operate without affecting the lives of non-Muslims. We believe that this approach will remove the apparent dichotomy".

Responding to the appeal of His Excellency, the Muslim Ummah wish to make the following clarification for our non-Muslim neighbours:

1.   That the Sharia'a legal system is not to be enforced on any non-Muslim in the State.

2.   That the system shall be for no one but, any person who professes faith in Islam.

3.   That its jurisdiction shall be covering Muslim related cases, be they personal, inter-personal, inter-group, civil or criminal.

4.   That it shall work within the frame work provided for in the 1999 Constitution.

5.   That the Shari'a Court is optional for non-Muslims, they can only be tried under the system on their free volition and request.

6.   That the legal system, while in operation has no any implication on any ethnic groups, who are residing in the State and are non-Muslims.

7.   That the system shall operate side by side with other conventional and customary courts as exist today in the State.

8.   That many of the precepts in the Shari'a legal system could still be found within the Penal Code of Northern Nigeria, since 1955/1956.

9.   That the non-Muslims are free to be judged by whatever laws they desire, as provided for within our democratic setting, and they can call for any system that can meet the need of their cultural heritage.

10. That the argument by some un-informed non-Muslims that 'Islam is built upon five pillars, viz;
     (1)   Believing in one God (Allah) and His Prophet and Messenger, Muhammad (PBUH).
     (2)   The Five daily Prayers
     (3)   Alms Giving (Zakkat)
     (4)   Ramadan fast

(5)   Pilgrimage; and that none of the above is denied to any Muslim by the government or the Non-Muslims in Nigeria. And then, why are Muslims calling for Shari'a ?.

We want to make it clear for those who take the above excuse for not supporting or tolerating the Muslims legitimate request for Shari'a; that Shari'a is the instrument that checks , assesses and evaluates the Muslim's spiritual link with his/her creator and the remaining inter-personal dealings with other human beings, as the Prophet of Almighty Allah to all mankind confirmed that "Al-Islam Huwal Mu'amalah" i.e Islam should manifest in all our social relationship. Secondly, Allah has categorically told the Muslims, that they can never be believers in Him, until they adjudicate their life by the standard of the Shari'a, without any rancor in their mind. (The Qur'an 4:65).

11a. That Qur'an has categorically made it clear that, there is no compulsion in religion, (the Qur'an 2:256) and That Muslims are taught to live peacefully with their neighbours in village, city, town or country of their sojourn. We can interrelate in business transactions and other areas of social development with non-Muslims, without intimidation, humiliation or deformation of their honour, dignity, religion or cultures. As prophet Muhammad (PBUH) lived with Jews, Christians and Pagans in the city of Madinah, and joined hands with them in many things of common interest.

1 b. That the Shari'a Court of Appeal in place now on the country would be deceptive if one aspect of Islamic law i.e criminal aspect should be excluded or modified to suit any un-Islamic legislation.

Cur Position: That as our due rights and privileges, as fellow citizens of Nigeria and as provided for within the nation's 1999 Federal Constitution, we wish to declare:

1.   That Nigeria is not a secular State as section 10 of the 1999 Constitution is mis-interpreted, thus:
> " The Government of the Federation or of State shall not adopt any religion as State religion".

However, the said section 10 did not say that Shari'a shall not be applicable as legal system, after all the constitution which provides for the section is the same constitution that provides for the right to practice one's religion.

2.   That the constitution provided freedom to belief, propagate, and practice one's religion in section 38 of the 1999 constitution which reads:

> "Freedom of thought, conscience and religion ... to manifest and propagate his religion or belief in worship, teaching, practice and observance.

3. That the constitution begins with a declaration in the preamble that reads:

   "WE ARE A NATION UNDER GOD"

4. That the constitution provides in the Seventh schedule for oath of office and oath of allegiance (Sworn to by the Holy Qur'an and Holy Bible) and concluded with ... ' So help, me God'. This proved that Nigeria conclusively is far from being a secular state but a multi-religious country.

5. That we demand Friday as a work free day, just as Saturday and Sunday are allowed for other religions.

6. That a Muslim cannot observe and practice his/her religion effectively without the Shari'a legal system in place. Therefore, the 1999 constitution, established the Shari'a Court for the Muslims, in pursuant to sections 275 and 316.

7. That by section 277 of the Constitution, the Shari'a Court is competent to decide among other things.

   I. Any question of Islamic law regarding marriage concluded under Islamic law.

   ii. Any question regarding validity of dissolution of Islamic law marriage or guardianship of an ..

iii. Any question of Islamic personal law regarding a wakf, gift, will or succession where the endower, donor, testator, or deceases person is a Muslim.

iv. Where all the parties to the proceedings are Muslims, they request the Court that hear the case in the first instance (i.e the Area Court or the upper Area Court) to determine the case in accordance with Islamic law.

8. The 1999 Constitution recognizes 3 set of Courts of Superior records in Nigeria i.e
   a. . The High Court .
   b. The Shari'a Court of Appeal
   c. The Customary Court of Appeal

9. That the Islamic Legal system is one of the three legal system, the Nigerian nation recognised i.e

i. The received English Law (of Christian origin, famously called "Common law" though some of pour uniformed non-Muslims disagree with the notion that the English Common law is not of Christian origin. Hereby are fact as revealed by a Christian English Jurist of the Supreme Court of England thus:
   > "In the case of Bowman V. Secular Society ltd. (1917) Ac 406, where Lord summer said, referring to England ' and English law:

Ours is, and always has been a Christian state. The English family is built on Christian ideas, and if the natural religion is not Christian, there is none. English law may be called a Christian law..."

In the same Lord Chancellor finely (as he then was said on p. 425 said:

"There is abundant authority for saying that Christianity is part and parcel of the law of the land (England)..."

Indeed, this law is the same brought for us from by colonial authority, which is hereby refer to as the "Common Law" in Nigeria.

ii. Islamic law: this is one of the three recognised Nigeria legal system because the colonial authority found it in existence when they arrived and leaved the system after the Creation of Nigeria with some modifications.

iii. Customary law: This is part of the three of the recognised legal system which also the colonial authority found in existence among the non-Muslim indigenous communities in Nigeria and enshrined in our constitution.

10. That by section 68 (2) of the Penal Code Applicable to Kaduna State, offenders who are of Muslim faith may in addition to other punishment provided by the Code be liable to the Haddi-Lashing prescribed by Islamic law for the following offenses:

    a.   Adultery by man under section 387 of the Penal Code

    b.   Adultery by woman under section 388 of the Penal Code

    c.   Deformation under section 392 of the Penal Code

    d.   Injurious falsehood under section 393

    e.   Drunkenness in public place under section 402 of the Penal Code

    f.   Drinking alcoholic drink under section 403 of the Penal Code.

11. That as a result of the above facts it is proved beyond reasonable doubt that the Shari'a as a legal system has been in existence before the creation of Kaduna State, and the inception of the then Northern Region of Nigeria.

12. That the history of Shari'a legal system in Kaduna State has never been the instruments of instability, dis-integration, violence and retrogression but it reveals our strength and cultural heritage in our multi-religious, multi-ethnic and multi-cultural society.

13. That as good Muslims who believe in the corporate existence of Kaduna State and Nigeria; and recognize the differences in our ethnicity, culture, tradition and religious system hereby

acknowledge and respect freedom of thoughts, believe and practice of non-Muslims as much as we respect that our fellow Muslims.

14. That as a result of the lapses in the present common law system of adjudication in which a case over a plot of land could last for between 1-10 years in our High courts, Shari'a should be allowed to be implemented in full, on Muslims.

15. That the request for the application of the Shari'a legal system in the State is not meant to intimidate or manipulate any one, but to avail our individual and collective constitutional rights for Sharia, by the Nation's Constitution.

16. That the Muslim Ummah of Kaduna State are not hereby requesting for Islamic State, but for, the application and practice of Shari'a legal system, as provided for by the 1999 Constitution.

Our appeal: Our appeal to our fellow Christians in the State is that, as Muslims tolerate some of the Christians traditional system imposed on us for years to date e.g Pope Gregory's Calendar; the symbol of the Cross in our public Hospitals etc let them tolerate and support our call for Shari'a which is not to be imposed on them.

1. That Islam teaches us that the nearest in love and affection to Muslims are those who say: *we are Christians.* (The Qur'an 5:82:85). And on this, observed by sincere Muslims respects Christians, and the respect will be more under an Islamic legal system. Therefore, we hope that our fellow Christians will reciprocate this gesture by tolerating our legitimate struggle for Shari'a legal system.

2. That as much as we recognize and respect the freedom, aspiration and rights of Christians and other non-Muslims in the State and the Country at large; we strongly felt they also would tolerate, recognize and respect our freedom, rights and aspiration as expected in a democratic setting, like ours.

3. That we pray that our Christian neighbours who share common beliefs with us in Almighty Allah, and in the spirit of accountability on earth and before Almighty Allah in the hereafter and the belief in love for mutual co-existence in our multi-religious and multi-ethnic society, would support our quest for progress , peace and stability in Kaduna State and Nigeria.

4. We also pray and appeal that our Christian neighbours would strongly support our struggle for returning people back from extreme materialism life style, to a spiritually and moderated one, for a better future and survival of democracy in Nigeria.

5. That the Muslim Ummah is appealing to the State Executive, the Legislature and the Judiciary to speed up, in giving us this constitional right of ours.

Conclusion: Finally, the Muslim Ummah appreciates and thanks the efforts of the Kaduna State's Chief Executive, His Excellency, Alh. Ahmad Muhammad Makarfi; the State Legislature and the Judiciary for establishing various committees to address the aspiration of the Muslim Ummah and other Communities in the State, through the positive and effective usage of democratic structures in the State.

Long live Kaduna State,
Long live Federal Republic of Nigeria.

SIGNED:

_____   _____
AL H. JA'AFARU MAKARFI   SHEIKH ZUBARI SIRAJO

                                                  17/2/2000

SHEIKH YUSUF SAMBO RIGACHIKUN

PRESBYTERIAN CHURCH OF THE SUDAN
WOMEN DEPARTMENT

PRISON PROGRAM ON 2nd JULY 2004
TIME FROM 10:00 _ 12: 00 AM.

- *PROGRAM :*

1. General song .
2. Opening Prayer   by Mrs . Joy Mathew .
3. A word of welcoming   by Rev. Khamis
4. A word from Secretary of Women Department .
5. General song .
6. A word from SCC National Women Coordinator.
7. Words from visitors .
8. Readings from the Scripture :
    a) Isaiah 42 : 22 by Mrs. Rejoice Daniel.
    b) Gosple of John 3 : 14 _ 21 by Mrs. Suzana Andria .
9. General song .
10. Preaching from Mrs. Mary Kur Deng .
11. Prayer for the prisoners / SUK.
12. Offertory song .
13. Blessing of the offerings by Mrs. Rebecca Amot
14. Benediction by Rev. Khamis .

GOD BLESS YOU

INTERNATIONAL CHRISTIAN UNION

الإتحـاد المسـيحى العـالمى

500 SUMMIT AVE.UNION CITY. NJ 07087   TEL: 201-902-9997   FAX: 201-863-4111

www.ICU-us.org   Tax ID # 203-411-854

You are cordially invited to attend the
International Conference on "Democracy in the Middle East
and Preserving Christians and Other Minorities' Future Existence"
At the Holiday Inn, Newark Airport Hotel on June 19th and 20th, 2006
160 Frontage Road, Newark, NJ 07114,

This event is sponsored by the **International Christian Union** and **Copts United**
with the support of other allied organizations.

International Christian Union   Copts United
UNION CITY.NJ 07087   Zurich, Switzerland
www.icu-us.org   **www.copts-united.com**

As a special conference-sponsored attendee, your expenses, including transportation and dining, will be complements of the International Conference. The conference will provide local transportation within the North Jersey region.

The Conference will convene International Politicians and Human Rights Activists, as well as noted Middle Eastern scholars and religious freedom experts. Topics to be addressed include discussions concerning the neglected history that brought Christians to today's lack of equality within the Middle East. Topics to be covered will also include what needs to be done to provide a better and respectable lifestyle within the democratic development in the Middle East. Minorities, human and civil rights, and the U.S. and other governments' roles in supporting democracy in The Middle East and throughout the region will be a major issue. The conference will conclude with a "Minorities Rights Forum." The resolutions of the conference will be forwarded to the United Nations and added to the documents that currently exist in support of the case pending with the human rights department.

Should you require special handling of your Visa, you must take this invitation to the U.S. Embassy. Please contact our office as soon as possible if assistance is needed.

This is a date to be marked in HISTORY. Please join us and help us have our voices heard. Your suggestions on these matters are highly appreciated. You can fax, email, etc. documents and facts to help us make this event fruitful. Please let us know if you are attending as the seats are limited. All names must be in by **June 13th 2006.**

International Conference on Democracy in the Middle East and Human rights of Christians and other minorities

Schedule

First Day 19th 2006

8:30 to 9:30 am Registration and breakfast
First Session
9:30 to 10:30 am

Dr. Monir Dawoud,
Mr. Adly Abadir Youssef
Mr. Cameel Halim

Break 15 Minutes
Second Session
10:45am to 12:45 pm

The honorable Senator Mr. Robert Menandez
The Honorable Congressman Mr. Steven Rothman
Mr. Adly Abadir Youssef
Dr. Gehad Auda
Dr. Saad Eldeen Ibrahim
Dr. Daniel Pipes
Dr. Wafaa Soultan
Mr. Mayer Richard Bohann

Lunch 12:45 to 2:00 pm
Third Session
2:00 to 4:00 pm

The Honorable Rabbi Dr. Eugene Korn
Father Keith Roderick
His Grace Bishop Dr. Marvin Heyboer
Mr. John Mccurdy
Dr. Shaker El Naboulsy

Break 4:00 – 4:30 pm
Fourth Session
4:30 to 6:30 pm

Dr. Ibrahim Habib
Dr.Walid Phares
Mrs. Elham Manea*(written speech)*
Dr. Ahmed Matter*(written speech)*
Miss Sera Ghali – Australia *(written speech)*

Dinner 6:30 pm